Heroes of the American
Reconstruction

Heroes of the American Reconstruction

Profiles of Sixteen Educators, Politicians and Activists

STANLEY TURKEL

McFarland & Company, Inc., Publishers
Jefferson, North Carolina, and London

LIBRARY OF CONGRESS CATALOGUING-IN-PUBLICATION DATA

Turkel, Stanley, 1925–
    Heroes of the American Reconstruction : profiles of sixteen educators, politicians and activists / Stanley Turkel.
       p.   cm.
    Includes bibliographical references and index.

ISBN 0-7864-1943-1 (illustrated case binding : 50# alkaline paper) ∞

    1. Reconstruction (U.S. history, 1865–1877) — Biography.
I. Title.
E668.T87   2005
973.8'092'2 — dc22   2004020954

British Library cataloguing data are available

On the cover *(from left clockwise)*: Albert R. Parsons (1848–1887), John R. Lynch (1847–1939), *Chicago Historical Society;* Robert B. Elliott (1842–1884), Albion W. Tourgee (1883–1905), *Library of Congress*

Manufactured in the United States of America

McFarland & Company, Inc., Publishers
  Box 611, Jefferson, North Carolina 28640
  www.mcfarlandpub.com

To my dear wife, Rima Sokoloff, whose life-giving love sustained me during the eight years it took to write this book.

To my children: Marc, whose professional knowledge secured the photographs, and Allison, whose missionary work to help abused children inspired me.

To my stepchildren: Joshua, who made important recommendations to improve the narrative, and Benay, who provided unstinting encouragement.

And to my grandchildren: Samantha, Juno and Anaya, whose curiosity and creativity stimulated me.

Contents

Contents

Preface

In 1956, I attended a six-lecture course entitled "The Reconstruction Period" given by the famous black historian W. E. B. Du Bois, who was in his eighties but still keen of mind and passionate about his subject matter. His presentation was a revelation filled with pertinent historic material that had not been taught during my college years at New York University. Some twenty years earlier, Du Bois wrote his classic *Black Reconstruction in America: An Essay Toward a History of the Part which Black Folk Played in the Attempt to Reconstruct Democracy in America, 1860–1880.* The opening sentence of the book sets the tone: "Easily the most dramatic episode in American history was the sudden move to free four million black slaves in an effort to stop a great civil war, to end forty years of bitter controversy and to appease the moral sense of civilization."[1]

Since that time, I have been studying the Reconstruction period, learning, questioning, and writing about this wondrous period of rebirth of American democracy. The surprising and inaccurate conclusion reached by most historians in the one hundred years after the Civil War was that Reconstruction was a tragic disaster and a dreadful decade.

Southern historian Francis Butler Simkins wrote in 1963, "A biased interpretation of Reconstruction caused one of the most important political developments in the recent history of the South, the disenfranchisement of the blacks. The fraud and violence by which this objective was first obtained was justified on a single ground: The memory of the alleged horrors of Reconstruction…. Historians, sensing that the discrediting of the period in which the Negro most freely participated in politics justifies his subsequent exclusion from those activities, have condemned Reconstruction measures as sweepingly as have the Southern politicians. They have called the military rule by which these measures were inaugurated 'as brutish a tyranny as ever marked the course of any government whose agents and organs claimed to be civilized'; and they have described the enfranchised freedmen as belonging to a race 'incapable of forming any judgments upon the actions of men.'"[2] The article on South Carolina in the eleventh edition of the *Encyclopedia Britannica* in all seriousness concludes that "all the misfortunes of war

1

itself are insignificant when compared with the sufferings of the people during Reconstruction."

Simkins went on to say, "It seems that the worst of which they [the Reconstructionists] have been adjudged guilty was the violation of the American caste system. The crime of crimes was to encourage Negroes in voting, office-holding and other functions of social equality."[3] Such conclusions derive out of the belief that blacks are innately inferior. The historian John W. Burgess expressed the essential prejudice: "A black skin means membership in a race of men which has never succeeded in subjecting passion to reason."

Until recent years, the history of Reconstruction was written with a strong anti-black bias. As Dr. Howard O. Lindsey wrote:

> In order to justify the post-Reconstruction policies, white Southerners launched a propaganda attack on the entire history of black Reconstruction, painting its short-comings in the most luridly negative colors possible and falsifying facts where necessary. The myth makers aimed their venom at three groups:
>
>   1. Northern Whites — a large and diverse group of people ("so-called carpet-baggers"), many very good, was defined solely in terms of its worst elements — a classic propaganda tactic.
>   2. Southern Whites — who supported Reconstruction were labeled "scalawags" and were uniformly vilified as corrupt thieves aiding and abetting the rape of the south by a vengeful north.
>   3. Blacks — keynote of the attacks was to stress the innate stupidity and gulli-bility of blacks and to shed crocodile tears over the ruthless way in which they had been manipulated by evil carpetbaggers and scalawags. The clear implication was that since blacks were congenitally inferior, they were incapable of self-government.[4]

However, it was not corruption but honesty, not ignorance but brilliance that frightened racists during Reconstruction. Southern whites feared good black government more than bad black government and a brilliant black politician more than an ignorant one.

Subsequently, revisionist historians have corrected our knowledge of the glorious experiment known as Reconstruction. We now know that the passage of the Thirteenth, Fourteenth and Fifteenth amendments to the Constitution represented a second Bill of Rights. We now know that after 200 plus years of slavery in the United States, the four million freed black slaves struggled against overwhelming odds for equality and broth-erhood with too little economic assistance, no land, and too much violence.

My years of research have turned up dozens of unknown American heroes of the Reconstruction whose exploits warrant recognition and commemoration. Sixteen of them caught my attention for reasons that will become clear when you read their biographies. Seven were black men who struggled in a dangerous Southern environment filled with racism and violence. They tried to give credence to the American dream that once slavery was ended, and they became citizens, they could aspire to be free and equal. All seven were elected to Congress from Southern states. One of my heroes was an educated free black woman who relocated from Massachusetts to South Carolina in 1866 to teach illiterate blacks how to read and write. Two were white politicians who belied the terrible reputation of carpetbaggers. Both struggled against Southern hatred to deliver the promise of the Fourteenth and Fifteenth amendments to all Americans, black and white alike. Another was a white abolitionist who founded the first integrated college in the United States and later served as Lincoln's ambassador to Russia. Two were veterans of the Confederate Army, one a famous general who was Robert E. Lee's second-in-command at Gettysburg and who later became a Republican and promoted equal rights for blacks. The other Confederate veteran married an African American woman after the Civil War and became a labor agitator who was unjustly hanged after the Haymarket riots. Another hero was a white minister abolitionist and soldier who led the first black regiment in battle against the rebels and later wrote *Army Life in a Black Regiment.*

For these heroes, it was a tough, uphill battle even though the Union Army was victorious in the bloodiest war in America's history. Their stories are lost in the dust-bin of the past and deserve instead to be reported and celebrated.

We have the record of kings and gentlemen ad nauseum and in stupid detail; but of the common run of human beings, and particularly of the half or wholly submerged working group, the world has saved all too little of authentic record and tried to forget or ignore even the little saved. With regard to Negroes in America, in addition to the common neglect of a society patterned on assumed aristocracy, came also the attempt, conscious or unconscious, to excuse the shame of slavery by stressing natural inferiority which would render it impossible for Negroes to make, much less leave, any record of revolt or struggle, any human reaction to utter degradation.

—W. E. B. Du Bois, 1951

1

Background of Reconstruction

One hundred and thirty years ago, a dramatic seating took place, which even now sounds like fiction. On February 25, 1870, a black clergyman named Hiram Rhoades Revels of Mississippi became the first black to serve in the United States Senate. Unbelievably, Revels was elected to the seat formerly held by Jefferson Davis, the president of the Confederate States of America, just defeated in the Civil War.

In the intervening years, black men and women had been excluded from election to the Congress so systematically that each isolated success was described as "the first since Reconstruction." What in the world was Reconstruction anyway? Was it anything more than some vaguely defined period after the Civil War when carpetbaggers and scalawags abused the South? If Mississippi elected a black man to the U.S. Senate in 1870, what else was going on?

As Columbia University Professor Eric Foner wrote:

> Reconstruction was a time of momentous changes in American political and social life. In the aftermath of slavery's demise, the federal government guaranteed the equality before the law of all citizens, blacks as well as white. In the South, former masters and former slaves struggled to shape the new labor systems that arose from the ashes of slavery, and new institutions — black churches, public schools, and many others — redefined the communities of both blacks and whites and relations between them. But no development during the turbulent years that followed the Civil War marked so dramatic a break with the nation's traditions, or aroused such bitter hostility from Reconstruction's opponents, as the appearance of large numbers of black Americans in public office only a few years after the destruction of slavery.[1]

Within a year after the Hiram Revels election, Joseph H. Rainey of South Carolina and Jefferson F. Long of Georgia broke the color line and were seated in the House of Representatives. By 1875, the following black men served in the House: Robert C. DeLarge, Robert B. Elliott, Richard H. Cain, Robert Smalls of South Carolina; Benjamin S. Turner, James T. Rapier and Jeremiah Haralson of Alabama; John R. Lynch of Mississippi; Josiah T. Walls of Florida; John A. Hyman of North Carolina; and

Charles E. Nash of Louisiana. Senator Blanche K. Bruce of Mississippi was the first African American to serve a full six-year term as a U.S. senator (from March 5, 1875, to March 3, 1881). Senator Bruce was also the first black man to preside over the Senate and the first whose signature appeared on all the country's paper currency (as Registrar of the Treasury starting on May 18, 1881).

How strange were these elections to the majority white population? Professor Foner described the dramatic and radical changes that altered the American political stage for the first time in more than 200 years:

> Before the Civil War, blacks did not form part of America's "political nation." Black officeholding was unknown in the slave South and virtually unheard of in the free states as well. Four years before the outbreak of Civil War, the Supreme Court decreed in the Dred Scott Case that no black person could be a citizen of the United States. In 1860, only five northern states, all with tiny black populations, allowed black men to vote on the same terms as white.
>
> During Presidential Reconstruction [1865–67 under President Andrew Johnson] voting and elective office in the south continued to be restricted to whites, although a handful of blacks were appointed to local offices and federal patronage posts. Black officeholding began in earnest in 1867, when Congress ordered the election of new southern governments under suffrage rules that did not discriminate on the basis of race. By 1877, when the last Radical Reconstruction governments were overthrown, around 2,000 black men had held federal, state, and local public offices, ranging from member of Congress to justice of the peace.[2]

How strange was freedom to the newly liberated slaves? Dr. Howard Lindsey described the change of status from subhuman chattel slavery to full citizenship in about twelve months:

> It produced much disorientation and psychological stress. Suddenly, for example, the master was no longer head of the freedman's household; now the black man of the house had to assume the role of protector and provider — no easy task for people without money, and barely with shelter, cast adrift in a land devastated by war. Families had painfully to try to reassemble themselves [which was often impossible] and make a new beginning.[3]

When the Civil War ended, much of the South looked as barren as the landscape of the moon. Cities lay in ruins, fields and crops were destroyed, 700,000 Americans died (out of a total United States population of 30 million) — all the result of the bloodiest war in history. Many families, black and white, wandered in search of food and shelter. But though their hardships were momentous, ex-slaves felt freedom for the first time in more than 200 years. Thousands left their former masters and their plantations, sometimes just to prove they had the right to move about freely. The needs of the ex-slaves were enormous. Where would they work? What would they be paid? How could they get food and clothing, a home, and schooling for their children and themselves? Few could look to the ex-slaveholders for help, for they had been embittered by defeat in the Civil War.

What, then, should be done about the freedmen? This was one of the two big questions the country had to decide. The other question, inseparable from the first, was what should be done about the defeated Southern whites? As the Civil War came to its end, a great national debate rose around these two questions.

White Southerners did not believe in racial equality. They thought the black man was inferior as did most Northern whites. Many states in the North had laws that drew a line based on color; in voting, in education, in jobs, in transportation, in churches and in clubs, blacks were excluded and not given equal treatment. When freedom came, blacks demanded the vote to protect their new status. The vote meant political power. Without it they would be helpless against the bitterness and hatred of the ex-slaveholders. The old masters had rebelled against the Union and been beaten in war. Should they be allowed back in power? Should their land, the economic base of their power, be taken away? Should the common people of the South, black and white, be given a chance to govern themselves? These were the problems of Reconstruction. The answers would decide how the South would be rebuilt.

President Andrew Johnson's Reconstruction Plan

A national debate on these crucial issues took place, centered in Washington. The Republican Party, which was in power, was split over Reconstruction. The radical wing of Lincoln's party — built around the abolitionists — had no faith in the South's old leaders. It wanted to rebuild the South by opening the gates of government to blacks and poor whites.

Before the debate was ended, Lincoln was assassinated. Vice President Andrew Johnson of Tennessee, a southern Unionist, took his place. The new president gave pardons liberally to the Confederate leaders if they merely signed a loyalty oath, and he offered easy terms for Southern states to return to the Union. He withdrew federal troops from much of the South and restored vast lands to the wealthy planters who had previously held the blacks in bondage and had fought the bloodiest war in history against the U.S. government.

This was a signal to the old rulers of the South: they grabbed the reins of power again. In state after state whites gathered to write new constitutions. They slammed the door on the blacks. The freedmen protested and they told President Johnson and the country that all men must have the right to vote, regardless of color. Southern whites moved swiftly to crush the protest. They rode through the countryside, burning black homes, beating, robbing and killing. Even state militia were used to terrorize the freedmen. President Johnson's agents in the South sent him reports that the whites were trying to put blacks into slavery again. Appeals to end the violence poured into Washington — and were ignored.

After state constitutions were drafted, new state legislatures were elected. Only whites were allowed to vote and run for public office. Therefore, only whites were elected, many of whom were ex-rebels, including former Confederate officers. They adopted "Black Codes"—sets of laws that regulated the life and labor of the freedmen. The codes read much like the old slave laws. They differed in details from state to state, but essentially they imposed rigid controls and harsh penalties upon the blacks. Most had these typical provisions:

- Blacks could not meet without a white being present.
- Blacks could not sit on juries or testify against whites.
- Blacks could be hanged for stealing a bale of cotton, a horse, or a mule.
- Blacks could not buy or rent farm land. They must have a special license to take any job but farm labor.
- Unemployed blacks could be arrested as vagrants and auctioned off or hired off to planters willing to pay the fine.
- Blacks leaving jobs before the end of a contract could be forced to return to their employers.
- Blacks were forbidden to marry whites.
- Blacks could not possess weapons of any kind.
- Blacks must be off the streets after dark.

This was what the ex-Confederates meant by restoring "home rule." According to the governor of South Carolina his new state government was "a white man's government and intended for whites only." To Radical Republicans this was a flat denial of reality. The Thirteenth Amendment to the Constitution, adopted in 1865, had outlawed slavery once and for all. Did it mean nothing? They refused to stand by while the white planters fastened new chains on black laborers. Northerners were shocked by the murders of freedmen reported regularly in the newspapers. The Congress, led by such men as Representative Thaddeus Stevens (Pennsylvania) and Senator Charles Sumner (Massachusetts), decided it would not accept the credentials of any of the southern congressmen-elect until the matter was considered by a joint committee. The resolution creating this committee stated the following:

> Resolved by the House of Representatives (the Senate concurring), that a joint committee of fifteen members shall be appointed, nine of whom shall be members of the House and six members of the Senate, who shall inquire into the condition of the States which formed the so-called Confederate States of America, and report whether they, or any of them, are entitled to be represented in either House of Congress; with leave to report at any time, by bill or otherwise.[4]

The Committee resolved itself into four subcommittees, which took testimony on conditions in Tennessee, North Carolina, South Carolina, Virginia, Alabama, Arkansas, Georgia, Mississippi, Florida, Louisiana, and Texas. Testimony was received on five topics: conditions of blacks in the South, conditions of whites in the South, effects of Johnson's plan of Reconstruction, the problem of Negro suffrage, and the need for congressional interference. From January through May 1866, testimony was heard from blacks, Southern leaders, members of the Union and Confederate armies, officers of the Freedmen's Bureau, provisional governors, etc. While these hearings were going on, serious race riots took place in Memphis and New Orleans. Congress established committees to investigate these riots and issue reports.[5]

The evidence from these various hearings led to majority reports condemning conditions in the South. In summary, the reports said, much of the white South still hated the Union. The feeling against the blacks — who were speaking up for their rights — was even more overtly violent than in slavery times. The reports stated that the army and the Freedmen's Bureau must stay in the South to protect the blacks and that the recent state elections could not be accepted as valid. If civil rights were not guaranteed for all citizens, then democracy in the South would never be born. It had been a disastrous mistake for President Johnson to restore the ex-Confederates to power.

The report stated that

> looking still further at the evidence taken by your Committee, it is found to be clearly shown by witnesses of the highest character and having the best means of observations, that the Freedmen's Bureau, instituted for the relief and protection of freedmen and refugees, is almost universally opposed by the mass of the population and exists in an efficient condition only under military protection, while the Union men of the south are earnest in its defense, declaring with one voice that without its protection the colored people would not be permitted to labor at fair prices, and could hardly live in safety. They also testify that without the protection of United States troops, Union men, whether of northern or southern origin would be obliged to abandon their homes. The feeling in many portions of the country towards emancipated slaves, especially among the uneducated and ignorant, is one of vindictive and malicious hatred. This deep-seated prejudice against color is assiduously cultivated by the public journals and leads to acts of cruelty, oppression and murder, which the local authorities are at no pains to prevent or punish."[6]

In addition, the Joint Committee reported what finally became the Fourteenth Amendment to Congress. It became the committee's most lasting achievement.

Congressional Plan for Reconstruction

In the fall elections of 1866, Northern voters showed that they opposed Johnson's policy. They sent still more Radical Republicans to Congress, thus providing the votes to put through the Radicals' own program for Reconstruction.

The new Congress began by extending the life of the Bureau of Refugees, Freedmen and Abandoned Lands (called the Freedmen's Bureau) and bypassing a Civil Rights Bill — both over President Johnson's veto. Then, cementing civil rights into the Constitution itself, Congress adopted the Fourteenth Amendment. It declared that blacks were citizens entitled to equal treatment before the law. This action affected the whole country, for there were still several Northern states that denied blacks the right to vote.

The Congress divided the South into five districts, placing them under military rule to guarantee peace and security. Then it ordered the South to hold elections again.

It took the vote away from many rebel whites and allowed blacks to vote and hold office. The newly elected black and white officials were to write new state constitutions that would be truly democratic. For the first time, black men elected to public office worked with white men to make the laws of the new South. While most blacks had been illiterate slaves, some had been born free and were well educated. Many were artisans, teachers, preachers, barbers, and waiters. They were elected to almost every kind of office in city, county, and state governments.

Mayors, sheriffs, policemen, county clerks, treasurers, supervisors, school superintendents, and justices of the peace were some of the local positions held by blacks during Reconstruction. Mississippi had twelve black sheriffs at one time. At the state level, blacks became not only legislators but also held such posts as speaker of the house, lieutenant-governor, secretary of state, treasurer and Supreme Court justice.

Twenty-two black men were elected to the U.S. Congress in the 19th century, usually after serving in their state constitutional conventions or state legislatures. They were elected by districts in which black voters had the power to insist on a share of federal offices. Thirteen had been slaves and nine had been born free. Two were United States senators: Hiram R. Revels and Blanche K. Bruce of Mississippi. The others served in the House of Representatives, most for only one or two terms, two for five terms. South Carolina, with the largest and most politically active black population, sent six men to Congress. But nine of the fifteen ex-slave states elected no black congressmen at all during Reconstruction. Nor was any black elected to Congress from any Northern state.

Most of the African Americans had served in state legislatures or had been state or local officials before going to Congress so they were not without parliamentary experience. Their education was better than other politicians of their day.[7] They took their positions seriously and their voting records showed that they were not only interested in civil rights for blacks but also in all of the leading issues of the times. Few became involved in the scandals of graft and corruption that swept the country in those years. The Republican leader James G. Blaine said of them, "They were as a rule studious, earnest, ambitious men, whose public conduct — as illustrated by Mr. Revels and Mr. Bruce in the Senate, and Mr. Rapier, Mr. Lynch and Mr. Rainey in the House — would be honorable to any race."[8]

An analysis of the twenty black congressmen and the two United States senators who were elected during the 19th century shows that ten of them were men with some college education and that the others had by self-instruction acquired varying levels of education.[9] The early black officeholders were made the objects of scorn, ridicule and hatred.[10] White Southerners rationalized their abusive behavior by acting as they always had when white supremacy was the law of the land. To Southern whites, black suffrage seemed an intolerable punishment for losing the war. Their dismay at what happened is illustrated by the following quotation, which is typical of any number of contemporary accounts: "The maddest, most unscrupulous and infamous revolution in history has switched the power from the hands of the race which settled the country ... and transferred it to its former slaves, an ignorant and feeble race."[11]

Congress shut the blacks out of the major committees where the most important legislative work was done. Still, black congressmen spoke up for the needs of their people and fought for civil rights and aid to education. It should be stressed that blacks never dominated the South in Reconstruction, not even in South Carolina, Louisiana and Mississippi — the three states where they had majority populations. Inexplicably, they did not seek revenge for the wrongs done them in slavery but cooperated willingly with whites who were their fellow Republicans.

The whites in that party were of two groups. One group was the Northerners who recently came to live in the South: Union Army veterans, mostly, who were trying to make a living there. The Democrats labeled them "carpetbaggers," supposedly bad men trying to take advantage of the freedmen to gain power and wealth. They aroused hostility because they upheld the equal civil and political rights of the blacks.

"Scalawags" was what the Democrats called the other group they hated: white Southerners willing to work with blacks. A popular definition ran as follows: "A scalawag is a white man who thinks that he is no better than a Negro and in so thinking makes a correct appraisal of himself." "Scalawag" was a contemporary term for shabby, verminous cattle. "Therefore," wrote a Southern news article, "there is a manifest fitness in calling the native southerner, of white complexion, who adopts the politics of the Radical party, a Scalawag."[12] Such men were seen as traitors not only to their region, but to the white men as well. Many had opposed secession. Now they aimed to create a better kind of life than the old rulers had permitted them.

Controlling the vote throughout the Southern states, the Republicans struggled to build a more equitable Reconstruction. They scrapped the Black Codes. They opened both the ballot box and the jury box to blacks and to thousands of whites who had been barred for lack of property qualification. They reorganized the courts and pledged equal treatment for blacks and whites before the law. Under their regimes, new roads, hospitals and schools were built. Taxation was established on a progressive basis and an amount of money was raised to pay for social services that the South had never known before. Orphanages, homes for the aged, and insane asylums were opened.

The most vital change was the creation of the South's first public school systems. The ex-slaves eagerly welcomed the schools that were opened by the Freedmen's Bureau. Northern missionary societies sent thousands of teachers, books, slates, pencils and paper to the freed territories even during the war. Most of the teachers — white and black — came from the North. The poor whites were often included in these early schools. Under the Bureau, education expanded rapidly with day and night schools, Sunday schools, and job training schools and colleges. In five years, the Bureau built some 4,000 schools staffed by 10,000 teachers. In one of the most successful mass educational efforts ever, a quarter of a million blacks were able to begin their formal education.

It is against this background that the heroes of the Reconstruction emerged and made their mark. In the post–Civil War world of uncertainty, excitement and revolutionary change, these people struggled to fulfill the lofty American dream. Even in the context of our current American society, it is almost impossible to realize the tremendous difficulties that they had to overcome.

Seven of these heroes were born slaves whose chances for freedom and success at birth were nil. They lived through hell, survived, and thrived. In the lives of each of these people, there is something so wonderful, so moving, so human that we can only feel enriched for learning about their achievements. Ultimately, white society's prejudice and violence overwhelmed them and their very existence.

2

Adelbert Ames (1835–1933): Medal of Honor Winner, General, Senator, Governor

On November 7, 1991, the *New York Times* reported that "Kirk Fordice became the first Republican Governor [to be elected in Mississippi] since a carpetbagger, Adelbert Ames, presided in the statehouse during Reconstruction more than 110 years ago." That brief reference to Adelbert Ames demeans and obscures the dramatic story of a young man from the North who fought through "the war to save the Union" and to abolish the evils of slavery in the United States of America.

Adelbert Ames became the most prominent Republican in Mississippi during the Reconstruction period, having been sent there by President Andrew Johnson on military duty. Later, appointed military governor by President Ulysses S. Grant, he was influential in efforts to have the state readmitted to the Union. He was subsequently elected U.S. senator and governor of Mississippi and served through the disputed presidential election of Rutherford B. Hayes at the end of the Reconstruction period. His life story should be remembered, memorialized and celebrated.

Adelbert Ames was born in Rockland, Maine, on October 31, 1835, and was the son of a sea captain. He attended public schools and was admitted to the West Point Military Academy, whose superintendent was Robert E. Lee of Virginia. Ames graduated West Point in 1861, fifth in his class, and was immediately commissioned as first lieutenant as the Civil War commenced.[1] Ames's first battle experience began on July 16, 1861, when Union forces left Washington D.C. to attack the Confederates at the Battle of Bull Run. In heavy fighting, Ames was severely wounded by a bullet in his thigh. His fearless gallantry was described by his superior who wrote in his report: "In addition, I deem it my duty to add that Lieutenant Ames was wounded so as to be unable to ride a horse at almost the first fire; yet he sat by his command directing the fire; being helped on and off the caisson during the different changes of front or position, refusing to leave the field until he became too weak to sit up."[2]

The Congressional Medal of Honor was awarded to Ames for his heroism on the field of battle. When he recovered, Ames commanded the Battery A during the entire Virginia Peninsula Campaign and was promoted to brevet lieutenant-colonel for gallant and meritorious services at the Battle of Malvern Hill, Virginia. Ames's record for gallantry and skill at the battles of Chickahominy, Gaines' Mill and Malvern Hill led to a new assignment which took him back to his native state of Maine. By the order of General McClellan, Ames accepted command of the 20th Regiment of Maine Volunteers. One month later, he led the newly recruited 20th Maine into the field of action at Antietam. In drilling his troops, Colonel Ames earned the reputation of being a stern disciplinarian. When he first saw the 20th Maine, the military posture and bearing of his men was so poor that he barked, "This is a hell of a regiment," and one man slouched so badly in ranks that Colonel Ames roared at him, "For God's sake, draw up your bowels!"[3]

Ames's capacity and devotion to duty gained him the confidence not only of his regiment but also that of his superior officers. An estimate of the respect held for him by the officers under whom he served was expressed by Major-General Joseph Hooker to Vice President Hannibal Hamlin: "I know of no officer of more promise, and should he be promoted, I feel no doubt but he will reflect great credit upon himself and his State." Brigadier General H. G. Berry also recommended Ames for promotion: "He has the benefit of an excellent military education, is brave, intelligent, intrepid and devoted — and is also an excellent disciplinarian." Unlike the stereotype of the typical professional soldier, Ames rarely smoked, seldom used profanity and drank very little. He was as close to Sir Galahad as was to be found in the Union Army.[4] Ames fought at Antietam, Fredericksburg and Gettysburg. He took part in the siege of Charleston, the attack on Petersburg, and the capture of Fort Fisher. During these battles, he was promoted to brigadier general of volunteers, and, for gallantry in action, was finally breveted as a major general.

When the war was over, Ames considered whether to remain in the regular army at reduced rank or seek better opportunities in civilian life. For about a year he stayed in uniform and served with the occupation forces in South Carolina. He wrote to his parents, "I am still at my duties which consist of little more than aiding the agents of the Treasury Department and the Freedmen's Bureau in trying white men for killing Negroes, of which work we have more than we can do well."[5] Ames liked the South Carolina winter weather but couldn't get used to the unfriendliness of the native whites. "Fire still burns in the hearts of the people," he wrote, "and our star spangled banner or our country's uniform are only needed to fan the flames into wrath."

Ames considered joining his father's flour-milling business in Minnesota or studying law. Instead, in the summer of 1867, he took a leave of absence and made a tour of Europe. When he returned, he was assigned to duty in Mississippi where he sympathized with the freedmen for the "barbarous treatment they were receiving at the hands of some of their white neighbors." He presided over a military commission to try a gang of whites who had killed some black men, burned their houses, and driven their families away. Such gangs continued to threaten, beat and murder black leaders to keep them from exercising their recently acquired political rights, while state and local officials condoned and even incited the outrages.[6]

Soon after his return to Mississippi, Ames's career choices were settled by his appointment as provisional governor of the state. Ames was only thirty-three years old. His order, dated June 15, 1868, instructed him to replace Benjamin G. Humphreys, a sixty-year-old ex–Confederate brigadier-general, whom the white voters had elected governor under the Johnson plan of restoration in 1865. Ames's orders came from General Irwin McDowell who was in charge of the military district including Mississippi. McDowell believed that Humphreys was sabotaging the congressional Reconstruction program.[7] The military regime in Mississippi combated crime, initiated action to protect the fundamental rights of blacks, intervened in planter-labor disputes, demonstrated a concern for the health and education of freedmen and set in motion the plan of political reconstruction devised by Congress.

Adelbert Ames (1835–1933) was a native of Maine, a graduate of West Point and a Medal of Honor Winner. Ames was a Union general, military governor of Mississippi, U.S. senator, and elected governor of Mississippi. He later made a fortune in Minnesota and Massachusetts as a businessman and lived to be ninety-eight years old. (©Medford Historical Society Collection/Corbis)

Departing from the military's usual nonpartisan stance, General Ames cast his lot with the Republican Party and assisted it in gaining political control of the state. Ames viewed with alarm the failure of Mississippi whites to accept the results of the Civil War. Now viewing his purpose in Mississippi as a "Mission with a large M,"[8] Ames explained to General-in-Chief William Tecumseh Sherman the reason for his decision to take sides in the local political struggles. He wrote:

> The contest [in Mississippi] is not between two established parties, as they are elsewhere, but between loyal men and a class of men who are disloyal — a class who are opposed to the principles which are generally conceded should prevail among us. I honestly believe that the success of the men who took this state from the Union will establish a reign of terror which will cause many of the white Union men, especially northern men, to leave the state at once. I am convinced that among the masses the

animosity to the "Yankee," northern or southern, is as strong now as it has ever been — defeat will make their lives and property highly insecure.... The number of murders and outrages taking place in this state at the present time is startling, nor are they the usual events of ordinary times. They are Ku-Klux outrages mainly based on political enmity and hatred.... It is my duty to protect all. It cannot be done by putting this state into the hands of ex-rebels. The war still exists in a very important phase here.[9]

When Ulysses S. Grant assumed the presidency in 1869, he appointed Ames to the command of the fourth military district (Department of Mississippi). Upon the readmission of the state of Mississippi to the Union, Ames was elected as a Republican to the United States Senate where he served from February 1870 until January 1874. He resigned to assume the governorship to which he had been elected in 1873. He served as governor of Mississippi from January 1874 until March 1876.

Adelbert Ames has received short shrift from historians. Only a few weeks before the surrender of Lee to Grant, when members of the Confederate Congress were about to flee, they put forth an inflammatory dispatch urging the South to continue the war and concluding with this warning: "Failure will compel us to drink the cup of humiliation even to the bitter dregs of having the history of our struggle written by New England historians."[10]

Instead, the exact opposite occurred. The history of Reconstruction was written for almost one hundred years after the event by historians sympathetic to the southern aristocracy. It seems inconceivable that the losers of the bloodiest war in history were allowed to wrap their traitorous acts in the description of their so-called noble cause. Ames's daughter wrote, "General Ames became the focus of vituperative attacks in the southern press. He was held personally responsible for the federal government policies so disliked by his opponents. His name stood for the whipping post in Mississippi. Impoverished veterans of secession wove around him fables and myths, used by political enemies to rouse former slave-owners to the white heat of a revolt against the laws of Congress and the Constitutional Amendments."[11]

After the 1875 gubernatorial election, violence escalated so severely that Ames's wife wrote, "At night in the town here, the crack of the pistol or gun is as frequent as the barking of dogs." Some shots were fired at the governor's mansion itself. Undeterred by this, Ames in his first message to the state legislature denounced the legislature as an illegal body, the product of force and fraud.[12] The legislature responded by taking the first steps toward an impeachment of the governor. The trumped-up charges included his frequent absences from the state, enabling criminals to go free, degrading the judiciary, etc. There were no accusations of corruption. Ames wrote, "Nothing is charged beyond political sins. Of course, with them that is a sin which to Republicans is the highest virtue. Their object is to restore the Confederacy and reduce the colored people to a state of serfdom. I am in their way, consequently they impeach me, which done, Jeff Davis will be restored to his former supremacy in this part of his former kingdom."[13] On February 15th, Ames wrote to James G. Blaine, "I think they will go on with my impeachment. A Republican and an ex–Union soldier cannot live in the

South. His position is similar to what would have been that of an abolitionist here in the days of slavery, or a Union soldier at Andersonville during the war. Our late election was a revolution. By it the legislature was gained. This is not a republican form of government."[14]

When Senator John F. Kennedy's *Profiles in Courage* was published in 1956, it was universally praised and won the Pulitzer Prize in history. In the introduction to the first edition, the historian Allan Nevins wrote, "Senator Kennedy treats a special kind of courage: the moral courage of a parliamentary leader who in behalf of principle confronts a chosen Governor by a majority composed of freed slaves and radical Republican sustained and nourished by Federal bayonets."[15]

One of those who was not enthralled by *Profiles in Courage* was Adelbert Ames's daughter, Blanche Ames, who was eighty in 1956. She disputed what she felt were misstatements about her father, and the seeds of her own book took root. When Blanche Ames, who had been called the foremost botanical artist of her time, began to write her first book, this matriarchal great-grandmother with four children and fifteen grandchildren undertook the enormous labor of a historian. In 1962, her 625-page book was finished; it recorded her father's role in the Civil War and Reconstruction, documented with original source material and contemporary photographs, illustrations and maps.[16]

After seven years of tireless and painstaking research, the eighty-six-year-old Blanche Ames had written the definitive biography of a great patriot and leader. This biography of Adelbert Ames is a dramatic and objective narrative of an unfortunately and unjustifiably little-known hero of our country. At the end of her biography, Blanche Ames writes vigorously and clearly about her sharp disagreement with John F. Kennedy. What follows is the heart of her position: "[T]here was first published in 1956 *Profiles in Courage* by Senator (now President) John F. Kennedy. This popular book of historical essays incorporates defamatory references to General Ames and other Massachusetts statesmen. Such untruths about General Ames told by the older writers of the Dunning School of Historians and by their modern followers again calls for refutation."

Profiles in Courage is a dissertation on the moral values of our democracy. In extolling courage (its dominant theme), it relates anecdotes about statesmen and politicians, weaving into these stories incidents that appeal to sectional pride. The chapter with Lucius Q. C. Lamar as the hero seems designed for the approval of southern readers. The author is highly critical of Charles Sumner and Benjamin F. Butler and he condemns Adelbert Ames's part in Reconstruction. In his *Profiles in Courage* Senator Kennedy writes:

> No state suffered more from Carpetbag rule than Mississippi. Adelbert Ames, first Senator and then Governor, was a native of Maine, a son-in-law of the notorious "butcher of New Orleans," Ben Butler. He admitted before a Congressional Committee that only his election to the Senate prompted him to take up his residence in Mississippi. He was chosen Governor by a majority composed of freed slaves and radical Republicans, sustained and nourished by Federal bayonets. One Cardoza, under indictment for larceny in New York, was placed at the head of the public

schools and two former slaves held the offices of Lieutenant Governor and Secretary of State. Areas of northern Mississippi lay in ruins. Taxes increased to a level fourteen times as high as normal in order to support the extravagance of the Reconstruction Government and heavy state and national war debts.[17]

Blanche Ames wastes no time in striking hard at Senator Kennedy's position. She accused Kennedy of pandering to southern readers who were critical of the civil rights granted to the recently freed slaves during Reconstruction. Blanche Ames called Kennedy's misstatements "pure buncombe," "name-calling," and "defamatory insinuations." Ames criticized Kennedy sharply for giving credence to "the same old myths and opprobrious epithets manufactured by his political opponents."

In his Preface, Kennedy assumed responsibility for "all errors of fact and judgment" and expressed his gratitude to Professor Allen Nevins, "one of the foremost political historians and biographers of our times for kindly consenting to contribute the Foreword and for offering criticisms which in the opinion of the author greatly improved the entire manuscript." Blanche Ames goes on to say that she wrote a letter on June 6, 1956, to John F. Kennedy highlighting his errors and asking him to make corrections in future editions of *Profiles In Courage*. "I asked Senator Kennedy whether he would think it just of historians to seize upon slander and repeat it over and over to defame his own good name, using the epithets of his political critics…. Senator Kennedy replied to me that it was 'not anticipated that *Profiles in Courage* will go through another printing and thus there will be no opportunity to make changes in the text. However,' he added, 'your letter has succeeded in stimulating me to further research with respect to the matters you mention. I hope to be able to pursue these investigations after the adjournment of Congress.'" Since the writing of that letter, *Profiles in Courage* has been reprinted more than thirty times,[18] but no changes in the chapter describing Adelbert Ames have ever been made.

Under the impression that Professors Nevins, Holcombe, Schlesinger and Johnson may have approved of the historical material set forth in the book, Ms. Ames sent them copies of her letter to Senator Kennedy. The reply from Dr. Nevins says in part, "My introduction to this book, written at his request, was in general terms and carried no endorsement of all the details of his admirable volume."[19]

Blanche Ames turned to Kennedy's bibliography to discover where he found authority for his slander of Ames. What she found was reference to Cate's biography *Lucius Q. C. Lamar, Stateman of Recession and Reunion*[20] as "one of the basic reference works which have been essential to my research." In turn Cate cited Lamar's son-in-law, Mayes, as the main source of his material. Blanche Ames comments, "Throughout the preparation of the study, the author has found particularly helpful *Lucius Q. C. Lamar: His Life, Times and Speeches,* a prejudiced and one-sided biography which maligns Ames. After all, Lucius Q. C. Lamar was a political enemy of General Ames, whom Lamar once threatened to lynch."

Blanche Ames then expresses her disappointment with Kennedy's inadequate and faulty research efforts. She wonders how Kennedy could have criticized an officer who fought with outstanding gallantry and courage throughout the entire period of the "War to Save the Union" in a book bearing the title *Profiles in Courage.*

Nearly 150 years after it ended, the Civil War remains a major event in American history and a source of public dispute. No less than in John F. Kennedy's time, the historical memory of the Civil War is highly political and depends on one's view of race in America. Many historians and professors who write about this period are themselves closely associated with one or another of our major political parties and are personally involved in the practical issues of party politics and political campaigns. After all, Horace Greeley's presidential campaign in 1872 for the Democratic Party called for the need to "clasp hands across the bloody chasm" and return political control of the defeated South to its "best men" (i.e., former slaveholders). Thus began the end of the idea of federal intervention on behalf of the recently freed four million former slaves. Blanche Ames's extraordinary seven-year research effort concluded that

> the search for truth has carried us through thousands of actions connected with the life of Adelbert Ames and the thoughts of his contemporaries. With this search has grown the conviction that there is much more at stake in this matter than the correction of blunders made by biased historians.
>
> Behind the concern that members of my family be represented accurately in history has been a strong motivation from other forces — a respect for integrity — and certainly, the conviction that our knowledge and plans for the future of our Country cannot be built on twisted and distorted history. When the sanctity of the oath to speak and to live by the truth is honestly observed, the foundations of our nation will be more secure.[21]

Adelbert Ames lived a long and fruitful life after leaving Mississippi in 1876 to join his father's Minnesota flour-milling business. He acquired textile mills in Lowell, Massachusetts, and patented a number of inventions ranging from flour-mill machinery to propulsion of canal barges to extension ladders for fire engines.[22] He lived to his ninety-eighth year and became "the Last General of the Civil War." Local newspapers announced each birthday, describing him as hale and hearty and straight as an arrow, even up to his ninety-seventh year.

Adelbert Ames is a genuine American hero whose life should be commemorated and celebrated. After his experience in Mississippi, he wrote, "I found when I was Military Governor of Mississippi, that a black code existed there; that Negroes had no rights, and that they were not permitted to exercise the rights of citizenship. I had given them the protection they were entitled to under the laws, and I believed I could render them a great service. I felt that I had a mission to perform in their interest, and I unhesitatingly consented to represent them and unite my fortune with theirs."

3

Samuel Chapman Armstrong (1839–1893): Union Army General and Founder of Hampton Institute

A private school for black students was opened in Hampton, Virginia, on a manual training basis in 1868. It was the Hampton Normal and Agricultural Institute, built on a site purchased by the American Missionary Association (AMA) largely through the efforts of Union General Samuel C. Armstrong. Liberal grants made by the Freedmen's Bureau and donations from northern friends were used to erect a large schoolhouse on a farm of 120 acres. In June 1870, the Institute was granted a charter from the General Assembly of Virginia creating a corporation with the power to choose their own successors and to hold the property without taxation with a deed from the AMA. In 1872, the General Assembly enacted a measure that gave to Hampton Institute one-third of the agricultural college land grant of Virginia, amounting to 100,000 acres. This property was later sold for $95,000, which was used to purchase the Wood Farm of 185 acres and to invest the balance.[1]

The founding of the Hampton Institute was a consequence of the dilemma in which the AMA found itself in 1865. Following the Civil War there were four million freedmen in need of education. The need for teachers far surpassed the resources of the AMA and other missionary societies. John W. Alvord of the Freedmen's Bureau reported that violent opposition to freedmen's education by barbaric white rebels endangered the lives of missionary teachers. In Virginia, as elsewhere throughout the South, schoolhouses were being burned and "nigger" teachers were being driven out of town.[2] A Norfolk paper proclaimed, "The negro schoolmarms are gone, going or to go, and we don't much care which, whereto, or how — whether it be to the more frigid regions of the northern zone; or to a still more torrid climate."[3]

The purpose of the Hampton Institute was described by General Armstrong as follows: "We are here not merely to educate students, but to make men and women out of individuals belonging to the down-trodden and despised races; to make of them

20

not accomplished scholars, but to build up character and manhood; to fit the best among them to become teachers, and apply the best educational methods, for the work is a rounded one, touching the whole circle of life and demanding the best energies of those who take it up."[4]

Hampton's enrollment gradually grew from 15 in 1868 to 323 in 1878 and 354 in 1880, of whom 68 were Indians.[5] It was estimated that, by 1880, 353 graduate teachers, both men and women, had taught between 15,000 and 20,000 children. The majority taught in country schools that paid them $25 to $30 a month, for five or six months a year.[6]

In 1879, a British visitor, George Campbell, described the progress at Hampton Institute:

> I principally came here to see the Hampton Agricultural Institute for blacks. I went over it under the guidance of General Armstrong, who has charge of it, and has made it what it is. It is not quite an Agricultural Institute, for it is more used to turn out schoolmasters than anything else. The justification for teaching them agriculture is that, as the schools are commonly open part of the year only, there is every opportunity for the practice of improved agriculture during the remainder of the year. Several trades are also taught. I believe that this is the only place in the Southern States where black printers are educated. The institution is primarily supported by funds subscribed in the North.... It is not a free school, not being looked upon as charitable. The students are expected to pay moderate fees, and by their work to earn something towards their own living. Besides the Negro students there are a good many Indians, sent by the United States government. They are Indians from the Western tribes; and it is intended that, after being civilized and educated, they are to go back, and to improve their countrymen. I was much interested in these Indians. They are not red, but rather yellow, and not all unlike some of the Indo-Chinese tribes to the east of Bengal. I had a good deal of talk with General Armstrong about the Negroes and about Southern politics. He is the son of a missionary who spent many years in the Sandwich Islands, but was a distinguished Federal soldier in the war. He thinks that the blacks are certainly inferior to the whites in intellect, but they are improvable. The Indians are decidedly stronger in intellect, but more difficult to manage.

Campbell concluded realistically that "considering the troubles and the ups and downs they have gone through, it is, I think, wonderful how beneficial this education has been to them, and how much these people, so lately in the most debased condition of slavery, have acquired independent ideas, and, far from lapsing into anarchy, have become citizens with ideas of law and property and order. The white serfs of European countries took hundreds of years to rise to the level which the Negroes have attained in a dozen."[7]

During the Civil War, it was in Hampton, Virginia, that the concept of "contraband of war" to describe fugitive slaves was created by Union General Benjamin Butler. This concept turned southerners' insistence that slaves were chattel property upon its head. Under wartime powers, Butler had the authority to seize property and deny its use to the enemy. It was said that Lincoln was somewhat uneasy over the "contraband" theory but didn't countermand it.[8] As the state of Virginia seceded from the Union in 1861, the Union Army decided that Fortress Monroe would be held and the rebels decided that Hampton could not be defended. While the white residents fled to the Confederate lines, hundreds of black slaves, refusing to believe their masters' stories of Yankee cannibalism, crossed the causeway to Fortress Monroe.

Out of the calamities and horrors of the Civil War came the major issue of was what was to be the fate of the emancipated Negro. Jefferson had believed that they must be sent back to Africa. Even Lincoln looked into this possibility but colonization proved to be impossible. The freedmen themselves refused to be transported en masse to Africa. What's more, had it been feasible, it would have stripped the United States of an essential working force. The South's basic assumption was that the Negro was intrinsically inferior and, therefore, must be kept subordinate to the white man. The North, in its congressional reconstruction, assumed that the Negro was equal to the white man. There was a third view of the matter: that the freedmen were at an inferior stage of development. It was this view that guided General Samuel Armstrong in conceiving, creating and operating the Hampton Normal and Agricultural Institute.

Samuel C. Armstrong was born on January 30, 1839, on the island of Maui in the Hawaiian islands to missionary parents Richard and Clarissa Armstrong.[9] His father was raised in central Pennsylvania of Scotch-Irish background. He graduated from Princeton Theological Seminary and decided on missionary work. He met and married Clarissa Chapman who was a graduate of Westfield, Massachusetts, Normal School. Richard, while delicate in health, was passionate and persuasive. He convinced Clarissa to join him in his missionary work. On their difficult trip to Hawaii on the brig *Thaddeus* they stopped for repairs in Rio de Janeiro. Clarissa later wrote:

> How delightful it was! The green grass, the fresh fruits! It was indeed paradise; but the trail of the serpent was there. On an open space I saw a long trail of black men, miserably clad, chained together, while besides them were others with great bags of coffee on their heads, chanting a mournful lay. From that day my sympathies went out to the poor slaves everywhere, but little did I think I should live to rear a son who should lead the freedmen to victory in the great contest which should come in future years.[10]

The Armstrongs were ultimately sent to Maui where they spent seven happy years. Edith Talbot (Samuel's wife) wrote that her father-in-law fulfilled his administrative and medical responsibilities by caring for 25,000 natives and by overseeing schools for 1,700 children. Because of him, the first sugar plantations and sawmills on Maui were started. He instructed the natives in the need for diversified crops and in the methods of tilling the land. Samuel later wrote about his father's work, remembering how his father used to tell him about the two churches he had built:

He planned and superintended the whole work without any carpenter. The timbers of the roof were hewn far up on the mountains, brought down on the backs of natives, and placed on the walls of broken stone laid in mortar made from coral brought up from the sea by native divers. Once, when a storm destroyed the work of months, the people, led by their chief, went willingly to the mountains and began again. Although my father nearly broke down here, yet afterward, when in the service of the Government, he spoke of these as the happiest days of his life, for his own hardships were forgotten in remembering how gladly the people heard and, in their weakness, followed like children.[11]

Armstrong's upbringing in Hawaii was idyllic and was best described in a journal he wrote of his vacations from his twelfth through his eighteenth year. At twelve, while on a school-inspecting trip with his father, he wrote,

July 15, 1851. Left for Kan in a canoe. We went to Keala and had a short meeting and then went on to Kaohe where he slept. In the morning we had a look about the country; it was very green. The house where we slept was an excellent native house; it was clean and neat.

July 16th. Father examined some schools. A great many canoes came in. In the afternoon, we started in the canoe for Kapua; we arrived a little before sunset. This place is very rocky. They have some goats here.

July 17th. About three o'clock in the morning we started for Kau on foot. Father was sick, and so he rode an ox; it was very lazy indeed. Our road was rocky, especially the first part. During the latter part we went through a large grove of trees. After a walk of about five and half hours we arrived at a native house, where we had a little rest and then started on....

July 22nd. The native schools were examined. They study principally reading and arithmetic. In the afternoon we went up on the hill to slide. We had bananas to slide on. We would balance ourselves and then shoot down the hill like race-horses.

July 24th. We had goat for dinner.

July 25th. We had some presents from the natives of fish, kalo and other things, we had some fun in the evenings running races.

July 27th. Started for the volcano on horseback.

July 28th. The smoke of the volcano soon began to appear; also Mauna Loa. After we had gone several miles we came to the pahoehoe, which is lava. We could distinguish the road for some way, but at last it got lost. A native came up and asked to be our guide. He took us away down in the woods and then up again. After a while we came in sight of the volcano; it looked awful. We went on to the house and slept.

July 30th. We went down about noon and visited the volcano. There was not any fire. We got some strawberries.

Armstrong's childhood was a balance between bodily exercise and improvement of mind. His wife said that "he never forgot the fun of being a boy; never, in fact, quite got over being a boy."[12] As Armstrong grew older, he studied the native Hawaiian character, which he called emotional, genial and unstable. He observed the success of the missionaries in the wholesale conversions to Christianity. After two years at Oahu College in Hawaii, Armstrong came to America in keeping with his father's dying wish and studied at Williams College where his mentor and spiritual father was President Mark Hopkins. A college classmate, Dr. John H. Denison, described Armstrong as "a sort of cataclysm of health, like other cyclones from the South Seas.... An islander with the high courage and jollity of the tar.... Extraordinary in his training and versatility, able to manage a boat in a storm, teach a school, edit a newspaper, assist in carrying on a government, take up a mechanical industry at will, understand the natives, sympathize with the missionaries, talk with profound theorists, recite well in Greek or mathematics, conduct an advanced class in geometry and make no end of fun for little children."[13]

Denison said that Armstrong was "a trifle above middle height, broad-shouldered, with a large, well-poised head, forehead high and wide, deep-set flashing eyes, a long mane of light-brown hair, his face very brown and sailorlike. He bore his head high and carried about an air of insolent good health.... Intellectually he was a leader. Spiritually he was religious, with a deep reverence for his father's life and work.... Sometimes he seemed to have little respect for the spiritual; he shocked people by his levity and irreverence.... Other men were original in thought; he was original in character; but above all things there was an immediacy of nature."[14]

At the start of the Civil War, Samuel Armstrong, as a Hawaiian, did not feel the call of patriotism. He continued his senior year at Williams College until graduation.

Samuel Chapman Armstrong (1839–1893), Union Army general, superintendent of schools in the Freedmen's Bureau, and founder of the Hampton Institute in Virginia. (©Medford Historical Society Collection/Corbis)

His judgment of Negro slavery was apparently softened by his recollection of the gentle paternalism that he had witnessed among the natives of the Pacific where the harsher methods of the American slavery system were unknown.

In 1862, Armstrong decided to join the Union Army, recruited one hundred men in Troy, New York, and was ultimately sworn in as a captain. After fighting at Harpers Ferry, Virginia, Armstrong's One Hundred and Twenty-fifth Regiment was captured by Confederate General Stonewall Jackson. Soon after, they were paroled and dispatched to a parole camp near Lake Michigan. Later, his regiment fought with General Burnside at the battle of Fredericksburg and General Hooker at the battle of Chancellorsville. At Gettysburg, Captain Armstrong wrote immediately after the battle,

On the second of July, we were drawn up between two batteries, and sustained a violent cannonade, lying on our faces in an orchard — that is, most of us. I preferred to take my chances standing and watching the fight. After some time our brigade was marched off to the left center, fell into line, and charged into a valley full of rebels, who were sheltered by a dense growth of underbrush. As we advanced with fixed bayonets and began to fire, they yelled out from the trees, "Do not fire on your own men." We ceased to fire and the "rebs" who had so deceived us gave us Hail Columbia, and dropped some of our best men. Those fellows were the famous Louisiana Tigers; but we rushed at them with fixed bayonets, drove them out of the bush, and plunged our fire into them as they ran. This was our first fight — my first — and a long curiosity was satisfied, men fell dead all around me; a sergeant who stood behind me in line was killed; and heaps were wounded in the charge. I was pleasantly, though perhaps dangerously situated. I did not allow a man to get ahead of me.[15]

On the following day, Pickett's infamous charge by the Confederate Army was witnessed by Armstrong, who described it in a letter to his mother:

We were ordered to charge the rebel skirmishers; it was a foolish order, a fatal one. I led that charge if any did, jumping on my feet and waving my sword for the men to follow.... The bullets flew like hail over my head, and it was not safe lying down.... Finally the rebels came out of the woods in three long lines several hundred yards apart, with glittering bayonets and battle-flags flying. It was grand to see those lines going up, and I trembled for our cause. I felt no fear, though I never forgot that at any moment I might fall. The responsibility and the high duty assigned to me sustained me, and it was wonderful that my own men did not shoot me, they were so excited. Well, we turned the rebel flank, and no wonder, for we did terrible execution. The first line broke and ran; the second came on and also broke and scattered, though they were brave as lions, and their dead lay close up to their line, and one of their color-bearers fell over one of our field-pieces.... Keep this letter in the family ... it is too egotistical to show.[16]

The Union victory at Gettysburg surely saved the North from further invasion by the Confederate Army. It also gained Armstrong the respect of his men. He again wrote in confidence to his mother about his troops, "At first for months they hated me;... it was because I was strict and paid no respect to their unmilitary and unmanly humors. But finally, especially after Gettysburg, all this changed.... And now I have the utmost confidence at almost every man in the regiment.... I know it and I love them. They have said that they would 'go to the devil' for me." Armstrong's bravery in the face of death and his daring leadership marked him for promotion. The regimental history of the One Hundred and Twenty-fifth says, "District record should go into general history of Captain Armstrong's brave and skillful action at that important point of battle.... Of the five officers who served with Captain Armstrong in his brave action, he was the only survivor."[17]

As a result of his bravery at Gettysburg, Armstrong was promoted to major. In October 1863, after the issuance of the Emancipation Proclamation, Armstrong applied for command in a black regiment and "passed a rigid examination for only men of special fitness were deemed qualified to lead in a service demanding not only intelligence, skill and patience, but unusual daring."[18] Armstrong knew that the Confederate Congress had adopted a joint resolution on May 1, 1863, that stated that "every white person, being a commissioned officer or acting as such, who during the present war shall command Negroes or mulattoes in arms against the Confederate States, or who shall arm, train, organize, or prepare Negroes or mulattoes for military service against the Confederate States, or who shall volunteer aid to Negroes or mulattoes in any military enterprise, attack or conflict in such service, shall be deemed as exciting insurrection, and shall, if captured, be put to death or otherwise punished at the discretion of the Court." Colonel Thomas Higginson stated that "officers who undertook this duty entered it with a rope round our necks and Negroes who served under them were liable to be hung, shot or returned to slavery." In November 1863, Armstrong was appointed lieutenant colonel of the Ninth Regiment of United States Colored Troops in Maryland. His first impression of the colored troops with their playfulness, strong emotion and love of music was a sharp contrast to his impression of the white soldiers. Armstrong was intensely moved one night when his men sang an old church hymn. He wrote his wife that when the men sang, "they look like men of war; all armed and dressed in uniform, they look like men of war. …It fitted the scene and their hearty singing of it sent through me a sensation I shall never forget. It became their battle-hymn. These were the dramatics of war; the dynamics came later."[19] His men needed recreation and regimental pride, which were both provided in athletic competition. Armstrong wrote,

> We officers subscribed money freely and bought an ox, which we roasted whole for the regiment. The day's sports with trials of strength at rope-pulling, the victors always receiving a prize and always being greeted with vociferous cheers. After this they ran races for prizes, and there was some wonderful running. Then they had a greased pole to climb, with $5 on top of it, which afforded rare sport. Next was a chase after greased pigs which had all their hair cut off and had been well oiled. The captor was to have the pig provided he caught him by the tail. A lot of bags had been furnished for a sack-race, which passed off with great success. After dinner the two regiments were drawn up facing each other, about ten rods apart, and the champion runners contested twice for a $5 prize. Also there was a blindfold race. My regiment won all the prizes and had during the day three times as much sport as any other. The men said they never had such a Christmas before. The roast ox was eaten for supper…. I have gotten along finely with my regiment. Have the finest camp in the brigade and the Ninth is acknowledged to lead the rest. The regiment next to us had six weeks the start of us, and today they are not over one week ahead of us in drill and far behind us in everything else. We expect to beat everything around in everything and we are in a fair way to do it.[20]

In March 1864, Armstrong sailed with 1,300 black soldiers for Hilton Head in South Carolina and wrote his mother about his change of heart. "Since entering this branch of the service, I have felt the high duty and sacredness of my position. It is no sacrifice for me to be here; it is rather a glorious opportunity, and I would be nowhere else if I could, and nothing else than an officer of colored troops if I could." That was a long way to come for the young man who had written just fifteen months before, "I have not learned to love the Negro." Most white officers in the Union Army held the conventional anti-black attitude. Only with exposure and experience with blacks as Union soldiers did these racist viewpoints change.

In August 1862 General Benjamin Butler recruited three regiments and two batteries of artillery in New Orleans from New Orleans and reported them as "intelligent, obedient, highly appreciating their position and fully maintaining its dignity."[21]

In November 1862, General Rufus Saxton at Beaufort, South Carolina, organized the First Regiment of South Carolina Volunteers and gave the command to Colonel T.W. Higginson of the Fifty-first Massachusetts Regiment who affirms that his regiment "was unquestionably the first mustered into the service of the United States."

In recalling his own experience with Negro troops, Colonel Thomas Wentworth Higginson wrote, "I have often asked myself why it was that, with this capacity for daring and endurance, they had not kept the land in a perpetual flame of insurrection.... The answer was to be found in the peculiar temperament of the race, in their religious faith and in the habit of patience that centuries had fortified.... They were the most affectionate people among whom I ever lived.... On the other hand, they rarely showed one gleam of revenge."[22]

In January 1863, the First Kansas Colored Regiment was mustered in and on January 26, 1863, the Secretary of War authorized the governor of Massachusetts to raise two Negro Regiments from that state.

Historian Francis Peabody wrote the following about black soldiers:

> The record of these and many later enlistments is one of the miracles of military history. What has appeared to so many observers a hopelessly submissive race, incapable of discipline, and tempted to savagery, provided a body of troops which was not only of unquestioned courage in battle, but self-restrained both in victory and among the more insidious temptations of camp life. There were enrolled in the northern armies 187,000 Negroes, 70,000 of whom were killed and wounded, and these recruits participated in not less than two hundred engagements. "No troops," General Banks reported after the siege of Port Hudson, "could be more determined or more daring." "By arming the Negro," Grant wrote to Lincoln in 1863, "we have added a powerful ally; they will make good soldiers."[23]

On the monument to Robert Gould Shaw in Boston, the following inscription by Harvard President Charles W. Eliot appears: "The Negroes who followed Shaw volunteered when desertion clouded the Union cause, served without pay for eighteen months till given that of white troops, faced threatening enslavement if captured, were brave in action, patient under heavy and dangerous labor, and cheerful amid hardships and privations. They gave to the nations of the world undying proof that Americans of African descent possessed the pride, courage, and devotion of the patriot soldier."[24]

Armstrong's expedition to Hilton Head, South Carolina, was made for the purpose of reinforcing Port Royal, a post which, though surrounded by rebels, had been in the hands of the Union Army since November 1861. Armstrong's longing for action was satisfied in August 1864, when his command was ordered to Petersburg, Virginia, to serve under General Benjamin Butler's Army of the James. Armstrong wrote that "the Union is to me little or nothing; I see no great principle necessarily involved in it. I see only the 4,000,000 slaves, and for and with them I fight."[25] On April 24, 1865, weeks after Lee surrendered, Armstrong fell from his horse and broke the bone of his right forearm. His recovery was incomplete so that his handwriting for the rest of his life was often illegible.

At about the same time, he was promoted as a brevet-brigadier-general of volunteers, and subsequently served in Texas at the head of the Eighth Colored Regiment. In October 1865 he and his men were sent North and discharged. The inactivity of Texas barrack life was in sharp contrast to his Civil War experience of trench fighting. However, on the voyage home to Mobile, Alabama, surrounded by his black soldiers, Armstrong had a life-converting vision. He wrote, "The western sky [is] draped in the most gorgeous cloud tapestry-the ship gliding swiftly through a glossy sea — a brass band discoursed rich music, and it was a scene of life and pleasure on board. The nights were warm and many of us slept on deck, subject, however to the inconvenience of being roused very early when the ship was washed down." It was here that his thoughts turned to his boyhood home and to the Manual Labor School at Hilo on the island of Hawaii where Hawaiian dark-skinned boys were trained in the mechanical arts.

After his discharge, Armstrong went to New York City and then to Washington, D.C., where he applied for a position with the Bureau of Refugees, Freedmen and Abandoned Lands. The Freedmen's Bureau was created by Congress in 1865 in response to the crying needs of the recently freed slaves who were helplessly adrift in the aftermath of the brutal Civil War. The Bureau was headed by General Oliver Otis Howard. In 1889, General Howard described the Bureau:

> The first consideration was how to do the work before us. The plantations were left uncultivated; some were abandoned, all had lost their slaves. People said, "We can't raise cotton with only free labor." Our task was to show them that they could. I started some joint stock companies from the North. Northern capital undertook the work. The result was, more cotton was raised the first year after the war than had been raised in any one year before. Other years were not as successful, but the point was proved and an impulse given to free labor.
>
> Another work we had to do was settle the relations between the former master and ex-slave. Troubles were continually arising. To settle these were established courts made up of one agent of the Freedmen's Bureau, one man selected by the whites and one by the Negroes. These courts settled all such difficulties till finally the courts themselves were transferred to the State and local authorities upon the condition of the reception of Negro testimony.
>
> Then there were land troubles. When the owners abandoned their plantations, the colored people settled on them — lived in their houses and used the land.

Most of the land was given back to the owners by the Government, under our direction and advice. It was often hard on the colored people. I was sorry for them and would have liked sometimes to do differently. Yet I believe it was on the whole better for them. It put them at the bottom of the ladder.

Then we had a hospital department. That was for the old and decrepit men and women and the sick and disabled who could not take care of themselves. We had also a department to establish asylums for the little children whose fathers had been killed in the war or who had strayed from their homes and been lost, as many had.

But the main point we had to attend to was the care of the schools.[26]

General Howard later wrote about his interview of twenty-seven-year-old Samuel Armstrong, "Though already a general, General Armstrong seemed to me very young. His quick motions and nervous energy were apparent then. He spoke rapidly and wanted matters decided if possible on the spot. I was then very favorably impressed with his knowledge and sentiment toward the freedmen and thought he would make a capital sub-commissioner."

Subsequently, Armstrong received a double appointment: as agent of the Freedmen's Bureau over ten counties in Virginia and also superintendent of schools over a large, loosely defined area. Armstrong described his work in a letter to his mother:

June 2, 1866

Dear Mother: I have been on duty in the bureau three months, and a singular experience it has been. Providence seemed to put me in just the place I wanted. The work is very difficult; there are here, congregated in little villages, some 5,000 colored people, crowded, squalid, poor, and idle. It is my work to scatter and renovate them; one in which much is expected, but very limited means are given. I think I have secured the confidence of the people as well as of my superiors, at least so far that I am the only civilian in the whole bureau occupying a position of superintendent, which is a special favor from General Howard.... I am uncertain of the future but still am confident that all will be well.

I am living in the so-called Massenburg House, one of the stateliest of the beautiful village of Hampton, now shorn of its glory — its greenhouse and garden destroyed and its rooms turned into offices and quarters. In the rear of the house is the bureau jail, where I summarily stow away all sorts of people when they are unruly. I have murderers, thieves, liars, and all sorts of disorderly characters — a squad of soldiers under my orders, who make quick work with any troublesome people. I am quite independent and like the position and the work.

I have about a dozen officers under me, though I am a civilian, and a glorious field of labor. I have some thirty-four lady teachers from the North. Some splendid people are helping me.... This Hampton has been the city of refuge of the Negroes throughout the war — here they came from all [over] Virginia to seek freedom, food and a home; hither caravans daily poured in for months with young, old and helpless, and here they built their little cabins and did what they could.

Here were raised several colored regiments, which took the men and left the women helpless and oh, the misery there has been — it can never be told! But the worst is over. The men came not back, since most were killed, disabled or died, and here are their families in my charge; and they are a great care; we issue 18,000 rations a day to those who would die of starvation were it not for this, and keep their children at school, and get them work and prevent injustice. Take us away and the Negroes might as well all be hanged at once.... General Howard told me it was the hardest position to fill he had; there is such ill feeling between whites and blacks, so many paupers, so much idleness, and such an enormous population.... The work is splendid, and if God leads me as He has done, I shall have nothing to fear — all will be well.[27]

Armstrong had not worked for the Freedmen's Bureau for very long when he devised a plan that promised relief for the immediate needs of the unemployed, uneducated and pauperized freedmen. He wrote to many people and organizations in the Boston area, saying, "There is another and most important field for philanthropic effort. It is the building up of industrial schools."[28]

Armstrong believed that putting a veneer of classic education on the plantation Negro would be a useless effort. He said that between a university education and no education was a middle course, which would offer hope for the freedmen. His vision was shaped by his Hawaiian experience and his years of work at the Bureau whose educational department continued to function until 1872. Armstrong worked in this department until the end and emerged a mature man settled in his outlook who had found his lifework. He wrote later about the history of the Hampton Institute:

Close at hand the pioneer settlers of America and the first slaves landed on this continent — here Powatan reigned; here the Indian was first met; here the first Indian child was baptized; here freedom was first given to the slave by General Butler's famous contraband order; in sight of this shore the battle of the Monitor saved the Union and revolutionized naval warfare; here General Grant based the operations of his final campaign. The place was easily accessible by railroad routes to the North and to a population of 2,000,000 of Negroes, the center of great prospective development, and withal a place most healthful and beautiful in situation.[29]

Samuel Armstrong's vision was an industrial school like the Manual Labor School at Hilo, which might be adapted to the needs of the Negro race. His Freedmen's Bureau experience brought him to the "Negro College" developed by the American Missionary Association at Hampton, Virginia. Armstrong described his conception and purpose of the new school: "The thing to be done was clear, to train selected Negro youths who should go out and teach and lead their people, first by example, by getting land and homes, to give them not a dollar that they could earn for themselves; to teach respect for labor, to replace stupid drudgery with skilled hands, and in this way to build up an industrial system for the sake, not only of self-support and intelligent labor, but also for the sake of character." The school opened on April 1, 1868, converting a former hospital barracks into temporary dormitories, employing one teacher and one matron with fifteen students and it was named The Hampton Normal and Agricultural Institute.[30] A few days later, Armstrong wrote to his mother, "Things here look well. My machine has just commenced to run. The anxiety and patient effort it has cost are great, but I am now satisfied with it all.... The buildings I have erected and repaired are insured for $15,000, less than their real value."

Armstrong immediately instituted his plan for combining work and study. The boys worked on the farm; the girls at housework. At the beginning the students worked two days a week and studied the other four.

Armstrong still had duties to perform at the Freedmen's Bureau where he was paid a salary from 1868 until 1872. His work creating the Hampton Institute was unpaid during these years. During the exciting start-up days, he fell in love with Miss Emma Dean Walker of Stockbridge, Massachusetts. Armstrong wrote to his sister in January 1868 that "[he] met a charming young woman there and you will hear more later" and again to his mother: "I am in love, of a truth; have seemed to meet as sweet a fate as ever befell a man. The difficulties of distance are great. She lives in a lovely village not far from Great Barrington. There is no engagement — there may never be — whether I win or lose remains to be seen. This is a family secret, of course." "When I look at her," he writes to his friend Hopkins, "I say, 'Angel'; when I look at myself, I say, 'Ass!'" The pair were married in October 1869 in Stockbridge and immediately relocated to the Old Mansion House on the Wood Farm in Hampton, Virginia. In the following happy nine years the Armstrongs had two children. Emma, while in failing health, gave spiritual sustenance to Samuel. He wrote from one of his frequent trips, "My cup has been richly filled [while] the only bitterness has been added by my own willful folly. You have come to me with such sacred sweetness and happiness as the world has not much of.... You are a daily strength and comfort, and I depend more and more upon you.... There are large blessings given to us and a power given to you to create peace and comfort and rest and make people happy that few possess."

Armstrong's inspiration was the driving force behind the creation and growth of the Hampton Institute. In short order, his enthusiasm and vitality attracted and transformed his students. George Merriam wrote,

> The subject answered to the experiment — those dark-skinned boys and girls came eager to learn. No one had believed in themselves, but they speedily learned self-respect and gained the respect of others. They did what was asked of them, earned most of their support, showed good workmanship and scholarship, were blameless in morals, caught the spirit of the place and went out to carry light into the dark places.... There was a working day of twelve hours, between the class-room, the work-shop, the drill-ground and the field, with rare and brief snatches of recreation. They met the demand with a resource inherited from their ancestors' long years of patient labor. The hard toil was a moral safeguard. The African race is sensuous and co-education might seem perilous. The danger was completely averted by the influence of labor, strenuous and constant, but diversified and interesting. The essentials of character — industry, chastity, truth and honesty, serviceable good will — were the aim and result of the Hampton training; and all ran back to the

homely root that man should be trained to earn intelligently and faithfully his daily bread.[31]

Support for Hampton Institute, through Armstrong's indefatigable efforts, was supported by many including General (later President) James A. Garfield, Dr. Mark Hopkins, the poet John Greenleaf Whittier and other educational and political figures and former abolitionists. One of Hampton's most famous graduates was Booker T. Washington who describes in his autobiography how hard he worked to be admitted to Hampton. Washington wrote, "I have spoken of the impression that was made upon me by the buildings and general appearance of the Hampton Institute, but I have not spoken of that which made the greatest and most lasting impression on me, and that was a great man — the noblest, rarest human being that it has ever been my privilege to meet. I refer to the late General Samuel C. Armstrong."[32]

Through Armstrong's great personal charm and energy, Hampton grew at an extraordinary pace. By 1899–1900, there were nearly 1,000 students of whom 135 were American Indians. By 1878, seventeen young Indians, former prisoners of war, had been brought from St. Petersburg where they had been incarcerated for three years.[33]

Armstrong persuaded Booker T. Washington to return to Hampton to oversee the Indian students in their dormitory, the Wigwam. He discovered that the average Indian felt himself far superior to the whites and immeasurably above blacks. Indians had never submitted to slavery and, in fact, some had owned large numbers of slaves. The Hampton Album introduction goes on to say, "Off the reservations, [Indians] hated to have their long hair cut, to abandon wearing blankets and smoking pipe tobacco. Washington succeeded as house-master, modestly if, ruefully adding as postscript: …no white American ever thinks that any other race is wholly civilized until he wears the white man's clothes, eats the white man's food, speaks the white man's language and professes the white man's religion."[34]

The Jubilee Singers at Fisk University had demonstrated the appeal of Negro spirituals to the American and European public. From 1873, the Hampton Student Singers and later the Hampton Quartet appeared all over the country, earning money for the Hampton building fund. These singers apparently took their schoolbooks with them on their tours and on their return finished their school courses with credit. Almost without exception they made excellent records after school life was done. The Hampton Singers gave about five hundred concerts and traveled thousands of miles through eighteen states and Canada. During their first year of travel they earned $10,000 as their net proceeds.

From these proceeds and various individual gifts, General Armstrong was spurred to further expansion in the curriculum to include shoemaking, carpentry, painting and blacksmithing. Building after building was added.

On one occasion, when the cornerstones of two buildings were to be laid by Bishop Potter of New York a sudden rainshower fell and someone said, "Had we not better wait? It will be soon over." "Oh, no," answered the bishop. "If I wait, General Armstrong will have another cornerstone ready!"[35]

Samuel Armstrong gave regular talks on Sunday nights. One of them sums up his philosophy and is therefore worth quoting:

> Spend your life in doing what you can do well. If you can teach, teach. If you can't teach, but can cook well, do that. If a man can black boots better than anything else, what had he better do? "Black boots!" Yes, and if a girl can make an excellent nurse, and do that better than anything else, what had she better do? "Nurse." Yes, she can do great good that way in taking care of the sick and suffering. Some of our girls have done great good already in that way. Do what you can do well and people will respect it and respect you. That is what the world wants of everyone. It is a great thing in life to find out what you can do well. If a man can't do anything well, what's the matter with him? A lazy man can't do anything well and no one wants him 'round. God didn't make the world for lazy people.... Go out from here to fight against sin. Fight the devil. Fight against badness, evil, and ignorance, disease, bad cooking. Help your people in teaching, in care of the sick, in improving land, in making better homes. Do what you can do well, and do it as well as you can.[36]

On May 11, 1893, Samuel C. Armstrong died. After his death, a memorandum was found among his private papers, which he wrote in 1890: "I wish to be buried in the school graveyard, among the students, where one of them would have been put had he died next. I wish no monument or fuss whatever over my grave; only a simple headstone-no text or sentiment inscribed, only my name and date. I wish the simplest funeral service, without sermon or attempt at oratory — a soldier's funeral."[37]

4

Blanche Kelso Bruce (1841–1898): First African American to Serve a Full Term in the U.S. Senate

Incredible as it may sound to a reader at the beginning of the 21st century, the Commonwealth of Mississippi was for six years ably represented from 1875 to 1881 by a distinguished African American senator, the Honorable Blanche K. Bruce. So inspiring is the story of Bruce's efforts in the fulfillment of the hard-to-achieve American dream that it ought not to be permitted to remain in obscurity. This brief biography is an attempt to recount some of the achievements of this statesman whose public career looms up as a monument to the African American's self-confidence, resolution and persistence in the face of overwhelming odds.

Senator Bruce's career in the upper chamber of Congress began on March 5, 1875, at the special session of the 44th Congress, called by President Grant. His name appears in the congressional record of that session as "Branch" K. Bruce, Floreyville, Mississippi.[1] Bruce was the first African American ever elected to a full six-year term. Bruce was born a slave.

Prior to his election to the United States Senate, Bruce had held positions of trust and honor in the state of Mississippi. He had been sheriff, tax collector, commissioner of the levees board and Bolivar County Superintendent of Education. Moreover, he had served as sergeant-at-arms of the first State Senate after the Reconstruction period and commissioner of elections in a county that was reputed to be the most lawless in the state. In all these positions, Senator Bruce displayed such integrity of purpose, sagacious statesmanship and tireless industry that his election to the U.S. Senate by the Mississippi state legislature followed as a logical and merited promotion.[2]

Senator Bruce's "maiden speech" in the Senate was delivered shortly after he took his seat in the special session. The speech was a vigorous protest against the proposed removal of troops from the South, Mississippi in particular, where the military authorities were still in control.

The speech made a profound impression on the Senate and clearly indicated the manly stand that Senator Bruce was preparing to take against the injustices practiced against black citizens in both the North and South.[3]

When the 44th Congress convened for its first regular session on Monday, December 6, 1975, the senior senator from Mississippi, James L. Alcorn, refused to follow tradition. It was presumed that Senator Alcorn, in accordance with the custom on such occasions, as senior senator would escort his colleague to the desk of the president of the Senate to be sworn in. This Senator Alcorn refused to do. When Mr. Bruce's name was called, Senator Alcorn did not move; he remained in his seat, apparently giving his attention to his private correspondence. Mr. Bruce, somewhat nervous and slightly unsure, started to the president's desk unattended. Senator Roscoe Conkling, of New York, who was sitting nearby, immediately rose and extended his arm to Mr. Bruce and escorted him to the president's desk, standing by the new senator's side until the oath had been administered, and then tendering him his hearty congratulations, in which all the other Republican senators, except Senator Alcorn, subsequently joined.[4] This was the beginning of a lifelong friendship with Conkling, who helped Bruce draw some good Senate committee assignments. Bruce later named his only son, born in 1879, for the New York senator. (Roscoe Conkling Bruce became an educator, orator, debater and scholar.) Early in the session, Senator Bruce presented a petition of the Sons of Temperance of the District of Columbia, proposing legislation for the prohibition of the importation of alcoholic liquors from abroad and that total abstinence be made a condition of the civil, military, and naval service. Later he introduced a bill "to provide for the payment of bounties, etc., to colored soldiers and sailors and their heirs."

His first important opportunity for valuable service came during the discussion of the resolution to admit former acting Governor P. B. S. Pinchback, an African American, as a senator from Louisiana. The resolution had been presented on March 5, 1875, at the special session of the Senate: "That P. B. S. Pinchback be admitted as a Senator from the State of Louisiana for the term of six years, beginning with the fourth of March 1873." Senator Bruce delivered the following address:

> When I entered upon my duties here as Senator from Mississippi, the question ceased to be novel, and had already been elaborately and exhaustively discussed. So far as opportunity has permitted me to do so, I have dispassionately examined the question in the light of the discussion, and I venture my views now with the diffidence inspired by my limited experience in the consideration of such questions and by a just appreciation of the learning and ability of the gentlemen who have already attempted to elucidate and determine this case.
>
> I believe, Mr. President, whatever seeming informalities may attach to the manner in which the will of the people was ascertained, Mr. Pinchback is the representative of a majority of the legal voters of Louisiana, and is entitled to a seat in the Senate....
>
> This view of the question is submitted not as determining the contest, but as an offset to the allegation that Mr. Pinchback does not fairly represent the popular will of the State, and as a presumption in favor of the legal title of the assembly that elected him.

The State government elected in 1872, and permanently inaugurated in January 1873, in the face of contest and opposition, obtained for its authority the recognition of the inferior and supreme courts of the State. When organized violence threatened its existence and the United States government was appealed to for troops to sustain it, the national Executive, in pursuance of his constitutional authority and duty, responded to the demand made for help, prefacing said action by an authoritative declaration, made through the Attorney General, addressed to Lieutenant-Governor Pinchback, then Acting Governor, of date of December 12, 1872, that said Pinchback was recognized as the lawful executive of Louisiana, and the body assembled at Mechanics' Institute as the lawful Legislature of the State"; and similar recognition of his successors was subsequently given. When in September 1874, an attempt was made to overthrow the government, the President again interposed with the Army and Navy for its protection and the maintenance of its authority....

Blanche Kelso Bruce (1841–1898), the first American to serve a full term in the U.S. Senate. Born in slavery, he attended Oberlin College; taught school; became a prosperous landowner and planter; was elected tax assessor, sheriff and tax collector in Bolivar County, Mississippi; and served with distinction as United States senator from 1875 to 1881. (©Corbis)

Now, sir, shall we admit by our action on this case that for three years the State of Louisiana has not had a lawful Legislature; that its laws have been made by an unauthorized mob; that the President of the United States actively, and Congress, by non-action at least, have sustained and perpetuated, this abnormal, illegal, wrongful condition of things, thereby justifying and provoking the indignant and violent protests of one portion of the people of that State, and inviting them to renewed and continued agitation and violence? Such action by us would be unjust to the claimant, a great wrong to the people who sent him here, and cruel even to that class who have awaited an opportunity to bring to their support the overwhelming moral power of the nation in the pursuit of their illusion — which has so nearly ruined the future of that fair State — a government based upon the prejudices of caste....

Under these circumstances, holding the question in abeyance is, in my judgment, an unconstitutional deprivation of the right of the State, and a provocation to popular disquietude; and in the interest of good-will and good government, the most judicious and consistent course is to admit the claimant to his seat.

I desire, Mr. President, to make a personal reference to the claimant, I would not attempt one or deem one proper were it not that his personal character has been assailed.

> As a father, I know him to be affectionate; as a husband, the idol of a pleasant home and cheerful fireside; as a citizen, loyal, brave and true. And in his character and success we behold an admirable illustration of the excellence of our republican institutions.[5]

This speech is an honest, frank, and convincing enunciation of republican truths. It is an unselfish and sober appeal for justice for another African American and may well pass for a masterpiece of logical thought and dynamic expression. It is an unfortunate fact that Pinchback, for all his great capabilities, was never seated in the Congress as representative or senator from Louisiana.

Long before Senator Bruce took his Senate seat, rioting in Mississippi had become prevalent with blatant acts of terrorism against blacks. In fact, his own county, Bolivar, was perhaps the only one in the state that had not furnished a stage for bitter race feuds. Even this county narrowly averted a calamity. Back in the early seventies, a report gained currency that in a few days there was to be a "shooting up" in Bolivar. Guns and ammunition were being stored and the outlook became menacing. The riot, however, was averted because Senator Bruce went personally to the controlling citizens and succeeded in arousing a strong sentiment against the threatening disorder.

In other sections of the state, violent brutality became so prevalent, especially on election days against black voters, that the returns of the elections were open to serious doubt. The United States Senate was forced to take cognizance of this condition. On Friday, March 31, 1876, a resolution was introduced appointing a committee "to investigate the late election in Mississippi." Senator Bruce embraced this opportunity to give a clear exposition of the condition of affairs in his state. His speech on this occasion reveals him as a broad-minded and courageous statesman free from the curse of narrow dogma. He began by announcing the basic principles of democracy:

> The conduct of the late election in Mississippi affected not merely the fortunes of the partisans — as the same were necessarily involved in the defeat or success of the respective parties to the contest — but put in question and jeopardy the sacred rights of the citizens; and the investigation contemplated in the pending resolution has for its object not the determination of the question whether the offices shall be held and the public affairs of the State be administered by Democrats or Republicans, but the higher and more important end, the protection in all their purity and significance of the political rights of the people and the free institutions of the country.[6]

He continued by referring to the evidence that proved that the black voters of Mississippi in the "late election" had not had an actual opportunity to cast their votes:

> The evidence in hand and accessible will show beyond peradventure that in many parts of the State corrupt and violent influences were brought to bear upon the registrars of voters, thus materially affecting the character of the voting or poll lists; upon the inspectors of election, prejudicially and unfairly, thereby changing the number of votes cast; and finally threats and violence were practiced directly upon the masses of voters in such measure and strength as to produce grave apprehensions for personal safety and as to determine them from the exercise of their political franchises.

It was in this speech that Senator Bruce replied to the erstwhile criticism that African Americans were cowards because they endured every kind of indignity without retaliating. Taking the prevalent view of progressive thought of the nineteenth century, he spoke as follows:

> It will not accord with the laws of nature of history to brand colored people a race of cowards. On more than one historic field, beginning in 1776 and coming down to the centennial year of the Republic, they have attested in blood their courage as well as a love of liberty. I ask Senators to believe that no consideration of fear or personal danger has kept us quiet and forbearing under the provocations and wrongs that have so sorely tried our souls. But feeling kindly towards our white fellow-citizens, appreciating the good purposes and offices of the better classes, and above all, abhorring war of races, we determined to wait until such time as an appeal to the good senses and justice of the American people could be made.[7]

This pronouncement of Senator Bruce exalting the virtue of patience, even in the face of grave injustices, was preeminently representative of the most highly educated blacks of the century in which Senator Bruce lived and must be interpreted in terms of philosophy of his day.

Perhaps the part of Senator Bruce's speech that has given most impetus to similar modern expression is contained in the following excerpt:

> The sober American judgment must obtain in the South as elsewhere in the Republic, that the only distinctions upon which parties can be safely organized and in harmony with our institutions are differences of opinion relative to principles and policies of government, and that differences of religion, nationality, or race can neither with safety nor propriety be permitted for a moment to enter into the party contest of the day. The unanimity with which the colored voters act with a party is not referable to any race prejudice on their part. On the contrary, they invite the political cooperation of their white brethren, and vote as a unit because proscribed as such. They deprecate the establishment of the color line by the opposition, not only because the act is unwise, but because it isolates them from the white men of the South and forces them, in sheer self-protection, and against their inclination, to act seemingly upon the basis of a race prejudice that they neither respect nor entertain. They not only recognize the equality of citizenship and the right of every man to hold without proscription any position of honor and trust to which the confidence of the people may elevate him; but owing nothing to race, birth, or surroundings, they above all other classes, in the community, are interested to see prejudices drop out of both politics and the business of the country, and success in life proceed upon the integrity and merit of the man who seeks it.... But withal, as they progress in intelligence and appreciation of the dignity of their prerogatives as citizens, they as an evidence of growth begin to realize the significance of the proverb, "When thou doest well for thyself, men shall praise thee"; and are disposed to exact the same protection and concession of rights that are conferred upon other citizens by the Constitution, and that too without humiliation involved in the enforced abandonment of their political convictions.

The speech closes with an enthusiastic expression of confidence in American institutions and in the newly enfranchised African Americans:

I have confidence, not only in my country and her institutions, but in the endurance, capacity and destiny of my people. We will, as opportunity offers and ability serves, seek our places, sometimes in the field of letters, arts, science and the professions. More frequently mechanical pursuits will attract and elicit our efforts; more still of my people — by surroundings, habits, adaptation, and choice will continue to find their homes in the South and constitute the masses of its yeomanry. We will therefore, probably of our own volition and more abundantly than in the past, produce the great staples that will contribute to the basis of foreign exchange, aid in giving the nation a balance of trade, and minister to the wants and comforts and build up the prosperity of the whole land. Whatever our ultimate position in the composite civilization of the republic and whatever varying fortunes attend our career, we will not forget our instincts for freedom nor our love for country.[8]

During the second session of the 44th Congress, Bruce confined his efforts largely to the relief of the legal heirs of black soldiers who had fought to preserve the Union. Consequently, he introduced a number of bills, urging that arrears of pensions be granted. He became the benefactor of many veterans who otherwise might never have received their pensions. In addition to such relief legislation, he presented for the second time a petition urging a general law prohibiting liquor traffic and introduced a bill for certain improvements along the Mississippi River.[9]

In the 45th Congress, Bruce continued to introduce bills for the relief of legal heirs of soldiers. During the second session of this Congress, he took an active interest in the Chinese Exclusion Bill, registering his vote against the measure which seemed to him to be contrary to American principles. His denunciation of the selfish policy of the United States toward the Indian was even more pronounced than that of his dissatisfaction with the restriction of the immigration of the Chinese. He believed that the attitude of the United States government toward Indians bred hatred and discontent. He believed that the government should do much more to civilize the Indian rather than to place restrictions. He advocated, therefore, that Indians should cease to be dealt with as tribes and should receive consideration as individuals, "subject to American law and [as] beneficiaries of American institutions."[10]

It was during the 46th Congress that Senator Bruce was most active. He did constructive work in advocating the improvement of the navigation of the Mississippi River. Senator Bruce kept this important problem before Congress, urging not only that the interest of the people in the valley itself be taken care of, but also that the river should be made the highway of interstate and foreign commerce. Toward this end, Bruce offered several bills providing for future needs. Unfortunately, the members of Congress did not appreciate this statesmanlike effort by Senator Bruce and his program, for these important internal improvements were not carried out.

Senator Bruce, moreover, had been watching, with increasing misgivings, the affairs of that notorious banking disaster known as the Freedman's Savings and Trust Company. To protect the rights of the depositors of the defunct institution, he offered the following resolution on April 7, 1879: "That the President of the Senate appoint a committee of five on the Freedman's Savings and Trust Company to take into consideration all matters relating to said institution, and that said committee be authorized to employ a clerk, and that the necessary expenses be paid out of the 'miscellaneous items' of the contingent fund of the Senate."[11]

The resolution was passed with unanimous consent. The vice president, the Honorable William A. Wheeler, subsequently appointed Senator Bruce as chairman of this committee. The other members were Senators Cameron, Gordon, Withers and Garland. To head such a committee was, indeed, an enviable privilege, but the real opportunity lay in the kind of service that the entangled affairs of the bank made possible. At that time, the affairs of the bank were in the hands of three commissioners, each receiving $3,000 a year, and no promise of winding down business of the bank was forecast. Thus the available assets were reduced annually by the total amount of these salaries at the expense of the depositors.

In order that his committee might have more power to go into the management of the bank, Senator Bruce offered the following resolution on May 16, 1879:

> That the Select Committee on the Freedman's Savings and Trust Company appointed by resolution of the Senate of April 7, 1879, is authorized and directed to investigate the affairs of said savings and trust company and its several branches, to ascertain and report to the Senate all matters relating to the management of the same and the cause or causes of failure, with such other facts relating thereto as may be important to a full understanding of the management and present condition of the institution and to a more economical administration and speedy adjustment of its affairs.

Following this resolution, Senator Bruce presented a petition on May 27, 1879, urging the passage of an act requiring the commissioners of the Freedman's Savings and Trust Company to close up the affairs of the institution and distribute the assets among the creditors.

The resolution and the petition had their desired effects. The services of the commissioners were dispensed with, thus saving $9,000 a year for the depositors; and the final settlement of the claims was turned over to the controller of the Treasury. To Senator Bruce's committee, therefore, goes the credit of bringing a speedy close to the affairs of this savings and trust company, without further loss to the depositors. Later, Senator Bruce made a strong, but vain, appeal to reimburse the depositors of the Freedman's Savings and Trust Company for losses incurred by the failure of the bank.

His final dealings with the company came in the second session of the 46th Congress, when he introduced the following bill:

> That the Senate authorize and direct the purchase by the Secretary of the Treasury, for public use, the property known as the Freedman's Savings and Trust Company, and the real estate and parcels of ground adjacent thereto, belonging to the Freedman's Savings and Trust Company, located on Pennsylvania Avenue between Fifteenth and Fifteenth-and-a-half Streets, Washington, District of Columbia.

The bill was considered, amended, and passed.[12]

Alert to the educational needs of the black youth, Senator Bruce introduced, among many other bills, during the second session of the 46th Congress, a bill "to provide for the investment of certain unclaimed pay and bounty moneys now in the Treasury of the United States and to facilitate and encourage the education of the colored race in the several States and Territories." The bill was referred to the Committee on Education and Labor, amended by Senator Pendleton of Ohio, and reported back adversely and postponed indefinitely.[13]

In January 1880, the Mississippi legislature, now controlled by Democrats, chose James Z. George to succeed Bruce. Before his term ended the following March, Bruce continued to be an activist senator, calling for a more equitable and humane Indian policy and demanding a War Department investigation of the brutal harassment of a black West Point cadet. At the 1880 Republican convention in Chicago, Bruce served briefly as presiding officer and received eight votes for vice president.

In the *Daily Democratic Statesman*, Austin, Texas, dated May 26, 1880, the following editorial appeared:

> The colored voters of the country, in convention at Washington, May 15, 1880, decided that it is due the colored race in the United States, with its 1,000,000 voters, that a colored man shall be placed on the presidential ticket. They declare in favor of Senator Blanche T. Bruce, of Mississippi, for the Vice Presidency, and their reasons for making the demand are given as follows:
>
> 1. He should be nominated because if the Republican party can afford to put a Democratic ex-rebel general in a Republican cabinet, it can afford to have a loyal colored Republican in the vice presidency.
>
> 2. He should be nominated because if the Irish and Dutch receive cabinet positions on account of their fidelity to the Republican party, the Negro should demand and receive some respectable recognition for his unswerving fealty to the party.
>
> 3. He should be nominated because he, of all men, can break the "solid South"; because if nominated, the black voters, to a man, would walk up to the polls and vote his ticket, though death and hell stared them in the face, and each voting precinct became a human slaughter house!
>
> 4. He should be nominated because he is the recognized leader of one million colored voters who, as a part and great factor of the Republican party, clamor for his nomination.
>
> 5. He should be nominated because his congressional record makes him worthy of it, and because race pride demands the honor.
>
> 6. He should be nominated because he is the most available colored man in the country and best reflects the sentiments and wishes of the colored people.
>
> 7. He should be nominated because he is a strong champion of education and of labor.
>
> 8. He should be nominated because he is an untarnished, pure and able statesman, and would not put the ticket on the defensive, but could make an aggressive fight.
>
> 9. He should be nominated because he was bold and brave enough to investigate and act which no other Republican dared to do.
>
> 10. He should be nominated because he is a conscientious and Christian statesman, worthy to fill any position which the people in their sovereign power see fit to bestow upon him.
>
> A circular containing these and other reasons why a colored man should be on the ticket are scattered broadcast all over the country.

Following the close of his Senate service on March 3, 1881, Bruce rejected an offer of the ministry to Brazil because slavery was still practiced there.

On May 23, 1881, President Garfield appointed Bruce the register of the U.S. Treasury; Bruce was the first black person to hold this position. For four years his signature made worthless paper legal tender. The nomination was confirmed without reference, after a complimentary speech from his associate, Senator L.Q.C. Lamar. Again, he demonstrated the executive adeptness that his previous life displayed. The former senator performed his work with such dispatch that co-workers and others were loud in their praise of his abilities.

When the Democrats gained control of Congress in 1885, Bruce was replaced at the treasury but still remained active in political and civic affairs. He was in charge of the Negro exhibit at the World's Cotton Exposition in New Orleans from November 1884 to May 1885. Again in 1888, Bruce was a delegate to the Republican National Convention in Chicago. He was nominated for the vice presidency on the Benjamin Harrison ticket and received eleven votes. President Harrison assumed office in 1889 and appointed Bruce as recorder of deeds for the District of Columbia. In 1896, Bruce campaigned for William McKinley. President McKinley reappointed Bruce as register of the Treasury again, an office he held until his death.

In later life, Senator Bruce developed his oratorical skills. His services for anniversaries and other special occasions rivaled those of the popular Virginia representative, John M. Langston, and Frederick Douglass. Bruce was made a trustee of the Washington Public Schools and served in this position for seven years. He was elected a trustee of Howard University and was later awarded an LL.D. degree from that school. A Democratic paper stated that Senator Bruce was equal in ability to the average cabinet officer of the day and had a higher character than many. He proved himself personally popular and officially successful.

On June 24, 1878, Bruce married Josephine B. Wilson, a schoolteacher of mixed ancestry. Mrs. Bruce, the daughter of an Ohio dentist, was culturally refined, wonderfully fitted to command the dignity and respect of her position. Josephine Bruce presided over her residence with true womanly grace, making it a fit rendezvous for the prominent political officials and Washington's black elite with whom they were so closely identified. Senator Bruce had befriended the prominent black leader Frederick Douglass, whom he shared an apartment with while Bruce was a bachelor. The Bruces were the only witnesses to the second marriage of Frederick Douglass.

On May 17, 1898, twenty years from the date of his marriage, Senator Bruce died, a victim of diabetes, at the age of fifty-seven.

The Evening Star, a Washington, D.C., daily newspaper, reported in an obituary on March 17, 1898, the death of Blanche K. Bruce as follows:

> Blanche K. Bruce, register of the United States Treasury, died at his residence at 8:15 this morning of a complication of diseases. He was in his fifty-seventh year.... Mr. Bruce was a man of national reputation. President McKinley appointed him to the office of register of the Treasury because he was recognized as a thorough representative of his race and known in all portions of the Country as able, brainy and

upright.... He was a convincing orator as well as an eloquent one.... Mr. Bruce was born in Prince Edward County, Va, March 1, 1841. He was born a slave and received the rudiments of his education from the tutor of his master's son. He was the companion and servant of his young master up to the breaking out of the civil war. The young master went from Missouri to join the Confederate Army.... Despite the scanty opportunities, Bruce was fairly well educated when he left his master. Toward the last of the war, Bruce taught school for a time at Hannibal, Mo., and then became a student at Oberlin. In addition, he pursued special studies at home.

At the close of the war, Bruce went to Mississippi, becoming a planter and engaging in politics. He quickly became prominent as a republican and safe leader of the Negro race. He first became Sergeant-At-Arms of the Mississippi Levee Board, Sheriff of Bolivar County in 1871–72 and County Superintendent of Education. Then his home record was crowned by election to the United States Senate in which body he took his seat March 4, 1875, serving six years. In the Senate, Bruce made a record which pleased his people and his race. He won the friendship and esteem of the most eminent statesmen and politicians in the country....

On March 21, 1898, *The Evening Star* reported on the Bruce funeral:

> ...following the casket were the honorary pallbearers, who were ex–Representative John R. Lynch of Mississippi, ex–Senator P.B.S. Pinchback and James Lewis of Louisiana, M.M. Holland of Ohio, W.A. Pledger of Georgia, John P. Green of Ohio, Representative George H. White of North Carolina, Lewis H. Douglas of New York, H.P. Cheatham of North Carolina, recorder of deeds for the District of Columbia; Rev. William Waring of Ohio, H.L. Chew, deputy register of the Treasury; Robert H. Terrell of Massachusetts, R.R. Church of Tennessee, Campbell L. Maxwell and Ralph W. Tyler of Ohio, etc....
>
> The floral offerings were numerous and many of them were of unusual richness and beauty. The card of President McKinley was attached to a large and exquisite wreath of white roses, lilies of the valley, white carnations, calla lilies and rare white orchids sprayed with feathery asparagus and lily leaves. A broad white satin ribbon was tied over two crossed leaves of palm attached to the wreath....

Blanche Kelso Bruce, the only black person to serve a full term in the United States Senate until the election of Edward Brooke in 1966 from Massachusetts, was described by Benjamin Brawley as "probably the most astute political leader the Negroes ever had." Former opponents in Mississippi remembered Senator Bruce as "always the gentleman, graceful, polished, self-assured, and never humble." Senator Bruce himself might have appreciated most the epitaph of the Raymond, Mississippi, *Gazette*, which recalled that he scorned the use of the phrase "colored men," often declaring, "I am a Negro, and proud of my race."

5

Cassius Marcellus Clay (1810–1903): Firebrand of Freedom, Abolitionist, Ambassador to Russia

Cassius Marcellus Clay was born on his father's plantation, Clermont, in Madison County, Kentucky, October 19, 1810, as the son of Revolutionary War veteran General Green Clay and Sally Lewis. (The greatest heavyweight boxer of all time, Muhammad Ali, was also born Cassius Marcellus Clay. His father, Marcellus Clay, a sign painter, and mother Odessa Grady Clay, a domestic worker, named their son for the white Kentucky abolitionist.)

This Cassius Clay fought for the abolishment of slavery, becoming one of Kentucky's greatest anti-slavery crusaders in the years before the Civil War. While attending Yale University, Clay had been deeply influenced by a pro-emancipation speech of William Lloyd Garrison. Clay became one of the most prominent American abolitionists and statesmen and was a proponent of Henry Clay's American System. He rejected measures pertaining to slavery and advocated gradual emancipation. In 1845 he founded a leading anti-slavery weekly newspaper, the *True American*. When his printing equipment was seized by local opposition, he continued to publish the paper from Cincinnati, Ohio. Later, changing its name to the *Examiner*, he moved the operation to Louisville, Kentucky. Clay served three terms in the Kentucky Legislature from 1835–1840. He helped found the Republican Party in 1854, and gave his support to its presidential tickets in 1856, 1860 and 1864.

Before the Civil War, Clay said, "For better or worse, the black people are among us.... We must educate them, for one day they will be part of our governing society." With these bold words he set himself apart from his neighbors and was called "lunatic," "traitor" and "madman" by his detractors. Remembering Clay, U.S. Supreme Court Justice John M. Harlan wrote: "There is a more striking combination of manly beauty and strength in his face than in the face of any man whom I ever saw. I always had the highest regard for his integrity of character, his manliness, and his fidelity to his own convictions."

Clay's father, Green Clay, a pioneer from Powhatan County, Virginia, settled in Madison County, Kentucky, and became a slaveholder. He built an imposing Victorian mansion in 1798–1799. Cassius Marcellus Clay was General Green Clay's third son, the youngest of six children. With his brother Brutus, Clay attended Madison Academy in Richmond and they were tutored by the celebrated teacher Joshua Fry in Latin, rhetoric, philosophy and the classics. In his thirteenth year, Cassius was sent to St. Joseph's College in Bardstown, the oldest Catholic college in Kentucky. While at St. Joseph's, Clay began a correspondence in French with his famous cousin, Henry Clay, secretary of state in President John Quincy Adams's cabinet.

Although Green Clay was one of the most prominent slaveowners in Kentucky, Cassius gradually became aware of and horrified by the vicious and inhuman side of slavery. In his biography of Cassius Marcellus Clay, H. Edward Richardson reports the following poignant incident.

Cassius Marcellus Clay (1810–1903). A white abolitionist, he was one of Kentucky's greatest anti-slavery crusaders before the Civil War. Clay was the founder of the interracial Berea College. He was also ambassador to Russia and was deeply involved in the purchase of Alaska. (©Corbis)

Mary, a comely mulatto girl of about eighteen who was a flower gardener at White Hall, helped Cassius and his sister make a miniature garden, and the children grew fond of her. Later, as a temporary arrangement, Mary was sent by General Clay to work in the house of one of the overseers. One day Cassius and Eliza, standing in their little garden, heard a piercing scream; it was Mary, coming into the yard. To the horror of all, she held a butcher knife in front of her, and her clothes were drenched with blood. The servants ran wildly from the fields and cabins and surrounded her, crying out with her in a communion of fear.

Cassius later came to understand that Payne, the drunken overseer, had attacked her. In self-defense she killed him with the knife, and then ran back to White Hall. Mary was taken to jail, later to be tried and acquitted. Nevertheless, in accordance with the custom of Kentucky and the other border slave states of that time, she was ordered to be sent into the Deep South. The innocence — the indifference — with which Cassius had viewed slavery was swept away. Years later he wrote:

"Never shall I forget — and through all these years it rests upon the memory as the stamp upon a bright coin — the scene, when Mary was tied by the wrists and sent from home and friends, and the loved features of her native land — the home of her infancy and girlish days — into Southern banishment forever; and yet held guiltless by a jury of, not her 'peers,' but her oppressors! Never shall I forget those ... faces —

the oppressor and the oppressed, rigid with equal agony! She cast an imploring look at me, as if in appeal; but meekly went, without a word, as 'a sheep to the slaughter.'"[1]

Soon after his father's death in 1828, Clay entered Transylvania University, in Lexington, Kentucky, known as the Athens of the West. Clay studied a wide range of subjects including philosophy, politics and oratory. In 1831, he enrolled in Yale University and expanded his horizons by seeking and interviewing many famous people of his time including Martin Van Buren, President Andrew Jackson, John Sargent, Daniel Webster, John Greenleaf Whittier, Julia Ward Howe, Edward Everett and Charles Sumner.

After hearing a speech by William Lloyd Garrison, abolitionist editor of the new *Liberator*, Clay wrote "so as to burn like a branding-iron into the most callous hide of the slave-holder and his defenders." Garrison's arguments were to him "as water to a thirsty wayfarer."

Clay graduated with honors and delivered the commemoration of the Washington Centennial on February 22, 1832, where he took the occasion to direct his first antislavery remarks to the distinguished audience: "The glove is already thrown down ... the northern and southern champions stand in sullen defiance."

As Richardson wrote,

> In the years to follow, his intelligence, rhetorical eloquence, and rare force of character were widely acknowledged by both friend and foe. His southern heritage, immense wealth, and northern education seemed to augur a distinguished political career, but his antislavery principles overrode personal ambitions. Many years later, a friend wrote Clay, "The real leaders of nations and races are never allowed to enter their promised lands, and therefore you are always coupled in my mind with regret."[2]

In August 1845, a committee of citizens in Lexington, Kentucky, delivered to Cassius M. Clay, one of the most pugnacious abolitionists of his time, an ultimatum that he "discontinue the publication of ... *The True American*, as ... dangerous to the peace of our community." Defiantly refusing, Clay mounted two brass cannons to guard his doors, armed his little band of friends with rifles and shotguns and prepared for battle. The Lexingtonians, however, avoiding blood and violence, held a dignified meeting and appointed a committee of sixty law-abiding men who quietly and with a sense of doing painful duty dismantled the press and equipment of Clay's paper and packed it to the station for exportation from the state.[3]

Focus on the slavery issue was heightened by the Nat Turner uprising in Virginia, which caused fear and hysteria among slaveholders. As Richardson wrote, "Clay argued that slavery was not only a violation of human rights but also a drain on the potential growth of the Commonwealth. From the outset of his career, Clay's support of the American System in Kentucky — gradual abolition, industry and free labor, internal improvements and progressive taxation, for example, over against agrarianism, slave labor, and low taxation — tended to set him apart from his own aristocratic, landowning class."[4] It was his abolitionist views that altered his otherwise predictable life of farming, business, politics and childrearing. After relocating to Lexington, Clay denounced slavery as an evil — "morally, economically, physically, intellectually, socially, religiously, politically — evil in its inception, in its duration, and in its catastrophe."

In denouncing slavery openly, Clay was subject to both verbal and physical abuse. He was challenged to a fight to the death by Samuel M. Brown, a paid assassin from New Orleans. Richardson quotes the report of an eyewitness:

> You have heard of the … fight at the Cave. It was not slow. It was the first Bowie Knife fight I ever saw, and the way … Cash used it was tremendous. Blows on the head hard enough to cleave a man's skull asunder, but Brown must have a skull of extraordinary thickness. He stood the blows as well if not better than most of men would do. Cassius … sprang in on him and used the knife with such power that Brown was either paralyzed by the blows, or forgot his revolver.[5]

Clay was saved when the bullet fired by Brown hit the scabbard strapped to his chest. Clay's only wound was a red spot over his heart.

Cassius M. Clay helped to start the famous anti-slavery, integrated school called Berea College, still in operation in Kentucky to this day. John G. Fee started a one-room school in 1855, which eventually became Berea College. Fee, a native of Bracken County, Kentucky, was a scholar of strong moral character, dedication, determination and great faith. He believed in a school that would be an advocate of equality and excellence in education for men and women of all races. Fee's uncompromising faith and courage in preaching against slavery attracted the attention of Clay, who felt he had found in Fee an individual who would take a strong stand on slavery.

In 1853, Fee built his home upon the ridge. In 1855, a one-room school, which also served as a church on Sundays, was built on a lot contributed by a neighbor. Berea's first teachers were recruited from Oberlin College, an anti-slavery stronghold in Ohio. Fee saw his humble church-school as the beginning of a sister institution "which would be to Kentucky what Oberlin is to Ohio, anti-slavery, anti-caste, anti-rum, anti-sin." A few months later, Fee wrote a letter, saying, "We … eventually look to a college — giving an education to all colors, classes, cheap and thorough."

Fee worked with other community leaders to develop a constitution for the new school, which he and Principal J.A.R. Rogers insisted should ensure its interracial character. It also was agreed that the school would furnish work for as many students as possible, in order to help them pay their expenses and to dignify labor at a time when manual labor and slavery tended to be synonymous in the South.

The first articles of incorporation for Berea College were adopted in 1859. But that was also the year Fee and the Berea teachers were driven from Madison County by Southern pro-slavery sympathizers. Fee spent the Civil War years raising funds for the school; in 1865, he and his followers returned. A year later, the articles of incorporation were recorded at the county seat, and in 1869 the college department became a reality.

The first catalog, issued for 1866–1867, used the corporate name "Berea College," but the title "Berea Literary Institute" was printed on the cover because it was thought to convey better "the present character of the school." Enrollment that academic year totaled 187: 96 black students and 91 whites. For several decades following the Civil War, Berea's student body continued to be divided equally between white and black students, many of whom went on to teach in schools established solely for African Americans.

In 1886–1887, the school had three divisions: primary, intermediate and academic. Students could pursue a college preparatory course, a shorter course, or a teacher's course. In 1869–1870, five freshmen were admitted to the college department, and in 1873 the first bachelor's degrees were granted.

Berea's commitment to interracial education was overturned in 1904 by the Kentucky legislature's passage of the Day Law, which prohibited education of black and white students together. When the U.S. Supreme Court upheld the Day Law, Berea set aside funds to assist in the establishment of Lincoln Institute, a school located near Louisville, for black students. When the Day Law was amended in 1950 to allow integration above the high school level, Berea was the first college in Kentucky to reopen its doors to black students.

By 1911, the number of students seeking admission to Berea was so great that the trustees amended the college's constitution to specify the southern mountain region as Berea's special field of service. The commitment to Appalachia, however, began as early as 1858 when Rogers, after a trip through the mountains, identified the region as a "neglected part of the country" for which Berea was founded to serve.

Curricular offerings have varied at Berea to meet changing needs. In the early 1920s, in addition to its college department, Berea had a high school that included ungraded classes for students who had not had educational opportunities, an elementary school, a vocational school and a Normal School for teacher training. Although the general mission of serving students with financial need continued, units and divisions were reorganized through the years. In 1968, Berea discontinued its elementary and secondary programs and focused entirely on undergraduate college education.

Berea's distinctive commitments and educational programs have brought the college national recognition. Above all, the excellence of Berea's academic program earns acclaim. *U.S. News & World Report* has repeatedly named Berea the No. 1 regional college in the South. *The New York Times, The Chronicle of Higher Education,* the *Philadelphia Inquirer, The Times of London,* and the "Solutions" segment of ABC World News have focused national and international attention on many aspects of the contemporary Berea experience. Full-tuition scholarships provided to all students, the effectiveness of the work program and students' involvement in community service projects are among the highlighted features. Such reports are expected to continue as Berea alumni distinguish themselves in all walks of life and in many parts of the world.

As the Civil War began, President Lincoln, who was well aware of Russia's intense desire to maintain political balance between the major powers, wanted to send a skillful ambassador to Russia. In order to offset the hostility of France and England, the United States needed Russian support. Lincoln finally selected Cassius Marcellus Clay, the eminent Kentuckian who was known as a strong Union man from a border state.

After Clay helped Lincoln get elected, he expected to be rewarded with an appointment to the Cabinet, most particularly as Secretary of War. Instead Lincoln gave the post to Simon Cameron who helped move Pennsylvania to support Lincoln. As Albert Woldman wrote in 1952,

> Bitterly disappointed, Clay then informed the President that, "Since the Cabinet was full, I will go to England or France as Minister." Lincoln replied that Seward had promised these two most important ministries to Charles Francis Adams and William L. Dayton. Undaunted, Clay expressed his next preference to be the post of Minister Plenipotentiary to Madrid, although he did not particularly care for "an old effete government like Spain." But here again political considerations thwarted the Kentuckian's wishes. A place had to be found for Carl Schurz. A political refugee, Schurz would not be acceptable in the Russian court. The Spanish post seemed to be the only spot in which he could be fitted.
>   Clay was angry, but Lincoln promised he would not forget him. Senator Baker of Oregon, with whom Clay had served in the Mexican War, interceded with the President on behalf of the Kentucky politician. What about appointing Clay envoy to Russia? Within a few days, a telegram reached Clay at his home in Lexington, Kentucky. It was from Montgomery Blair, Lincoln's Postmaster General. The President was prepared to offer him the post to Minister to St. Petersburg, Blair wrote. Would he accept? Quickly, on March 27, 1861, Clay telegraphed Blair his reply: "For the sake of the cause I accept the Russian mission."[6]

The story of Lincoln and Russia is not very well known. Lincoln knew Russia as a "country where they make no pretense of loving liberty." Nevertheless, he formed a firm alliance and working partnership with Czar Alexander's absolute dictatorship. The Russian-American agreement was based on a mutual fear and a common enemy: Great Britain. This alliance succeeded in preventing European intervention in the American Civil War on the side of the Confederacy. It also stopped the Anglo-French alliance from attacking Russia over the Polish question. Ambassador Clay was greatly moved by Alexander II's action in liberating Russia's millions of serfs.

Clay often boasted that Russia and the United States "were bound together by a common sympathy in the cause of emancipation. I did more than any man to overthrow slavery. I carried Russia with us and thus prevented what would have been a strong alliance of France, England and Spain against us and thus saved the nation."

Clay was very much involved in the purchase of Alaska from Russia. In the sale of Alaska — immensely rich in timber, fisheries, furs, oil and other mineral resources — Russia agreed to the peaceful transfer of 600,000 square miles of territory for a piddling sum. Charles Sumner, chairman of the Senate Committee on Foreign Affairs, urged ratification of the Alaskan purchase as follows: "Even if you doubt the value of these possessions, the treaty is a sign of amity. It is a new expression of that entente cordiale between the two powers which is a phenomenon of history." There was a popular belief in the United States that we purchased a "dreary waste of glaciers, icebergs, white bears and walrus fit only for Eskimos" because we were under some obligation to Russia for friendship during the Civil War. But there were more important reasons for the transaction. Russia was apparently eager to get rid of Alaska because it had become difficult to administer and because the czar was afraid that it might fall into the hands of Great Britain. So, inspired by hostility to England and friendship for the United States, plus $7,200,000 in gold, Russia agreed to sell Alaska to the United States.

Ambassador Clay was a strong proponent of the Alaska acquisition along with Secretary of State William Seward, who predicted in 1860, "The Pacific Ocean with its coasts and islands is destined to become in the future the great theater of the world's affairs." For the comparatively trifling sum of $7,200,000, the United States was able to add nearly 600,000 square miles of territory to her possessions — 369,529,600 acres, to be exact, at about two cents per acre! Critics referred to the acquisition as "Seward's Folly" and "Walrussia," a Godforsaken wasteland of "polar bear gardens, perpetual icebergs, eternally, cannonading volcanoes and destructive hurricanes."

Clay served as minister plenipotentiary to Russia in 1861, returning home when he received a commission to serve as major general in the Union Army. Clay returned to St. Petersburg, Russia, in 1863 to continue his diplomatic service as minister to Russia until 1869.

Clay had married Mary Jane Warfield on February 26, 1833. Mary Jane would bear eight of his ten children. It was rumored that Clay fathered a son with a famous Russian ballerina named Anna Marie. (Clay's wife, Mary Jane, found the Russian winters too cold and left him alone for several years.) Clay later adopted this son and brought him to the United States. According to Madison County Courthouse records, he was born in St. Petersburg, Russia, on March 22, 1866, and was originally named Leonide Petroff. His name was changed to Launey Clay and in 1876 he was included in Cassius Clay's will for an "undivided sixth interest" in the White Hall estate, which had been built upon the original estate house structure of Clermont.

When he was in his seventies Clay had a romantic involvement with a young woman in her mid-twenties. Later, when he was in his eighties, he married his sixteen-year-old servant, and once again the neighbor's suspicions of this "madman" were reconfirmed as were his ex-wife's who sought a court order to remove him from the three story White Hall mansion and have him placed in a mental institution.

A prominent journalist vindicated him, however, when assigned to cover the story by an eastern newspaper who no doubt felt that they were onto a juicy scandal. The young newspaper writer who later became one of Kentucky's leading novelists made the following observation: "I came to Richmond expecting to find a deranged old man holding a teenage girl captive against her will ... what I found instead were two people very much in love with one another ... the only thing I know for sure is that I no longer have the fear of growing old ... virile, romantic, macho, charming, intelligent, sensitive, caring, and courageous ... these are the things that Cash Clay was guilty of."

In his later years, Clay wrote an autobiography entitled *The Life of Cassius Marcellus Clay: Memoirs, Writings, and Speeches*. As his health failed due to advancing age, Clay confined himself more and more to White Hall. Cassius Marcellus Clay died July 22, 1903, in the older section of the house, where he had been born ninety-three years earlier.

6

Robert Brown Elliott (1842–1884): Distinguished Lawyer, Eloquent Orator, Racial Militant

One of the most talented and controversial politicians in the Reconstruction era was Robert Brown Elliott of South Carolina. Elliott made one of the great speeches of his time when he spoke out in Congress in favor of Senator Charles Sumner's Civil Rights Bill.

A dramatic highlight in the House civil rights debate came early in January 1874 when the aging, ailing Alexander Stephens of Georgia was wheeled into place to speak for an hour against the proposal. Not even a decade had passed since he had been vice president of the Confederacy. Now he was back in the U.S. House of Representatives to raise his voice on behalf of white supremacy. Denying racial prejudice, Stephens said that the measure was unconstitutional, that such things should best be left to the states, and that in any event, the blacks of Georgia did not want racially mixed schools.

By the time Stephens had finished, it was late in the afternoon. The House had agreed in advance to hear Elliott speak in rebuttal immediately afterward. Asked if he minded delaying his speech until the following morning, Elliott replied that he would abide by the wishes of the House. Some blacks objected to the postponement, but the majority of the members voted for adjournment. Forewarned, blacks and whites turned out in force to hear him the next day.[1] The stage was set when Stephens, elderly and ailing, was brought into the chamber in his chair. All eyes turned to Elliott.

He was an impressive man, deep-chested, broad-shouldered, with abundant hair worn *au natural* in the African style. "Face to face," a contemporary said, "stood the Anglo-Saxon and the undoubted African. The issue was between them; the contest began." "I regret, sir," Elliott began, "that the dark hue of my skin may lend color to the imputation that I am controlled by motives personal to myself in my advocacy of this great measure of national justice. Sir, the motive that impels me is restricted to no such narrow boundary, but it is as broad as your Constitution. I advocate it, sir, because it is right."

Elliott reviewed the history of blacks in America. They had shown their mettle in the Revolutionary War, had proved a decisive factor in the Civil War and had been praised by Andrew Jackson in the War of 1812. They had earned their civil rights in tears and blood. And what were civil rights? Like a teacher in a graduate seminar, Elliott explained civil rights, quoting Francis Lieber, Alexander Hamilton, and the French Constitution. He scornfully dismissed Stephens. It ill behooved a man who tried to wreck the Constitution to read lectures to men who fought for it. Elliott continued,

> I meet him only as an adversary; nor shall age or any other consideration restrain me from saying that he now offers his Government, which he had done his utmost to destroy, a very poor return for its magnanimous treatment, to come here and seek to continue ... the burdens and oppressions which rest upon five million of his country-men who never failed to lift their earnest prayers for the success of this government when the gentleman was seeking to break up the Union of these states and to blot the American Republic from the galaxy of nations. [Loud applause.][2]

Vitriolic opposition to the bill had come from John Harris of Virginia. Harris insisted that not even Abraham Lincoln, the idol of the black masses, had been convinced of the equality of the races. "I say there is not one gentleman upon this floor who can honestly say he really believes that the colored man is his equal," Harris continued. "I can," Alonzo Ransier, congressman and former lieutenant governor of South Carolina, spoke up. Harris's reply was that he was talking to white men. To John Harris, Elliott offered the back of his hand. "To the diatribe of the gentleman from Virginia, who spoke yesterday, and who so far transcended the limits of decency and propriety as to announce upon this floor that his remarks were addressed to white men alone, I shall have no word of reply. Let him feel that a Negro was not only too magnanimous to smite him in his weakness, but was even charitable enough to grant him the mercy of his silence." Elliott pleaded for the bill.

> The Constitution warrants it; the Supreme Court sanctions it; justice demands it.... The results of the war as seen in reconstruction, have settled forever the political status of my race. The passage of this bill will determine the civil status, not only of the Negro, but of any other class of citizens who may feel themselves discriminated against. It will form the capstone of that temple of liberty begun on this continent under discouraging circumstances, carried on in spite of the sneers of monarchists and the cavils of pretended friends of freedom, until at last it stands in all its beautiful symmetry and proportions, a building the grandest which the world has ever seen, realizing the most sanguine expectations and the highest hopes of those who in the name of equal, impartial and universal liberty, laid the foundation stone.[3]

The black South Carolinian sat down in triumph. For almost an hour he held court on the floor of the House. Even the Democrats were impressed. Ben Butler later compared Elliott to John Hancock, John Adams and that other famous South Carolinian, John C. Calhoun.

The *New York Tribune* said the thirty-two-year-old South Carolinian held the galleries spellbound with this speech, which finished with an appeal to the Anglo-Saxons' vaunted sense of fair play. The *Tribune* also praised him for his neat handling of the ungentlemanly gentleman from Virginia who had insulted a black colleague. *The New York Times* was impressed by the beat and cadence of Elliott's speaking style. *The New National Era* and *Citizen* of Washington thought the entire black race was indebted to South Carolina for sending this powerful, persuasive man to the House where he could appear in person as a refutation of black inferiority.[4]

The *Deseret Evening News* (January 7, 1874, Salt Lake City, Utah Territory) reported that Elliott "concluded with an eloquent peroration, which was loudly applauded on the floor and in the galleries and at the close of his speech he received many congratulations from the members. Elliott is from South Carolina and is the darkest of any of the colored members…. He was educated in England." Robert Brown Elliott served twice in Congress but he made his greatest impact as a South Carolina state official and party leader.

This British-educated Bostonian moved south to work for the *Charleston Leader*, a weekly newspaper, after the Civil War. Of West Indian parentage, he had attended school in Jamaica and in London, and he had a working knowledge of several languages acquired through widespread travel.

Robert Brown Elliott (1842–1884), one of the most talented and controversial black politicians of his generation. Educated in England, he studied law and was admitted to the South Carolina bar in 1869. Elliott was elected to U.S. Congress and in 1874 gained national attention for his brilliant speech in support of civil rights. (Library of Congress)

Elliott, who may have studied law in both England and America, started practicing law under the military occupation in South Carolina and continued in the civilian courts when the state reentered the Union. In great demand as an attorney, he amassed one of the best private law libraries in South Carolina.

From the beginning, he was a leader in the South Carolina Republican Party. He helped to formulate the 1868 state constitution and was one of the party organizers who turned out the necessary votes to get it approved. At the constitutional convention he fought against former slaveholders being compensated for their losses. He maintained there never was and never could be any legitimate claim to hold another person as property, and the delegates voted with him, despite insistence by some factions that bona fide contracts were thereby being abrogated.

He pushed for a liberal homestead tax exemption and for elimination of the poll tax, splitting with Joseph Rainey on the latter issue. Elliott's argument was that impoverished blacks, having been cheated out of their wages as slaves, could not afford to pay twenty-five cents, much less a dollar as Rainey suggested. He lost this tussle; the constitution as approved levied a tax of one dollar to help support the pubic schools.

Elections for a new legislature followed the convention. After turning down a chance to run for the state Senate, Elliott was elected to the lower House. He added excitement to the opening of the legislature by giving Franklin Moses, Jr., a well-to-do native white Republican, a close race for the speakership. Elliott lost, but he succeeded in consolidating his position in the party by becoming chairman of the state executive committee. At the close of his term in the legislature, Governor Robert Scott named him assistant adjutant general of the state militia. This group was on constant call as rioting and violence continued to erupt across the state.

Columbia, the South Carolina state capital, was the hub of a relaxed, desegregated social life revolving around Governor Scott and his wife. The gregarious Elliott, a very dark, trim man, was likely to be at these parties. The whites admired his wit and personality while respecting his intellect and his ability to inspire black audiences with his fiery speeches.

During this period, Elliott was planning his next step up to Congress. People in his district knew him well from the courts, the legislature, and the militia. With the backing of the party leadership, he gained the Republican nomination in the Third Congressional District in the summer of 1870. In the hard-fought general election, J. E. Bacon, the Democratic contender, accused Elliott of having used his position as a state legislator for personal gain. One allegation was that Elliott through his position on the legislature's railroad committee had lined his pockets with bribes. He surmounted these undocumented charges and swept the district by a margin of nearly 7,000 votes.

Elliott went to Congress in March 1871 to take the seat once held by Preston Brooks — the man who had caned Charles Sumner of Massachusetts into insensibility in the Senate chamber before the war. Arriving in Washington as the controversy over the disfranchisement of ex–Confederates was beginning to boil, Elliott opposed a hasty general restoration of political rights but was willing to consider petitions from individuals who demonstrated a change of heart in their attitude toward the federal government. He introduced such a personal petition for a friend who later became his law partner.

During the debate in the House he pointed out that people who were disfranchised had got in that unenviable fix by rushing "madly into rebellion against this, the best Government that exists under heaven." When John Farnsworth of Illinois painted a sad picture of the poor old white man who was barred from officeholding while his lowly, unlettered ex-slave could qualify, Elliott sarcastically noted that the "poor old man" was barred from office for the simple reason that he had once betrayed his oath to uphold the Constitution and now "would only curse the Government" and "murder its loyal adherents" while the ex-slave had put his life on the line to defend the Union.

Elliott maintained that granting general amnesty would be like paying a premium for treason. He said that recalcitrants in the South would take it as a sign of the federal government's weakness and as "evidence of the fact that this Congress desires to hand over loyal men of the south to the tender mercies of the rebels who today are murdering and scourging the loyal men of the southern States."

The congressman emphasized that he spoke not only for blacks but for his other constituents "whose complexions are like those of [the] gentlemen around me." He pointed out that he came to Congress from a Republican district backed by as large a majority as any man in the House. These voters, he said, expected the government to protect life and property in the South and would not otherwise continue to support the party.[5]

Whether in the constitutional convention, state legislature, or Congress, Elliott aligned himself with the Republican Party's radical faction. At the convention he successfully led the fight against articles requiring a literacy test for voters and a poll tax that would be used to fund public education. In each case he correctly predicted that the measure could be used by future hostile administrations to disenfranchise blacks and undermine the gains of Reconstruction. He was equally adamant in calling for the invalidation of debts contracted for the purchase and sale of slaves. In the legislature he strongly supported a successful bill to ban discrimination in public accommodations and public conveyances. As a congressman he gave a celebrated speech in favor of federal suppression of the Ku Klux Klan. As a sign of his growing national reputation, Boston blacks in 1874 invited Elliott to give the oration at the funeral ceremonies to honor the memory of U.S. Senator Charles Sumner.[6]

When he returned to South Carolina Elliott was acclaimed by blacks as a hero, but he realized that corruption and internal divisions within the state Republican Party were bolstering Democratic fortunes and endangering the prospects for black participation in politics. To lead the drive for reform effectively, Elliott needed to remain in South Carolina, and on November 1, 1874, he resigned his House seat and won a seat in the state general assembly.[7]

As speaker of the assembly, Elliott tried but failed to stem the tide of violence, intimidation and economic pressure undermining blacks' civil rights and their representation in state government. To make matters worse, the Republican governor, Daniel Chamberlain, was increasingly identified with the state's Democrats in spite of the fact that he had been elected with heavy support from black voters. In 1876 Elliott was elected state attorney general, but the withdrawal of federal troops and the collapse of the Chamberlain administration the following April made Elliott's position increasingly untenable. With the end of federal Reconstruction, Elliott was forced out of office in May 1877.

Elliott defended a number of former South Carolina Republican officeholders brought to trial by the Wade Hampton Democratic administration following its takeover at the state. John W. Cromwell, an early black historian, characterized Elliott's handling of some of those cases before the state supreme court as "models of forensic oratory and legal learning."

The former congressman continued to participate in Republican Party activities, but he could not put his heart into such an unrewarding cause. In 1878 he presided over a state convention for the last time. Then he told his friends that it was thankless work to dissipate energy and money in state offices, and he resigned.[8]

Elliott returned to his law practice but found business for black attorneys to be so meager that in 1879 he accepted an appointment as a special customs inspector for the Treasury Department, based in Charleston. While on an inspection trip to Florida he suffered the first of the malarial fever attacks that gradually undermined his health. He worked for Secretary of the Treasury John Sherman's presidential campaign, seconding his nomination and serving as manager of Sherman's black delegates at the Republican Convention of 1880. In May 1881, the Treasury Department transferred Elliott to New Orleans. His disenchantment with the move from South Carolina intensified and led to his dismissal in August 1882. He established another law partnership, but it failed to prosper.[9] He missed the stimulus of public life, but there was no place for an outsider in the shrinking Louisiana Republican Party.

Given Elliott's considerable power, visibility and outspokenness on controversial issues, it is not surprising that he became the object of frequent attacks by Democrats and even opposition within his own party. What is surprising was the viciousness of the attacks and the extent to which he was singled out for abuse.

There was also the strong strain of self-help ideology that permeated Elliott's speeches. Like the more conservative Bruce, he was a firm believer in the value of public education. Then, too, he frequently reminded black audiences of the responsibility they had in South Carolina since they were the majority. In a nationally reported speech in 1874, following his triumphant civil rights speech in Congress, Elliott told a Columbia audience of the need to clean up state and party governments because blacks were being judged by a different standard. Obsessed with fears about the fragility of the Reconstruction governments, conscious of the fact that "revolutions may go backward," Elliott called for federal support of southern blacks. But at the same time he argued that blacks themselves had their destiny within their own hands and should rise to the challenge.[10]

Yet more than color, power, and positions were involved. Elliott was singled out in large measure because of his style and lack of deference toward whites, whether friend or foe. To one Democratic newspaper he was "as big a rascal as can be found anywhere within the ranks of Radicalism and is besides, supremely insolent, arrogant and arbitrary." Elliott owed much of his reputation for being "uppity" and a "race first man" to his role in reversing the practice in South Carolina of blacks deferring to whites over nominations to major offices.[11]

While Blanche Bruce remained optimistic about eventual black assimilation into American life, Elliott became pessimistic, particularly as his health, political power and financial status declined. Malaria ended the life of this hard-driving, talented, controversial politician on August 9, 1884, just two days before his forty-second birthday. Unlike Bruce, Elliott was not given an elaborate funeral. Frederick Douglass gave the following tribute to Robert Brown Elliott in the *New York Globe:*

Living as I have done, in an atmosphere of doubt and disparagement of the abilities and possibilities of the colored race, early taught that ignorance and mental weakness were stamped by God upon the members of that race, Robert Brown Elliott was to me a most grateful surprise, and in fact a marvel. Upon sight and hearing of this man, I was chained to the spot with admiration and a feeling akin to wonder.

There was no doubt as to complexion, form or feature.... He might have been an ordinary Negro, one who might have delved as I have done, with spade and pickaxes. Yet from under his dark brow there blazed an intellect worthy of a place in the highest legislative hall of the Nation. I have known but one other black man to be compared with Elliott, and that was Samuel R. Ward, who, like Elliott, died in the midst of his years. The thought of both men makes me sad. We are not over rich with such men, and we may well mourn when one such has fallen. I, with thousands who knew the ability of young Elliott, was hoping and waiting to see him emerge from his late comparative obscurity and take his place again in the halls of Congress. But alas! He is gone, and we can only hope that the same power that gave us one Elliott will give us another in the near future.[12]

7

Charlotte Forten Grimké (1837–1914): Abolitionist, Educator, Journal Author

Charlotte L. Forten, abolitionist and teacher, might have known from early in life what she was called upon to do. After all, she was the granddaughter of James Forten, an inventor, renowned abolitionist, and one of the wealthiest black men of the 1700s. She was the daughter of the equally famous Robert Forten, and the niece of Robert Purvis, another prominent, wealthy black abolitionist.

The Fortens were one of the most well-known black families in Philadelphia. Wealthy sailmaker James Forten and his wife Charlotte Vandine Forten headed the family; their daughters were Margaretta (1815–1875), Harriet (1810–1875), and Sarah (1814–1883). The Fortens were active abolitionists who took part in founding and financing at least six abolitionist organizations, and their home was always open to visiting abolitionists.

James Forten was born free in 1766 and served in the Revolutionary War as a powder boy aboard the ship *Royal Louis*, commanded by Captain Decatur, father of the celebrated commodore. It was captured by the British ship *Amphion* and young Forten was transferred to the prison ship *Old Jersey*, then moored in New York Harbor. He finally was freed in a prisoner exchange after surviving a raging pestilence on board.[1] He became a lifelong abolitionist, dedicating his life to the battle against slavery. After the war was over, he went to work for a sailmaker where he became foreman at age twenty and then proprietor-owner twelve years later. He invented an improved device to handle sails for which he obtained a patent and, over time, he earned a good deal of money. Ultimately, his sailmaking business employed forty workers.[2]

He was admirable in his personal life as well. He ultimately married Charlotte Vandine, who gave birth to eight children. Forten protested the Fugitive Slave Law in 1793 and in 1813 attacked a bill to ban the entrance of free Negroes into Pennsylvania. Forten wrote: "Has the God who made the white man and the black, left any record declaring us a different species? Are we not sustained by the same power, supported by the same food, hurt by the same wounds, wounded by the same wrongs, pleased with the same delights, and propagated by the same means. And should we not then enjoy the same liberty, and be protected by the same laws?"[3]

Forten's outspoken and staunch opposition to the American Colonization Society set him apart from most reformers. His belief in the equality of the races helped convince William Lloyd Garrison and Theodore Dwight Weld that colonization was an evil and that true abolitionism was the right course.[4] Forten died in 1842, at the age of seventy-six. "His funeral procession was one of the largest ever seen in Philadelphia; thousands of people, of all classes and complexions, having united in this tribute of respect to his character."[5]

In December 1833, Charlotte Forten and her daughters helped establish the Philadelphia Female Anti-Slavery Society, the country's first biracial organization of women's abolitionists, which drew all of its black members from the city's elite. Margaretta was one of fourteen women who drafted the Society's constitution and was an officer throughout the organization's history. Sarah served on the organization's governing board for two years. Harriet frequently co-chaired the Society's anti-slavery fairs. The Fortens also represented the Society as delegates to state and national conventions.

Margaretta was a teacher for at least thirty years. During the 1840s she taught at a school run by Sarah Mapps Douglass; in 1850 she opened her own school. She supported the women's rights movement, working to obtain signatures for a Women's National League petition. Margaretta never married and lived in her parents' home as an adult, as did her two younger brothers, Thomas and William.

Sarah Forten Purvis was a writer. Starting at seventeen, she composed numerous poems and articles for the *Liberator*, under the names "Magawisca" and "Ada." At least one of her poems, "The Grave of the Slave," was set to music by black bandleader Frank Johnson. Two of James Forten's other relatives had great influence on his granddaughter Charlotte Forten. One was her father, Robert Forten, who inherited James's sail-making business and his lifelong commitment to the abolition of slavery.[6] The other was her uncle Robert Purvis, husband of Harriet Forten, the free-born son of a Moorish-Negro mother and an English father. John Greenleaf Whittier, after listening to Purvis speak at the American Anti-Slavery Society, said that he had "never seen a finer face and figure and his manners, words and bearing are in keeping."[7]

Sarah and Harriet both married into another family of prominent black Philadelphian abolitionists, the Purvises. Harriet married Robert Purvis in 1832; Sarah married Joseph Purvis in 1838. Both couples moved to an area about fifteen miles south from Philadelphia. In 1857 Joseph Purvis died, and Sarah moved with her children to the Forten family home.

The household of Robert and Harriet Forten Purvis became a major haven for abolitionists and fugitive slaves alike. In addition to raising her own children, Harriet pursued her public career as an abolitionist with her husband's wholehearted support. In her later years, Harriet lectured against segregation and for black suffrage. Robert

Purvis was known as the "Father of he Underground Railroad" for his founding of the Vigilance Committee of Philadelphia, which saved hundreds of fugitive slaves.[8]

Charlotte was born in Philadelphia in 1837. She led a protected life after her mother died when Charlotte was three years old. Her father sent her to Byberry to live with Robert Purvis and his wife Harriet (Charlotte's aunt). She was not permitted to attend Philadelphia's segregated schools. Instead, the Forten family wealth allowed her to have private tutors. In order to expand her education, her father later sent her to live with another prominent black abolitionist family, Charles and Sarah Remond of Salem, Massachusetts. Charlotte graduated from Higginson Grammar School in 1855.

In 1856, Charlotte received a teaching assignment at the integrated Epes Grammar School, making her the first black teacher of white students in Salem, Massachusetts. The next two years were happy and fulfilling for Charlotte. She was able to pursue her favorite avocations: edu-

Charlotte Forten Grimké (1837–1914), a black abolitionist and teacher of freed slaves on the Sea Islands, Georgia, during Reconstruction. Charlotte was the wife of the Reverend Francis J. Grimké, famous minister of the Fifteenth Street Presbyterian Church in Washington, D.C. (Photographs and Prints Division, Schomburg Center for Research in Black Culture, The New York Public Library, Astor, Lenox and Tilden Foundations)

cation and abolitionism. She read widely, attended lectures and educated herself, embracing everything from the classics to poetry.

Charlotte moved in elite intellectual cultural and abolitionist circles. Her role models included William Lloyd Garrison, Wendell Phillips, and John Greenleaf Whittier as well as her grandfather, father and uncle. No wonder, then, that she became active in the Salem Female Anti-Slavery Society. However, her fragile constitution was not strong enough for the burdens of teaching and studying. In 1858, Charlotte returned home to Philadelphia where she recuperated and began writing. She served as correspondent for the *Atlantic Monthly* and for the *National Anti-Slavery Standard*.[9]

Since 1854, Charlotte had been writing a journal which began with this first entry: "A wish to record the passing events of my life, which even if quite unimportant to others, naturally possess great interest to myself, and of which it will be pleasant to have some remembrance, has induced me to commence this journal." This unsuspicious entry hardly forecast the moving written record of the next ten years of a sensitive, literate black woman to the white world around her. Race was always foremost in Charlotte Forten's mind. She wanted to excel at everything and always found herself wanting. "I feel grieved and ashamed to think how very little I know to what I should know of what is really good and useful. May this knowledge be to me a fresh incentive to more earnest, thoughtful action, more persevering study."

The hypocrisy of the United States for sanctioning the institution of slavery finally drove Charlotte Forten to denounce her country and almost deny her God. Every Fourth of July celebration showed in sharp contrast the huge gap between the florid boasts of freedom and the grim bigotry of the slave system. She wrote in her journal, "The patriots, poor fools, were celebrating the anniversary of their vaunted independence. Strange, they cannot feel their own degradation — the weight of the chains which they have imposed upon themselves.... The celebration of this day! What a mockery it is. My soul sickens of it." In the next July 4th entry, she wrote, "Spent the afternoon and eve in trying to rest; but in vain. Patriotic young America kept up [such] a din in celebrating their glorious Fourth, that rest was impossible."

The next four years were quiet while Charlotte regained her health. She could hardly have foreseen the adventure that the outbreak of the Civil War would afford her. The capture of Port Royal, South Carolina, by the Union Navy at the end of 1861, only seven months after the firing on Fort Sumter, set into motion the "Rehearsal for Reconstrucion."[10] Like many young abolitionist women she was eager to go South to teach the recently freed slaves. Secretary of the Treasury Salmon P. Chase believed that education was the key to the successful integration of the freedmen into citizenship. The Department sent out a call to many northern missionary societies for teachers willing to relocate to the South. In August 1862 during a visit to Boston, Forten was encouraged to apply for a job as a teacher with the recently organized Boston Port Royal Educational Commission.

When the commission did not contact her for several months, Forten wrote in her diary that "they were not sending women at present." She applied to the Philadelphia Association and was quickly accepted because of the recommendation of the poet John Greenleaf Whittier. After notification on October 21, 1862, she quickly departed aboard the steamer *United States* a week later.[11]

Forten's new home was on St. Helena Island, one of the Sea Islands halfway between Savannah, Georgia, and Charleston, South Carolina. Like the rest of the Sea Islands, St. Helena was fertile for cotton and rice growing but was wet, hot and mosquito-infested. Her daily living conditions were strictly makeshift and far different from her accustomed upper middle-class upbringing.

Upon her assumption of teaching responsibilities Forten was not immediately embraced by the Gullah and Geechee Sea Islanders. She was the first black teacher they ever experienced and her style seemed strange to them. She wrote in her diary that the local people had "a barbaric" way of worship. The longer she stayed in the islands teaching reading, writing (which had been banned by the Slave Code of 1790) and arithmetic, the more the Gullah folks taught her about spirituality from an African perspective and about their lifestyle that was based in praise of a Higher Being. Forten later wrote that she "never before saw children so eager to learn, although I had had several years' experience in New England schools. Coming to school is a constant delight and recreation to them. They come here as other children come to play."

The Reverend Thomas Callahan, a missionary of the United Presbyterian Church, reporting from Louisiana, captured the spirit:

> Go out in any direction and you meet Negroes on horses, Negroes on mules, Negroes with oxen, Negroes by the wagon, cart and buggy loan, Negroes on foot, men, women and children…. Negroes in rags, Negroes in frame houses, Negroes living in tents, Negroes living in rail pens covered with brush, and Negroes living under brush piles without any rails, Negroes living on the bare ground with the sky for their covering; all hopeful, almost cheerful, everyone pleading to be taught, willing to do anything for learning. They are never out of our rooms and their cry is for "Books! Books!" and "when will school begin?"[12]

In addition, to the three R's, Forten taught history. She met Thomas Wentworth Higginson, colonel of the First South Carolina Volunteers, an all-black regiment, and Colonel Robert Gould Shaw, the white commander of the all-black Fifty-fourth Massachusetts Volunteer Regiment (made famous in the movie *Glory*). She was also lucky enough to meet Harriet Tubman, the famous black conductor of the Underground Railroad, then a scout and spy for the Union Army.

> Saturday, January 31 … we spent nearly all our time at Harriet Tubman's otherwise [known as] "Moses." She is a wonderful woman — a real heroine. Has helped a large number of slaves, after taking her own freedom…. My own eyes were full as I listened to her — the heroic woman! A reward of $10,000 was offered for her by the southerners, and her friends deemed it best that she should for a time, find refuge in [Canada]. And she did so, but only for a short time. She came back and was soon at the good brave work again….
> I am glad I saw her — very glad.[13]

Here are some entries from Charlotte Forten's diary while she lived in South Carolina:

> Thursday, November 13, 1862: Talked to the children a little while today about the noble Toussaint [L'Ouverture]. They listened very attentively. It is well that they should know what one of their own color could do for his race. I long to inspire them with courage and ambition (of a noble sort), and high purpose.
> Thursday, November 27, 1862: This morning a large number of Superintendents, teachers and freed people, assembled in the little Baptist Church. It was a sight that I shall not soon forget — that crowd of eager, happy black faces from which the shadow of slavery had forever passed. "Forever free!" Those magical words were all the time singing themselves in my soul, and never before have I felt so truly grateful to God. The singing was, as usual, very beautiful. I thought I had never heard my favorite "Down In the Lonesome Valley" so well sung.
> Sunday, November 30, 1862: I am quite in love with one of the children here — little Amaretta who is niece to our good old Amaretta. She is a cunning little kittenish thing with such a gentle demure look. She is not quite black, and has pretty close hair, but delicate features. She is bright too. I love the child, wish I could take her for my own.
> Thursday, New Year's Day, 1863: The most glorious day this nation has yet seen, I

think. I rose early — an event here — and early we started, with an old borrowed carriage and a remarkably slow-horse. Whither were we going? Thou wilt ask, dearest A. To the ferry; thence to camp Saxton, to the Celebration.... I cannot give a regular chronicle of the day. It is impossible. I was in such a state of excitement. It all seemed, and seems still like a brilliant dream.... The meeting was held in a beautiful grove, a live-oak grove, adjoining the camp.... As I sat on the stand and looked around on the various groups, I thought I had never seen a sight so beautiful. There were the black soldiers, in their blue coats and scarlet pants, the officers of this and other regiments in their handsome uniforms, and crowds of lookers-on, men, women and children, grouped in various attitudes, under the trees. The faces of all wore a happy, eager, expectant look.... [Dr. Brisbane] read the President's [Emancipation] Proclamation, which was warmly cheered.... Immediately at the conclusion, some of the colored people — of their own accord sang "My Country Tis of Thee." It was a touching and beautiful incident and Col. Higginson, in accepting the flags, made it the occasion of some happy remarks. He said that the tribute was far more effective than any speech he could make.... The men admire and love him.... After he had done speaking he delivered the flags to the color-bearers with a few very impressive remarks to them. They each then, Sgt. Prince Rivers and [cpl] Robert Sutton,[14] made very good speeches, indeed and were loudly cheered.

Charlotte eventually was no longer simply looked at as a "stuck up" (i.e., "sidity" in Gullah) black woman. She became a part of the community and was sadly missed when she had to leave the island in the latter part of May in 1864 aboard *The Fulton*. She arrived in New York on June 3, 1864, very ill and in need of rest. Charlotte had witnessed a miracle on the Sea Islands in the two years she was there: 2,000 students in school, thousands of adults receiving instruction in churches before the Sunday-morning services. By the close of 1863, almost 7,000 acres of former plantation land were owned by freedmen.[15]

Charlotte settled in Philadelphia and continued to write extensively. She served as a secretary of the Teachers Committee of the New England branch of the Freedmen's Union Commission where she coordinated, recruited and advised teachers working with recently freed slaves.

In 1871, she taught at the Robert Gould Shaw Memorial School in Charleston, South Carolina, and then at the highly rated prep school, the M Street School (later named the Paul Lawrence Dunbar High School). After two years, she took a job as a clerk in the United States Treasury Department.[16]

On December 19, 1878, Charlotte Forten married a black man, the Reverend Francis J. Grimké. She was forty-one years old, he was twenty eight but with similar political and cultural views; they lived together successfully for thirty-six years. Unfortunately, their daughter Theodora Cornelia, born on New Year's Day in 1880, died when she was only five months old. Except for this tragedy, the Grimkés' life together was an idyllic one. Charlotte worked alongside her husband in the Fifteenth Street Presbyterian Church where he was pastor. They shared lifelong interests in racial equality, intellectual pursuits, teaching, missionary work, and writing. Charlotte was a founding member of the National Association of Colored Women, founded in 1896.[17]

Who was Francis J. Grimké? How did he and his brother Archibald acquire the name Grimké? In order to answer these questions we need to refer back to pre–Civil War South Carolina. The story is fascinating and instructive.

The Grimké name goes back in South Carolina history to the aristocratic family of the wealthy judge John Grimké. Among John's eleven children were daughters Sarah and Angelina.

These two daughters, raised in a slaveholding family, made many remarkable decisions in their lives. One of the first was to leave the South, and slaveholding, behind. Moving North, they settled in Philadelphia, where they became active in the antislavery movement. Throughout their lives, they would pursue what were viewed as radical causes: not only abolition, but also educational opportunity for women.[18]

In February 1868, Angelina read in the *National Anti-Slavery Standard* an article written by Professor R. Bower of Lincoln University, a black college in Pennsylvania. Seeking to disprove the notion of black inferiority, Bower compared his black students favorably to any class he ever had. He identified one of these superior black students as "Grimkie who came here two years ago, just out of slavery."[19]

Despite the misspelling, "Grimkie" caught Angelina's eye. Perhaps this was a former Grimké slave who had taken the family name. Angelina wrote Mr. "Grimkie" to find out who he was, and his prompt answer amazed her.

Archibald Grimké's reply introduced himself as Angelina's nephew. He was the Negro son born of her brother Henry and one of his slaves, Nancy Weston, whom Henry Grimké had lived with after the death of his wife.

Archibald sketched his own life and that of his two brothers, who were also sons of Henry Grimké. When Henry Grimké died, his three colored offspring—Francis, Archibald, and John—were left under the guardianship of their white half brother, Montague. At the outbreak of the Civil War, Montague decided to sell the three boys. Archibald ran away. Francis did, too, but he was found and sold into slavery along with John. After the war the three were reunited and freed in Charleston. Agents of the United States Sanitary Commission working in Charleston were impressed by the obvious intelligence of Francis and Archibald and sent them to Boston to go to school. In 1866 the two young men, aged sixteen and seventeen, entered Lincoln University, where they were excellent students. In the course of pursuing his studies, Archibald Grimké's name had been mentioned in print and Angelina had seen it.

What was the reaction of Sarah and Angelina on learning of the existence of their black nephews? Angelina wrote them acknowledging the relationship and charging them to bear proudly the once honored name of Grimké. "I am glad you have taken the name Grimké. It was once one of the noblest names of Carolina. You, my young friends, now bear this once honored name. I charge you most solemnly, by your upright conduct and your life-long devotion to the eternal principles of justice and humanity and religion, to lift this name out of the dust where it now lies, and set it once more among the princes of our land."

In letters that followed, both Sarah and Angelina proffered their interest and concern for the welfare of Archibald and Francis. They also contributed to the boys' expenses despite the extremely modest Weld income. (Angelina's husband was Theodore Dwight Weld, a famous abolitionist.) When the young men graduated from Lincoln University, Angelina and her son attended the commencement exercises. Francis was valedictorian of his class, and Archibald ranked third.

The two young black men visited the Weld home and before long came to consider it their own. The Welds and Sarah Grimké, in turn, considered Archibald and Francis part of the family, and devoted time and attention to charting their future.

Archibald decided to become a lawyer. He stayed at Lincoln to earn his master's degree, then attended and graduated with distinction from Harvard Law School. An LL.B. in his hand, he stayed on in Boston, where his law practice thrived. For twelve years he published the leading Negro newspaper in the city and was an outstanding leader of his race. In 1894 Archibald became United States Consul to the Republic of Santo Domingo for four years. He later became president of the American Negro Academy in Washington, and during his busy lifetime wrote several books, including fine biographies of William Lloyd Garrison and Charles Sumner.

Francis Grimké's career was equally accomplished. He graduated from the Princeton Theological Seminary in 1878. For most of the rest of his long life he served as minister of the Fifteenth Street Presbyterian Church in Washington, D.C. There he ministered with distinction to the Negro people of his parish and of the whole nation, fighting for Negro rights through his sermons and his writings until his death in October 1937.

As Ray Allen Billington wrote,

> In the Reverend Francis Grimké, Charlotte Forten found the ideal husband. With social views and literary interests in common, they lived an idyllic life, marred only by the death of their one child in 1880. Charlotte Forten Grimké died on July 23, 1914, after a lingering illness that had kept her bedridden for thirteen months. Her bequest to humanity was a journal which could reveal to a later generation her undying belief in human decency and equality.[20]

8

Thomas Wentworth Higginson (1823–1911): Militant Abolitionist, Lifelong Activist, Man of Letters

In June 1904, when Thomas Wentworth Higginson was eighty-one years old, and lynching of blacks occurred at the rate of one hundred per year, when anti-black racism pervaded the United States, he wrote:

> There is no charge more unfounded than that frequently made to the effect that the Negro was best understood by his former masters. It would be more reasonable to say that the Negro as a human being was really least comprehended by those to whom he represented merely a check for $1,000, or less, from a slave auctioneer. This principle may be justly borne in mind in forming an opinion upon the very severest charges still brought against him. Thus a southern Negro has only to be suspected of any attempt at assault on a white woman and the chances are that he will be put to death without a trial, and perhaps with fiendish torture. Yet, during my two years' service with colored troops, only one charge of such assault was brought against any soldier, and that was withdrawn in the end and admitted to be false by the very man who made the assertion, and this in a captured town … does anyone suppose for a moment that the mob which burns him on suspicion of such a crime is doing it in defense of chastity? Not at all; it is in defense of caste.[1]

Thomas W. Higginson was born in 1823 in an eminent New England family. He was the youngest of ten children whose father was a successful Boston merchant who became the steward of Harvard College. He was deeply interested in Unitarianism and organized the Harvard Divinity School.

When Thomas was ten years old, his mother wrote, "He has genuine refinement and delicacy, with manliness and power of controlling himself and a sense of right, governing his thoughts and actions — which command my respect as much as if he was a grown man…. I never [saw] one who was more thoughtful and considerate of others — though he has been the youngest and an object of uncommon interest."[2]

Higginson rejected his family's plan to become a lawyer and instead attended the Harvard Divinity School to become a Unitarian minister. By then, Higginson was invested in two causes which were to guide him for the rest of his long life: abolitionism and women's rights.

After being ordained a minister, he worked at the Newbury Unitarian Church until his outspoken views on abolition got him removed by the pro-slavery members of his seaport congregation. Higginson was one of the signers of the Call for the First National Women's Rights Convention. He officiated at the wedding of Lucy Stone and formally joined the newly married couple in endorsing on the marriage certificate a protest against the ineligibility of married women to own property under existing laws.[3]

Higginson supported the ten hour bill, land reform, penal legislation, temperance, anti-slavery and women's rights. In 1853, at the World Temperance Convention in New York City, he supported the appointment of Susan B. Anthony to the Committee on Arrangements, which caused an uproar of hissing and catcalls.[4]

Higginson led a walkout of the convention, which resulted in the formation of the Whole World's Temperance Convention, supported by some of the most important leaders: Susan B. Anthony, Abby Foster, Lucretia Mott, Elizabeth Cady Stanton, Lucy Stone, Wendell Phillips, Horace Greeley, Theodore Parker and William Lloyd Garrison.[5]

But Higginson yearned for "one occasion worth bursting the door for — an opportunity to get beyond this boy's play."[6] He found that opportunity on May 24, 1854, when Anthony Burns, an escaped slave, was captured in Boston. A Vigilance Committee made up of Higginson, Parker, Phillips, Samuel Gridley Howe, Austin Bearse, Martin Stowell and William Kemp debated a forced rescue of Burns. On May 26, Higginson led a failed attempt to rescue Burns from the courthouse. Higginson escaped and later wrote Mary that "there has been an attempt at rescue and failed. I am not hurt except a scratch on the face which will prevent me from doing anything more about it, lest I be recognized."[7]

Ultimately, Burns was returned to the South; Higginson, who prepared his defense on the immorality of the Fugitive Slave Law, was never tried. Novelist Richard Henry Dana confessed his surprise at Higginson's conduct in his journal: "I knew his ardor and courage but I hardly expected a married man, a clergyman and a man of education to lead the mob."[8]

During the 1850s the issue of slavery in the territory of Kansas flashed into open warfare. Many of the free soil settlers were being harassed by the pro-slavery border ruffians from Missouri. "Higginson supported the recruitment of men, arms and ammunition for Free Soil northerners wishing to emigrate to Kansas, and even went West to report on the welfare of the New England men who had settled there. His 'Letters from Kansas' depict the open insurrection constantly threatening, as marauding bands of southerners plundered the wagon trains and settlements of the northerners."[9] Tuttleton continues, "[Higginson] rode shotgun on a wagon train bound across the prairie for Topeka, telling his mother: 'Imagine me also patrolling as one of the guards for an hour every night, in high boots amid the chewy grass, rifle in hand and revolver in belt.'"[10]

In Lawrence, Kansas, Higginson preached on the text of Nehemiah 4:14: "Be not afraid of them: remember the Lord, which is great and terrible, and fight for your brethren, your sons and daughters, your wives and your houses."[11] Sometime in 1858, John Brown contacted Higginson and requested money for his "secret service." Brown was about to implement "the perfecting of by far the most important undertaking of my whole life."[12] Brown was secretive about this undertaking but Higginson believed that the project was to rescue fugitive slaves in Virginia and transport them to safe haven in Canada.

Higginson was one of the "Secret Six," important backers of John Brown, who was the first American ever hanged for treason at Charlestown, Virginia (now West Virginia), on December 2, 1859. The Secret Six were vigorous and, for their time, extremist abolitionists. They were Theodore Parker, the great and well-known theologian preacher; Dr. Samuel Gridley Howe, world-famous

Thomas Wentworth Higginson (1823–1911). A renaissance man, he was a militant abolitionist; a supporter of workers' rights, penal legislation, temperance, anti-slavery, women's rights and John Brown; and colonel of the first American regiment of freed slaves during the Civil War. He wrote *Army Life in a Black Regiment.* (©Corbis)

physician and psychologist; Gerritt Smith, greatest American landowner of his day; George Luther Sterns, industrialist and inventor; Franklin Benjamin Sanborn, educator, editor and biographer; and Thomas Wentworth Higginson.[13]

Other famous supporters of Brown, both in Kansas (1856) and in his raid on Harpers Ferry, Virginia (1859), were Henry David Thoreau, Ralph Waldo Emerson, John Murray Forbes, Thaddeus Hyatt, and Amos A. Lawrence.

Brown's plan was, of course, the futile assault on the federal arsenal at Harpers Ferry. Of the Secret Six, only Higginson remained in the country in the expectation of arrest for his support of Brown's failed scheme. Higginson tried to persuade Brown's wife to agree to an armed attempt to rescue her husband, but Brown refused to approve that plan and after his trial he was executed on December 2, 1858. Surprisingly, Higginson himself was never arrested and was never called to testify before the Mason Committee. The Congress, he concluded, where "white men are concerned, would yield before the slightest resistance and dared not try to arrest him in Worcester."[14]

When the Civil War began, Higginson was thirty-seven years old and, after a decade of political demonstration, insurrection, and the promotion of revolution, he was physically exhausted. Nevertheless, he remained vigorously anti-slavery, writing a series of articles in the *Atlantic Monthly Magazine* on Nat Turner's insurrection, Denmark Vesey, Haitian emigration and ordeal by battle. He started to "read military books, took notes on fortifications, strategy, and the principles of attack and defense. He took fencing lessons and began a drill club. All this self-taught military preparation enabled him to become ready for what was to be, to one who had been such an ardent abolitionist, the supreme opportunity of his life."[15]

After raising a group of Worcester volunteers in August 1862, Higginson was appointed captain of a company of the 51st Massachusetts Regiment. This gave him the opportunity to learn the military manuals and to have hands-on experience in training inexperienced volunteers. Soon thereafter, the following letter was delivered to Higginson:

> Beaufort, S.C., November 5, 1862
>
> My Dear Sir — I am organizing the First Regiment of South Carolina Volunteers, with every prospect of success. Your name has been spoken of, in connection with the command of this regiment, by some friends in whose judgment I have confidence. I take great pleasure in offering you the position of Colonel in it, and hope that you may be induced to accept. I shall not fill the place until I hear from you, or sufficient time shall have passed for me to receive your reply. Should you accept, I enclose a pass for Port Royal, of which I trust you will feel disposed to avail yourself at once.
>
> I am, with sincere regard, yours truly,
>
> R. Saxton
> Brig.—Genl. Mil. Gov.

Higginson was absolutely surprised by this invitation. He wrote, "Had an invitation reached me to take command of a regiment of Kalmuck Tartans, it could hardly have been more unexpected. I had always looked for the arming of the blacks, and had always felt a wish to be associated with them.... But the prevalent tone of public sentiment was still opposed to any such attempts ... and it did not seem possible that the time had come when it could be fairly tried."[16]

There had always been doubt as to the wisdom of arming former black slaves. Could they be trained properly to be Union soldiers? Could they be counted on when under fire? Would they turn their guns on all whites? Ultimately, 192,000 blacks served successfully in the Union Army to win the war against the secessionist and traitorous Confederate government.

In order for the Union Navy to reinforce a blockage of the Confederacy it needed a sea base behind southern lines on the Atlantic Ocean. In late 1861, a joint Union force under Admiral Samuel Du Pont and General Thomas Sherman conquered Port Royal and Beaufort, South Carolina, and held this base and anchorage until the end of the war.

Many thousands of slaves were freed from the plantations located on the Sea Islands. A special agent of the Treasury Department, Edward L. Pierce, was given the responsibility of feeding the newly freed blacks. He also was charged with the responsibility of organizing civilian activities such as employment contracts and education. Pierce was unique in that he believed that ex-slaves were human beings who, if treated well, could become useful and productive citizens of the United States.

Perhaps no better description of this exciting event has ever been written than the following description by C. Vann Woodward in the Introduction to *Rehearsal for Reconstruction*:

> The Port Royal Experiment ... began not long after the war started, seven months after the fall of Fort Sumter, and developed behind Confederate lines while the war thundered away on the mainland Virginia and along the Mississippi, hundreds of miles away. The stage was cleared for the experiment by the United States Navy on November 7, 1861, long remembered by the slaves as "the day of the big gun-shoot." Under the command of Admiral Du Pont, a fleet sailed into Port Royal Sound, opened a bombardment, quickly reduced the defending batteries, and on the following day landed troops to occupy the islands.[17]

As soon as Du Pont's guns ceased fire, the slaveowners and planters, as well as the entire white population, hurriedly loaded a few possessions and a few house servants on flatboats, set fire to piles of cotton bales, and sailed away to the mainland. Behind them they left their mansions, meals cooking on stoves, along with their slaves and virtually all their possessions. When the troops arrived in Beaufort, the only town of consequence, they discovered only one white man, and he was too drunk to move. Some 10,000 slaves, more than eighty percent of the island population in 1860, remained behind—some to loot the mansion houses, but they all welcomed the invaders and set about to determine—gradually and painfully—whether the troops came as liberators or as a new set of masters. The troops and their commanders were by no means clear on this point themselves. The old regime had collapsed as suddenly as any in history, but the new regime was not ready to take its place.

Into this island limbo between the old and the new sailed "Gideon's Band." The steamer *Atlantic* landed them at Beaufort in March 1862. The Gideonites, a band of fifty-three missionaries, were mostly young anti-slavery people, about half of them from Boston and its vicinity and half from New York. They were united in their determination to give shape to liberation and guidance and help to the liberated. At Beaufort, South Carolina, the abolitionists and the slaves confronted each other on slave territory for the first time.

It was a dramatic coincidence that abolition and reconstruction should have struck first in the Sea Islands. The northern newspaperman who called the islands "the exclusive home of the most exclusive few of that most exclusive aristocracy" was guilty of some overstatement. But old Beaufort and its vicinity was the seedbed of South Carolina secessionism. Robert Barnwell Rhett, fire-eating secessionist, made his home there, and so did William J. Grayson, poet and champion of the slavery cause. The mansions of the Elliotts, the Heywards, the Coffins, the Fripps, the Barnwells and the Seabrooks stood abandoned among their stately live oaks and festoons of Spanish moss. The old masters had vanished quickly and completely, but they had left behind them a slave culture and social discipline that was the product of two centuries and that would be slow to yield to the newly imported culture of freedom and free enterprise.

In August 1862, it became necessary to reinforce General McClellan's Army of the Potomac, so U.S. Cavalry forces were withdrawn from the Port Royal Harbor area. The overcrowding of the freedmen brought from three evacuated islands helped to change long-standing Union policy regarding the arming of Negro troops. Under General Rufus Saxton, military governor of the Department of the South, the First South Carolina Volunteers was organized.

"Gentlemen, the question is settled; Negroes will fight." So spoke the Union General George H. Thomas as he rode over the 1864 battlefield of Nashville and saw "the bodies of colored men side by side with the foremost in the very works of the enemy." General Thomas, a Virginian from a slaveowning family, was a little behind the times.

Black soldiers had begun fighting and dying for the Union in late 1862, as soon as President Lincoln would let them. They included northern freemen and southern slaves who joined the invading Union forces. At the end of the Civil War, there were 149 black regiments, one tenth of the Union Army. Saxton's choice of Thomas Wentworth Higginson as colonel of this very first American regiment of freed slaves was a brilliant one. One of Higginson's junior officers wrote, "He was a born commander.... He met a slave and made him a Man."[19] Higginson wrote later about his feelings when he took command, "[I] had been an abolitionist too long, and had known John Brown too well, not to feel a thrill of joy," upon finding himself at the head of a black regiment.[20] Howard Meyer wrote, "No one could have been chosen who was better suited to lead and understand, to teach and learn from, to educate and inspire, a group of 800 men who had either been slaves from birth, or came to this country, unlike every other immigrant group, not to escape oppression but to find it.... The new colonel was strong on drill and military appearance, qualities of great importance to a group whose status as free men was only of recent origin, and who had been forbidden, under penalty of the lash, ever to read and write before their liberation. The recruits he led lacked neither courage nor native ability, and justified his faith in them."[21]

The South Carolina Volunteers acquitted themselves well in battle. The men suffered casualties but drove off the Confederates in a stand-up fight against rebel guerrillas on St. Simon's Island. In another excursion to the Georgia coast, they demolished enemy saltworks, took prisoners and freed slaves and property. Saxton praised his Negro regiment strongly.[22]

On the Emancipation Day ceremonies at Camp Saxton in 1862, General Saxton was planning a gala celebration for some 5,000 ex-slaves, their missionary friends, 800 of the newly trained First South Carolina Volunteers and invited guests. Willie Lee Rose wrote, "The white tents of Higginson's regiment were spread in orderly array on the grounds of the Smith plantation, located on a picturesque point about three miles south of Beaufort on the site where the French had build a fort in the sixteenth century.... Great stores of molasses, hard bread and tobacco were laid by for the guests, and a dozen oxen were roasted on spits."[23]

Eyewitness accounts of the ceremonies reflected the significance of the day for the people of the Sea Islands. After all, nowhere else could the Emancipation Proclamation have so much meaning than to the recently freed slaves who dressed in their holiday best. The weather was perfect: a cloudless sky, the blue river, and the warm South Carolina sun lent a festive air to the more than three-hour-long service. After speeches, singing and prayers the highlight of the event was the reading of Lincoln's Emancipation Proclamation by Dr. William H. Brisbane, a native Sea Island abolitionist who freed his slaves many years earlier. The most moving part of the ceremony came after Dr. Brisbane concluded his reading of the Proclamation. Higginson wrote,

> Then the colors were presented to us by the Rev. Mr. French, a chaplain who brought them from the donors in New York. All this was according to the program. Then followed an incident so simple, so touching, so utterly unexpected and startling, that I can scarcely believe it on recalling, though it gave the key-note to the whole day. The very movement the speaker had ceased, and just as I took and waved the flag, which now for the first time meant anything to these poor people, there suddenly arose, close to the platform, a strong male voice (but rather cracked and elderly), into which two women's voices instantly blended, singing, as if by an impulse that could no more be repressed than the morning note of the sang sparrow.
>
> > "My Country, 'tis of thee,
> > Sweet land of liberty,
> > Of thee I sing!"
>
> ...Firmly and irrepressibly the quavering voices sang on, verse after verse; others of the colored people joined in.... I never saw anything so electric; it made all other words cheap; it seemed the choked voice of a race at last unloosed. Nothing could be more wonderfully unconscious; art could not have dreamed of a tribute to the day of jubilee that should be so affecting; history will not believe it; and when I came to speak of it, after it was ended, tears were everywhere.[24]

The first South Carolina Regiment had a distinguished service: they conquered Jacksonville, Florida, in March 1863 and liberated hundreds of slaves from the plantations along the Edisto River in South Carolina. In July 1863, Higginson was wounded with a concussion when enemy shellfire hit the pilothouse of his boat. Because he didn't respond favorably to treatment, Higginson was discharged in April 1864 with a medical disability. Higginson was given a hero's welcome in Boston and later wrote in *Army Life in a Black Regiment*, "[We] had touched the pivot of the war ... till blacks were armed, there was no guarantee of their freedom. It was their demeanor under arms that showed the nation into recognizing them as men."[25]

Army Life in a Black Regiment was considered a forgotten masterpiece by Howard Mumford Jones, who wrote, "Its supreme appeal is as an expression of yearning of the North for the South, for color, for warmth, for a simpler and healthier way of life than that of industrialized cities"; yet there is no doubt that "a lively humor, a fine eye for the picturesque, indignation against injustice and real affection for his men create one of the few classics of military life in the national letters.... The pen of its writer was touched with the incommunicable power that turns writing into literary art."[26]

In a letter that Higginson retained until the end of his life, one of the black rank and file privates wrote: "I meet many of the old soldiers. I spoke of you — all hailed your name with that emotion (that become you) of the Soul when hearing of one who when in darkness burst light on their pathway."[27]

After the war, the admirable Thomas Wentworth Higginson resumed the life of a New England man of letters. He led the committee to raise funds for the defense of Susan B. Anthony when she was arrested in 1872 to test the theory that the right of women to vote was covered by the Fourteenth Amendment.

Among many other progressive activities in his later years, Higginson

• demanded an end to the segregation of Negro children in the public schools of Newport, Rhode Island;

• wrote that "it hardly embarrassed a professor's position if he defended slavery as a divine institution; but he risked his place if he denounced the wrong";

• wrote in 1899, "The whole history of free states consists in rebellion against the interference of other states which think themselves wiser and stronger.... The men who are remembered in history the longest are sometimes those who raise their voices against such aggressions, even when their own government commits them"[28];

• and expressed in his autobiography *Cheerful Yesterdays* (1898), written in his seventieth year, the wish "that he would live to see international arbitration secured, civil service reform completed, free trade established; to find the legal and educational rights of the two sexes equalized;... to see natural monopolies owned by the public, not in private hands;... to live under absolute as well as nominal religious freedom."

His final words, which perhaps reflect the hallmark of his life, were "Let my memory perish, if only humanity may be free."[29]

9

John Mercer Langston (1829–1897): Lawyer, Minister Resident and Consul-General, Dean and Professor of Law at Howard University, Member of Congress

Ten years after Reconstruction ended, an African American was elected to Congress from Virginia for the first time. This event can only be explained in light of the personality of this remarkable man who was almost sixty years old at the time. By the time this election took place, John Mercer Langston had held numerous important public positions of trust and confidence. While never a member of a state legislature, Langston was elected as a member of the Council of Oberlin, Ohio, and in other township offices. Langston served as dean of the law department of Howard University and in 1873 became vice president and acting president of that institution. In 1885, he became the president of the Virginia Normal and Collegiate Institute. He served earlier as inspector-general of the Freedmen's Bureau, as a member of the board of health of the District of Columbia, and as minister resident and consul-general to Haiti and chargé d'affaires to Santo Domingo. Election to the U.S. House of Representatives was the crowning achievement of his distinguished career.

The *Montgomery* (Alabama) *Herald* wrote,

> It is impossible for the Fourth Virginia Congressional District to elect a man that would reflect more credit upon his constituents and race, or American statesmanship, than Mr. Langston. He is undoubtedly the highest type of Afro-American citizenship. All through his long, eventful, venturous course, leaping with giant-like strides, from the valley of obscurity to the summit of human grandeur and manly excellence, not one act of his has tended to reflect dishonor upon himself, his people, or his country.

Another Negro journal added this comment:

> This country has never yet produced a more remarkable man than Hon. John M. Langston. He is a man of observation, and nothing escapes his keen and penetrating eye, with knowledge of human nature that it would be almost impossible to deceive him. The life and services of no man will fill a brighter page in history than his. The future historians will record the remarkable fact that he has been equal to every emergency, and used only honorable means to attain his ends.[1]

It is unfortunate to report that "future historians" did not take much notice of John Mercer Langston. In writing the biography of Langston, William J. Simmons said, "One of the greatest Negroes in America is the subject of this sketch. His name has become a household word, especially among the younger generation, and his deeds shine brightly alongside of those of even older men."[2] Langston is not a household word, and indeed, few today have ever heard of him even though at the time of his death in 1897 he attained prominence as a black leader second only to Frederick Douglass.

In 1852, John M. Langston, just twenty-two years old, spoke on behalf of Dr. Norton S. Townsend, a white anti-slavery candidate for Congress. The location was a pro-slavery, rural backwater called French Creek, Lorain County, Ohio. Earlier, a heckler had yelled out to a white speaker, "Are you in favor of nigger social equality?" Later, when Langston finished speaking, the same heckler cried out at the top of his voice, "You learned that at Oberlin." When Langston admitted this statement to be true, the heckler screamed, "You learned another thing at Oberlin. You learned to walk with white women there!" That was true, Langston replied. Advancing to the edge of the platform and looking straight at his tormenter, he said, "If you have in your family any good-looking, intelligent, refined sisters, you would do your family a special service by introducing me to them at once." In the midst of the sudden surprising outburst of popular applause following this remark and in approval of it, an old gray-headed Democrat addressed his vanquished friend, saying, "Joe Ladd, you damn fool, sit down! That darkey is too smart for you. Sit down!" These last words convulsed the audience and Mr. Langston retired from the stand in triumph. French Creek was carried on election day by a large majority for Dr. Townsend.[3]

Who was this black man who even at age twenty-two had the courage, wit and audacity to speak out in a repressive society? In their biography of John Langston, William and Aimee Lee Cheek wrote,

> During a multi-faceted career in black protest, politics, education and law lasting a half a century, John Mercer Langston became the first black lawyer in the West, the first Afro-American elected to public office, a recruiter of black troops for the Union Army, an inspector for the Freedmen's Bureau, the first law dean of Howard University, the U.S. minister to Haiti and Santo Domingo, the president of the Virginia State College for Negroes at Petersburg, and the first and only black representative of Virginia in Congress.[4]

In the spring of 1855, John Mercer Langston became the first black American elected to public office by popular vote in the United States when he won the post of township clerk in Brownhelm, Ohio. The jubilant officeholder reported his victory in a letter to Frederick Douglass, who published it in his newspaper:

> I have a news item for you. On the 2nd of this month, we held our elections. In our township, we had three district parties, and as many independent tickets. The Independent Democrats were wise for once, at least, in making and sticking to their own nominations. But more than this, and a thing which also exhibits their wisdom and virtue; they put upon their ticket the name of a colored man, who was elected clerk of Brownhelm Township, by a handsome majority indeed. Since I am the only colored man who lives in this township, you can easily guess the name of the man who was so fortunate as to secure this election. To my knowledge, the like has not been known in Ohio before. It argues the steady march of the Anti-Slavery sentiment and augurs the inevitable destruction and annihilation of American prejudice against colored men. What we so much need at this junction, and all along the future, is political influence; the bridle by which we can check and guide to our advantages, the selfishness of American demagogues. How important, then, it is, that we labor night and day to enfranchise ourselves. We are doing too little in this direction. And I make this charge against Anti-Slavery persons, as well as colored ones. I hope that before a great while, we will all amend our ways in this particular.[5]

In his time, his name became a household word, especially among the younger generation. As well as he was known then, he is almost completely forgotten today.

John Mercer Langston was born in Louisa County, Virginia, on December 14, 1829, with Indian, Negro and Anglo-Saxon genes. It was said that he had the fortitude of the first, the pride of the second and the progressiveness of the third. He was the son of Captain Ralph Quarles, a white plantation owner and his slave mistress Lucy Langston, daughter of an Indian mother and a father of mixed blood. Langston remembered her as "a woman of small stature, substantial build, fair looks, easy and natural bearing, even and quiet temper, intelligent and thoughtful, who accepted her lot with becoming resignation, while she always exhibited the deepest affection and earnest solicitude for her children." Captain Quarles, a veteran of the Revolutionary War, was a large landed slaveholder who had unusual views as to the management of his slaves. No white man was allowed to oversee them; this work was done by other slaves. Upon his death in 1834, Captain Quarles freed all his slaves and appointed trustees to relocate them to Ohio with liberal provisions for those recognized by him as his children. Lucy died soon after Quarles and was buried beside him on the family land. Langston could recall being brought when he was five to his mother's deathbed. In those days it was not uncommon for free Negroes to be kidnapped in northern states and sold into slavery. John was saved from such an attempt by an older brother and the legal skill of a white family lawyer, Allen G. Thurman (later a senator from Ohio). John went to live with William Gooch, one of the executors of the estate. He stayed with the Gooch family for five years, until they decided to move to Missouri, a slave state. Langston lived with another white family before moving to Cincinnati to attend a private school conducted in the Baker Street Baptist Church by two white schoolteachers. In due time, young John Mercer entered Oberlin College and lived with the family of George

Whipple, one of the professors. Whipple was better known as Secretary of the American Missionary Association, which later did phenomenal work in the education of freed slaves in the South during Reconstruction. Langston graduated with honors from Oberlin in 1849.

John Langston, upon his graduation from Oberlin College, married Caroline Matilda Wall, also an Oberlin graduate. Caroline was the daughter of Colonel Stephen Wall, a white planter, and his slave Priscilla (Prissy) Ely. Langston wrote about Col. Wall in 1880, "A noted man of superior intelligence and business enterprise remembered even to this day by those of his old neighbors who still live."[6] Wall mated with at least three of his slaves, all of whom bore him children. Sometime before his death in 1845, Wall freed his four children by the Ely sisters and sent them to southwestern Ohio where, in Harveysburg, a progressive black settlement flourished under the direction of the abolitionist-supporting Hicksite and Orthodox friends societies.[7] In 1850, Caroline came to Oberlin and after a year in the preparatory course, entered the ladies collegiate literary course and graduated in 1854. On October 25, 1854, John Mercer Langston, twenty-four, was married to Caroline Matilda Wall, twenty-one. Together, they bore and raised three sons and a daughter. In a book published in 1914, author John Cromwell described an interesting phenomenon in the Langston family:

> The traditional influence of the family for education may be seen in these coincidences: In 1849, in his twenty-first year, he [John Mercer Langston] graduated from

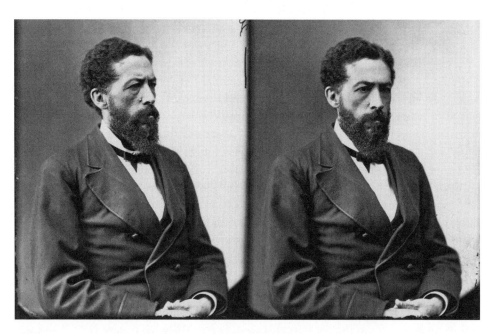

John Mercer Langston (1829–1897). A distinguished black lawyer who served as dean of the Howard University law school, he was inspector-general of the Freedmen's Bureau, minister resident and consul-general to Haiti and chargé d'affaires to Santo Domingo, and the first African American member of the U.S. House of Representatives from Virginia. (©Corbis)

Oberlin College. Nearly thirty years after, his eldest son, then twenty-one, took the same degree, A.B., from the same spot, and following their examples, the grandsons, John Mercer Langston, Second, and Carroll Napier Langston, in turn, when twenty-one, followed in the steps of their immediate predecessors. This is an example unique in the history of the colored race in America where three generations have graduated from the same college and at the same age.[8]

Langston sought admission to the Albany Law School but was refused on account of his color. He was advised to pass his way into the school by claiming that he was a Frenchman or Spaniard coming from the West Indies or Central America for he could well have passed as either. But Langston scorned such a trick. He next tried to gain admission to a law class in Cincinnati whose president said that as a young "colored man" he could not find himself at home with white students. That man never made a greater mistake.

Langston ultimately read for the law after graduating from the theological department of Oberlin College in 1853. He finally was admitted to the Ohio bar under the guidance of the Hon. Philemon Bliss of Elyria, Ohio, a lawyer-politician noted for his anti-slavery sentiments as well as his commanding influence in the community. Before the special committee appointed for the purpose would admit this "colored man" to the Ohio bar they determined that Langston had more white than Negro blood. He was finally sworn in by the court as a lawyer on October 24, 1854. Thus he began his remarkable legal career. Langston relocated to Lorain County, Ohio, nine miles from Oberlin, to a town called Brownhelm, a rich and progressive community of white people. He was the only black residing in that part of Ohio and began to practice with a bootlegger as his first client.

Langston's election as Brownhelm township clerk brought him a speaking invitation that he later referred to as one of the most important in his life. It was from the American Anti-Slavery Society, which held its annual meeting in New York City in May 1855. Other speakers were William Lloyd Garrison, Wendell Phillips and the theologian Theodore Parker, codefendants in the black fugitive Anthony Burns's celebrated rescue case.[9]

On May 9, 1855, 3,000 persons gathered at the Metropolitan Theater in New York for the American Anti-Slavery Society meeting. On the platform sat the best-known anti-slavery advocates in the United States: Gerrit Smith, Wendell Phillips, Henry B. Stanton, Henry Wilson; women suffrage leaders Antoinette Brown and Lucy Stone; ministers Henry Ward Beecher and Theodore Parker; and famous abolitionists William Wells Brown, C.C. Burleigh, Abby and Stephen Foster, Oliver Johnson, Samuel May, Jr., James and Lucretia Mott, Robert Purvis, Charles Lenox Redmond and H.C. Wright. After his welcoming remarks, William Lloyd Garrison introduced twenty-five-year-old John Mercer Langston as the "colored lawyer recently elected as Clerk of Brownhelm Township in Ohio."[10] Langston delivered a speech that was widely praised and reported in the daily papers of New York and the leading journals of the various anti-slavery societies. Its logic and conclusions resonate strongly some 148 years later. His opening sentences are unforgettable:

Some great man has remarked that a nation may lose its liberty in a day and be a century in finding out. Does our own nation afford illustration of this statement? There is not, within the length and breadth of this entire country, from Maine to Georgia, from the Atlantic to the Pacific Oceans, a solitary man or woman who is in the possession of his or her full share of civil, religious and political liberty. This is a startling announcement perhaps made in the heart and center of a country loud in its boasts of its free institutions, its democratic organizations, its equality, its justice and its liberality. We have been in the habit of boasting our Declaration of Independence, of our Federal Constitution, of the Ordinance of 1787, and various enactments in favor of popular liberty for so long, that we verily believe that we are a free people; and yet I am forced to declare, looking the truth directly in the face and seeing the power of American slavery, that there is not within the bosom of this entire country, a solitary man or woman who can say, "I have my full share of liberty." Let the president of this society ... stand up in the presence of the people of South Carolina and say, "I believe in the sentiments contained in the Constitution of my country, in the Declaration of Independence and in the Word of God, respecting the rights of man," and where will be his legal protection? Massachusetts will sit quietly by and see him outraged; the president of the United States will not dare to interfere for his protection; he will be at the mercy of the tyrant slaveholders. Why? "Because slavery is the great lord of this country, and there is no power in this nation today strong enough to withstand it."

Moving to Oberlin in 1856, Langston was twice elected to the Oberlin village council and was a member of its Board of Education for eleven years. When the policy of Negro enlistments was settled, he became a successful recruiting officer of three black regiments: the Fifth, Fifty-fourth and Fifty-fifth. His first visit to Washington was to suggest the propriety of obtaining a colonel's commission in one of these regiments. General James A. Garfield, subsequently president, accompanied him to the White House and introduced him to President Lincoln.

During these formative years Langston was able to develop his speaking and writing skills mostly on behalf of oppressed black Americans, demanding educational and political opportunities.[11] Langston studied the speeches of the great American orators: Daniel Webster, Henry Clay and John C. Calhoun. He said that

many times he had been lost in wonder and admiration of the grace, eloquence and power of their best utterances [which].... cultivated in matchless diction the broadest and most liberal sentiments with respect to free principles and equal rights.... These latter made the speeches which realized at last the highest, truest and noblest image of eloquence dedicated to a holy, sacred purpose, when speech alone demonstrates the height and depth, the power and effect of which in its best estate it is capable. When a man pleads the cause of justice, liberty, humanity with his heart earnestly, sincerely, deeply imbued with the conviction of his duty, his soul pure in its consecration thereto, and his understanding illuminated by the light which is divine, he is eloquent.[12]

In 1867, at the recommendation of Chief Justice of the Supreme Court Salmon Chase, Langston was appointed Inspector-General of the Bureau of Freedmen, Refugees and Abandoned Lands, reporting to General Oliver Otis Howard. After extended trips through Maryland and Virginia, Langston was offered the position held by General Howard by President Andrew Johnson. Langston refused and, after telling Howard that the president was no friend, met with Secretary of War Ulysses S. Grant. Subsequently, President Johnson offered Langston the ministership to Haiti, which Langston declined. He continued to act as Inspector-General of the Freedmen's Bureau, traveling throughout the South.

When Howard University[13] was established and a law department opened, the task of heading it was given to Langston who had been admitted to practice before the U.S. Supreme Court on January 17, 1867 on motion of General J.A. Garfield.[14] Young black men came from all over the country to study law at Howard University, an opportunity universally denied them at most law schools.

In 1871, at the first Howard University commencement exercises, Langston prevailed on Senator Charles Sumner to deliver the commencement address. His acceptance was an act of respect to Langston and an encouragement to black men to study law. Subsequently, Sumner got Ralph Waldo Emerson to deliver one of the Sunday morning course of lectures on ethics given to law students.

President Grant appointed Langston as a member of the first Washington Board of Health, a position Langston held for seven years. This Board had almost absolute powers in the areas of municipal sanitation and hygiene. As the only lawyer on the Board, Langston's legal abilities were constantly needed. During a visit to a northern city to get the benefit of other local health boards, the following incident displayed Langston's wit and repartee: "You have a Negro on your board?" "Yes," answered Professor Langston, "and he knows as much of sanitation as any of them; he has as much common-sense, is as eloquent and"— turning to the darkest one in the party, said —"allow me to introduce him, Dr. Bliss." Taking the joke, Dr. Bliss said, "I may be darker than you, Professor Langston, but your hair is not so straight as mine."

Professor Langston was also a trustee of the Freedman's Savings and Trust Company until it went out of business in 1874. On the resignation of General Howard from the presidency of Howard University, Professor Langston was chosen vice president and acting president. This was in 1873. On his failure to be elected to the presidency Langston retired from the institution in 1875 and the law department suspended operations for two years. In 1877 President Hayes tendered Langston the position of minister resident to the Court of Port au Prince in Haiti. It was accepted and held for eight years, when he resigned, as there was a change of administration. President Cleveland sent for Minister Langston and asked him to remain Haitian minister. With characteristic honesty, Mr. Langston replied: "Mr. President, I actively opposed your election and cannot conscientiously remain in your administration."

Langston was in great demand as a popular orator especially during political campaigns and celebrations of emancipation. An army officer who was stationed at Gordonsville, Virginia, reported a Langston speech in the *Washington Star* while Langston was minister to Haiti:

It was given out that John M. Langston the colored orator ... would speak at Louisa Court House. The result was an unusually large attendance of colored people, so that the town was full.... Although a long while free, and honorably distinguished there never had been a time before when Mr. Langston could safely visit his native county. Now he was to come back, a leading man of his race, to speak in public, and to revisit the scenes and recall the memories of his childhood. It was therefore a great occasion for him and for the freedmen of Louisa County. The white people, however, took little note of it or interest in it, although I had tried among the lawyers and some of the merchants, and other principal citizens, to convey the impression that Langston was a man they should recognize and respect. I remember particularly trying to convince General Gordon, then County Attorney, and an excellent man, that he might be pleased with Langston, and would be interested if he came over and heard him talk. The feeling that the Negro was, in all cases necessarily inferior and totally uninteresting was, however, too strong and the General and several others manifested impatience, if not a little indignation at my commendatory observation about Langston. They would not have it that any "nigger" could talk law, politics, reconstruction or anything else with a degree of ability and intelligence to merit their attention; and they could not imagine that they themselves were soon to attest in a remarkable manner the folly of settled enmity or contempt of an entire race or class of men.... Langston began by referring to old Virginia and Louisa County as the place of his birth, and spoke in the happiest vein and with all the eloquence, elegance and oratorical art that distinguished him of the genuine affection he felt for his native State and town, and of the pleasure it gave him to come back again to the home of his boyhood. In a few minutes he had the mastery of every man within his voice. He pictured the greatness of the State in its earliest days, referred to its distinguished men, and its history and national influence, spoke touchingly of its present temporary depression and distress, and most hopefully and glowingly of its future promise and possibilities as a free state. Then with admirable taste and tact he fell naturally into a discussion of the living questions of the day, avoiding all irritating points and expressions. In a little while I looked about me and saw the platform and all avoidable space near it and around it packed with white people. The blacks accustomed to yielding precedence had given up all the best places and a white man was wedged into every one. More eager interest I never saw in the faces of any audience. There was General Gordon crowding near Langston with irrepressible confession of homage springing from his eyes and pouring down his cheeks, while the beautiful periods, paying honor to Old Virginia, fell from the orator's lips. The address continued for two hours with unflagging interest on the part of the audience, and closed with an admirable peroration. Then followed a scene of spontaneous enthusiasm that is seldom witnessed.... He was borne by the pressure into the dining room of the hotel, and a grand dinner was forthwith ordered in his honor, at which General Gordon presided, and many of the best citizens sat at the board. He was at once a guest of the town, and no attention of honor seemed too great for its good people to bestow upon him. All prejudice against his color was totally extinguished.[15]

While performing a special mission to Haiti for the merchant John Wanamaker in 1885, Langston was chosen president of the Virginia Normal and Collegiate Institute at Petersburg. Here his college training, his experience as educator at Howard University, his service as Inspector-General of the Freedmen's Bureau and his long tenure in the diplomatic service stood him in good stead. Langston said that he took the $1,500 post at the small Negro state college in 1885 in order to return to his native state and help black students. Langston had success in increasing the school's enrollment and in training teachers.

The Institute had been established three years earlier by the Virginia General Assembly as a reward to the blacks who supported Senator William Mahone's Readjuster Party. Mahone, a former Confederate general, was the powerful Republican boss of Virginia. The Readjuster Party, created from discontented Conservatives, Negroes and Republicans, elected majorities to both houses of the General Assembly in 1879. In 1881, the party elected a Readjuster governor and sent Mahone to the U.S. Senate. Under Mahone's control, the state legislature readjusted the state debt, increased public school appropriations 50 percent, abolished the whipping post and the poll tax, established an insane asylum for blacks and created the Virginia Normal and Collegiate Institute. For a brief period, Virginia enjoyed this populist experience as Boss Mahone tried to consolidate and expand his political control. In 1885, the Democratic Party regained control of the state by smearing Mahone with charges of undue Negro influence in the Republican Party.[16]

Langston's efforts at Virginia Normal were thwarted by the split between an all-white state Board of Education and the black Board of Visitors. When his contract was not renewed in 1887, he decided to run for Congress for Virginia's Fourth District.

Langston held an advantage that no previous black candidate had in his race for Congress: he had been widely known for at least a generation. He was, after all, the first black man to be elected to public office in the United States. He had been a long-time leading member of the Republican Party; he had served as minister to Haiti.[17] Virginia was his home state and he knew Virginia politics well from his work in the Freedmen's Bureau. Furthermore, while twenty black men had been elected to Congress from other southern states during Reconstruction, Virginia had never been represented by a Negro in the House or Senate. But Langston's best reason for becoming a candidate for Congress was the nature of the Fourth District. Its 8,000 square miles contained 107,071 Negroes and 56,194 whites (according to the 1880 census) in eleven counties. Its major city, Petersburg, was the home of the Virginia Normal and Collegiate Institute.[18] Of the city's 3,000 free Negroes, many were educated, self employed and owned real estate. The census recorded the following professions: one physician, two attorneys, six ministers and thirty barbers, carpenters, contractors and grocers. These leaders organized a successful boycott of three black schools in 1882, demanding black teachers.[19]

Blacks had been trying unsuccessfully to secure a nomination to Congress from the Fourth District since 1868. In 1884, former slave Joseph P. Evans of Petersburg ran on an independent ticket and was beaten badly. A journal, the *Virginia Lancet*, edited by George Bragg (a twenty-one-year-old Negro), commented sarcastically, "It is no use for any colored man to make an attempt to go to Congress unless he has plenty of money to buy up the leaders."[20]

"Little General" William Mahone held on to his power in the Republican Party by convincing Negroes that his policies of incremental improvement offered the greatest benefit for equal rights. His authoritarian ways alienated many black and white Readjusters who walked out of the state convention and elected their own delegates to the Republican national convention. Langston pulled out all the stops and contacted Senator John Sherman, presidential hopeful and brother of Union General William Tecumseh Sherman, for support.[21] Langston clubs were started throughout the Fourth District and a carefully written biographical brochure with a photograph was distributed widely. Langston purchased a large building and converted it into his campaign headquarters. Many political rallies were held in Langston Hall during the hard-fought campaign. Some white politicians expressed their dislike of Mahone by supporting Langston, who named seven of them in his autobiography.[22] On the other hand, Mahone got Frederick Douglass to write a letter critical of Langston. Douglass wrote, "You know his history. He came among you ... as an educator ... not a politician.... He was on the finance committee of the Freedman's Bank when most of its bad loans were made.... He remained with Howard University so long as there was a chance of making himself its president.... No encouragement should be given to any man whose mad political ambition would imperil the success of the Republican party."[23] While the Douglass letter was circulated widely, it evoked pro–Langston reactions from the Negro press. The *Washington Bee* commented, "Awake colored citizens and upon this charge cry good for Langston and universal liberty." The *People's Advocate* said "the Douglass letter was as unfortunate as it is mischievous." The *Star of Zion* said that Douglass "exhibited his malignity" against Langston.[24]

Just before the congressional nominating convention scheduled for September 19th, Mahone said, "It was not time for a Negro Congressman from Virginia yet and even if the time had come Langston was not the man." Langston backers walked out of the convention to the adjacent Opera House and proceeded to put Langston's name up for nomination. The Richmond Whig reported that "men stood up on chairs and shouted themselves hoarse. They wrung each other's hands and the excitement was so great that tears welled up in the eyes of many of the delegation."[25] The Glee Club sang "Langston for Congress" with this refrain: "Sing for Langston, loud and free, He is true to you and me." Langston spoke for almost an hour: "I am in rebellion against tyranny and am the upholder of the dignity of my race." Next door, the Mahone Republicans nominated Judge A. W. Arnold of Sussex County as the regular Republican candidate. A week earlier, the Democrats nominated E.C. Venable, heir to a family tobacco company, which employed eight hundred workers and produced three million pounds of tobacco annually.

Mahone brought outside Negro speakers into the campaign to castigate Langston as "hypocritical, selfish and snobbish to his own people." Langston campaigned vigorously and encouraged his supporters to make copies of Negro registration records and undertake house-to-house canvasses to get out the vote. He wrote, "I want the people everywhere, in every house, on every road, in every shop, at every lodge, at every schoolhouse, at every church, at every Sunday School, at every marriage gathering, in every factory, at every meeting ... all time, to be taking, thinking about and working for the success of our cause on election day.... The father should interest the son; the son his father;... in my present great struggle for my people and for the proper advancement of my race.[26]

Langston faced enormous odds in this election campaign. The Democrats had almost limitless campaign funding. The pro–Democratic *Richmond State* editorialized, "We've got the rocks and we expect to win." Senator Mahone's forces expended large sums for their candidate.[27] Langston spent $15,000 of his own fortune, which was estimated between $50,000 and $100,000.

Aside from his sterling reputation, Langston's campaign had three other features that were unique and beneficial. First, his campaign workers were young, well educated and experienced in political campaigns. David Batts, campaign committee chairman, served as a police officer in Washington, D.C., and as a city councilman in Danville, Virginia. Matt N. Lewis, secretary, was an attorney who had been deputy collector of internal revenue in Petersburg, Virginia. Scott Wood, a Howard Law School graduate, and Ross Hamilton, sixteen years in the Virginia House of Delegates, were former students at Virginia Normal.[28]

Another advantage was his speaking ability on the campaign trail. On Monday at county court, he spoke to crowds of 200 to 1,000 who gathered for oratory, whiskey and barbecue. While his main appeal was to blacks in his "desperate struggle to establish the manhood, honor and fidelity of the Negro race,"[29] Langston was apparently careful not to antagonize the Democrats into an anti–Negro stance.

The Langston local clubs were a third advantage — the Harrison, Morton and Langston Invincibles and Female Invincibles. The *New York Times* judged the women's clubs the campaign's "most remarkable feature," urging the men to new levels of political activity.[30]

Historian William Cheek described the end of the political campaign as follows:

> In the closing weeks of the campaign, the corruption and cynicism of southern politics were on full display. Mahone's men offered five dollars to each Langston Club president and one dollar to each club member; Negro leaders were paid in installments on their promises to bring in votes. Langston and Venable spent freely, according to a Mahone aide, who added that Langston paid local leaders "much larger sums than you would think of paying." Bribe money generally knew no color distinctions. At the rate of a dollar a vote, Mahone instructed his agents to buy up every Democratic vote possible.
>
> Intimidation took many forms. One of Mahone's Negro workers called Langston's tactics a "system of organized ostracism"; Negro ministers threatened to expel members of their congregations if they voted against Langston. Mahone's "collar around his neck" prevented Negro W. H. Ashe, and many like him, from voting for Langston. Some Negroes were told to vote for Venable or not at all. Fear of retaliation lasted until well after the election. Asked about his political views, one colored man replied: "Well, Sir, I am afraid to state.... I am afraid some bad enemy or mob or something of the kind will come after or against me."[31]

On election day, November 6, the weather was clear and pleasant but the opportunity for a fair election was cloudy and dismal. All the electoral judges and poll watchers were controlled by Mahone. For example, one gross miscarriage of justice occurred in the Petersburg sixth ward where Negro voters outnumbered whites by nearly three to one. A wooden barrier was located at the door to segregate the voters, blacks to the left, whites to the right with the lines voting alternatively. When the voting ended, 252 of the 265 whites voted; only 401 of the 709 blacks voted. At the end of the day, there were still 125 blacks in line holding Langston ballots. The U.S. examining supervisor later testified that the delay was caused by the difficulty of finding the names of the colored men in the registry because so many had the same name.[32]

The election results reflected the fraud and cheating that was rampant:

Venable	13,300
Langston	12,657
Arnold	3,207

Four days after the election, Langston wrote to President Benjamin Harrison to congratulate him for his victory. He took the occasion to describe his own election:

> I am so situated ... by reason of the precautions taken, with regard to the conduct of the election, the manipulation and count of the votes, that I shall be able, should I be denied my seat in Congress ... to show in a contest beyond a reasonable doubt my right thereto. I am a colored man. I am, however, and I have always been, a true and loyal Republican. I do not understand why any Republican or Democrat, should deny me the right and privilege of representing the people of this or any other District in the United States Congress, though I be a colored man, when duly accredited upon their vote to such duty and honor, and I will not submit to any such thing.[33]

Over the next nineteen months the battle was waged in the Congress until September 23, 1890, when John Mercer Langston was finally sworn in as the first black man ever elected to the House of Representatives from Virginia. Historian William Cheek wrote,

> For a few months a Negro represented Virginia in the national legislature. He was there because of his own experience, wealth, and personality, because of a remarkable group of capable and dedicated young Petersburg Negroes, and because he appealed to something deeper and more basic in Fourth District Negroes than their need to sustenance or their fear of reprisal. Eventually a momentarily idealistic Republican party and a ruthless parliamentarian had seen that their votes were counted....
>
> The most significant result of the 1888 campaign may have been psychological. No memoir writers of the period even mention John Mercer Langston. It appears that white Virginia, shocked a Negro could ever have represented it in the national legislature, was able in time to convince itself he had never existed. It is likely that black Virginia remembered. For years afterward colored men sitting outside country stores could recall how, for a brief time, the nobody Negro going nowhere was the somebody Negro going somewhere.[34]

10

James Longstreet (1821–1904): Confederate General, Critic of Robert E. Lee, Political Realist

The Confederacy may have lost the Civil War on the battlefield but they won the war in the history books. Southerners mobilized what Virginia newspaper editor Edward A. Pollard called "the war of ideas." This hugely successful campaign wiped out the memory of slavery, transformed the Civil War into the "War between the States" and enabled the traitorous rebellion of the Confederate Army to call itself the "Lost Cause." It obliterated the memory of 192,000 blacks who fought in the Union Army, and managed to shift the blame for the bloodiest war in history from the seceding southern states to the failure of the North to recognize state rights. In the late 19th century, thousands of Civil War monuments were built throughout the country. You can count on one hand those that contain even an image of a black soldier. Is there any other country in the world who would permit the canonization of traitorous rebel soldiers into icons of heroism? After all, the Confederate Army tried to trample the American flag. It killed American soldiers and fought the bloodiest war in history against the duly elected United States government. The Gettysburg battlefield, site of the Union Army's greatest victory, has been transformed into a shrine celebrating Pickett's charge. Memorial Day, which was first celebrated in 1865 when black South Carolinians placed floral wreaths on the graves of Union soldiers, soon became an occasion for expressions of sympathy for fallen rebel soldiers. Even before Reconstruction ended in 1877, white historians were writing off the extraordinary gains made by the four million freed slaves and decrying how the South suffered under so-called Negro misrule.

Blacks were not the only ones who were forgotten by selective memory of the Reconstruction period. General James Longstreet, Robert E. Lee's second-in-command at Gettysburg, made three mistakes that denied him his deserved place in southern posterity. He argued with Lee's strategy at Gettysburg, he became a Republican, and he had the nerve to support the civil rights of blacks after the Civil War. The general's reputation was only worsened when, in reaction to an organized and malicious effort, he wrote a number of articles in which he criticized the generalship and judgment of both Robert E. Lee and Stonewall Jackson.

Gary W. Gallagher, professor and chair in history at Pennsylvania State University, wrote a foreword to the 1985 reprint of *James Longstreet: Lee's War Horse* first published in 1934, in which he said,

> James Longstreet stood with Robert E. Lee and Stonewall Jackson in the great triumvirate of the Army of northern Virginia. The title of his memoir, "From Manassas to Appomattox," indicates the span of his service in the war. He commanded the First Corps of Lee's army from its creation in 1862 to the surrender in 1865 and critical roles were his at Second Manassas, Fredericksburg, Gettysburg, Chickamauga and the Wilderness. His magnificent conduct at Sharpsburg won him a sobriquet from Lee, who, when Longstreet reached headquarters late in the evening of that long and bloody day, grasped his lieutenant by the shoulders and said warmly, "Ah, here is Longstreet; here is my Old Warhorse."[1] A stout fighter who took good care of his men, Longstreet was popular among soldiers in the ranks, who knew him affectionately as "Old Pete." He was Lee's most trusted subordinate after Jackson's death, on the battlefield a calm presence who, in the words of a member of his staff, "was like a rock in steadiness when sometimes ... the world seemed flying to pieces."[2] Combative to the end, he was with Lee at Appomattox when a Union officer approached bearing a message from Grant. "General," said Longstreet to his chief, "unless he offers us honorable terms, come back and let us fight it out."[3]

James Longstreet (1821–1904), R.E. Lee's "War Horse" and Confederate general, supported the civil rights of blacks during Reconstruction. He wrote *From Manassas to Appomattox* and was sharply criticized and ostracized by Southern veterans and historians. (©Bettman/Corbis)

In his 658-page autobiography Longstreet writes about his birth and upbringing:

I was born in Edgefield District of South Carolina, on the 8th of January, 1821. On the paternal side, the family was from New Jersey; on my mother's side, from Maryland. My earliest recollections were of the Georgia side of Savannah River, and my school-days were passed there, but the appointment to West Point Academy was from North Alabama. My father, James Longstreet, the oldest child of William Longstreet and Hannah Fitzrandolph, was born in New Jersey. Other children of the marriage, Rebecca, Gilbert, Augustus B., and William, were born in Augusta, Georgia, the adopted home. Richard Longstreet, who came to America in 1657 and settled in Monmouth County, New Jersey, was the progenitor of the name on this continent.

My father was a planter. From my early boyhood he conceived that he would send me to West Point for army service, but in my twelfth year he passed away during the cholera epidemic at Augusta. Mother moved to North Alabama with her children, whence in my sixteenth year I made application through a kinsman, Congressman Reuben Chapman, for appointment as cadet, received the coveted favor, and entered with the class that was admitted in 1838.

As cadet I had more interest in school of the soldier, horsemanship, sword exercise, and the outside game of foot-ball than in the academic courses.

Longstreet continues his recollection of his West Point days and reports on the Civil War careers of some of his classmates.

There were sixty-two graduating members of the class of 1842, my number being sixty. I was assigned to the Fourth United States Infantry as brevet lieutenant, and found my company with seven others of the regiment at Jefferson Barracks, Missouri, in the autumn of 1842.

Of the class graduating the year that we entered were G. T. Beauregard and Irvin McDowell, who, twenty-three years later, commanded the hostile armies on the plains of Manassas, in Virginia. Braxton Bragg and W. J. Hardee were of the same class.

The head man of the next class (1839) was I. I. Stevens, who resigned from the army, and, after being the first governor of Washington Territory, returned to military service, and fell on the sanguinary field of Chantilly on the 1st of September, 1862. Next on the class roll was Henry Wager Halleck, who was commander-in-chief of the United States armies from July, 1862, to March, 1864. W. T. Sherman and George H. Thomas, of the Union army, and R. S. Ewell, of the Confederate army, were of the same class (1840). The class of 1841 had the largest list of officers killed in action. Irons, Ayers, Ernst, Gantt, Morris, and Burbank were killed in the Mexican War. M. Lyon, R. S. Garnett, J. F. Reynolds, R. B. Garnett, A. W. Whipple, J. M. Jones, I. B. Richardson, and J. P. Garesche fell on the fields of the late war.

Of the class of 1842 few were killed in action, but several rose to distinguished positions — Newton, Eustis, Rosecrans, Lovell, Van Dorn, Pope, Sykes, G. W. Smith, M. L. Smith, R. H. Anderson, L. McLaws, D. H. Hill, A. P. Stewart, B. S. Alexander, N. J. T. Dana and others.

Longstreet remembers Ulysses S. Grant fondly:

But the class next after us (1843) was destined to furnish the man who was to eclipse all — to rise to the rank of general, an office made by Congress to honor his services; who became President of the United States, and for a second term; who received the salutations of all the powers of the world in his travels as a private citizen around the earth; of noble, generous heart, a lovable character, a valued friend — Ulysses S. Grant.[4]

After secession, James Longstreet first offered his services to the Confederacy through the state of Alabama after resigning his commission as a major in the United

States Army. He expected nothing more prestigious than a job as paymaster, his last appointment in the Federal army, but to his surprise he received a colonel's commission commanding infantry. By 1st Manassas (Bull Run) he had already been promoted to brigadier-general in command of three Virginia infantry regiments (1st, 11th, and 17th) which covered Blackburn's Ford during that battle. With an odd bit of irony, General Longstreet was supported by the brigade under Colonel Jubal Early who wrote in his official report of the action at the ford that Longstreet "was actively engaged in the thickest of the fire in directing and encouraging the men under his command, and I am satisfied he contributed very largely to the repulse of the enemy by his own personal exertions." This was likely the first and last compliment Early ever directed at Longstreet, and one might be pardoned for musing as to whether or not Early even remembered making this comment in the years after the war as he mounted a premeditated smear campaign against General Longstreet.[5]

After the Confederate victory at Manassas, Longstreet continued to rise in rank and stature in the Confederate command structure. He formed close associations with P. G. T. Beauregard and Joseph Johnston, the latter desiring Longstreet to be given the distinction of second in command. This appointment was not securable, however, because several generals outranked Longstreet and because of Johnston's own squabbles with the Richmond government. By the time McClellan invaded the Virginia Peninsula, Longstreet was a major-general, and he performed an important and well executed rear guard action at Williamsburg during Johnston's retreat toward Richmond.

From that point forward, with the single exception of Seven Pines, Longstreet gave exemplary service to the Confederate Army. When Robert E. Lee took command and formed the Army of northern Virginia, Longstreet found in him both a friend and a valuable guide through his career as a soldier. With Lee's unqualified recommendation, he rose in rank to the senior lieutenant-general in the Confederate Army and was given command of the 1st Corps of the Army of northern Virginia, the premier subordinate of the premier army of the Confederacy. All across Virginia, into Maryland and Pennsylvania, Longstreet led his soldiers into battle after battle and received the love and affection of his men and the appreciation of his fellow generals. During the Seven Days and 2nd Manassas campaigns, Longstreet displayed his brilliance on the offensive and at the defensive as well. He was known as the bulldog, the staff in Lee's right hand, and the Old Warhorse, and as the war progressed, he would live up to each of these titles. But Longstreet could hear the guns of war echoing all across the Confederacy, not just in Virginia, and as 1863 opened, he found himself seeding the controversy that followed him for the rest of his life. He disagreed with Robert E. Lee.

Prior to the campaign that resulted in the battle at Gettysburg, Longstreet offered a plan to Lee and the Richmond government designed to relieve pressure on the important Mississippi River port to Vicksburg, then under attack from the forces under U.S. Grant. The loss of this port would have the disastrous effect of closing the Confederacy's overland link to the states of Arkansas, Texas, and most of Louisiana, and sealing the Mississippi from use by the Confederacy. Additionally, Braxton Bragg and his Army of Tennessee were being pushed back toward the important rail center of Chattanooga, a loss which would further strangle the already suffering Confederacy. "Old Pete" knew that this possibility had to be countered as well.

Longstreet's plan was not adopted that June. The strategy employed was Lee's plan to invade the North, designed to relieve Virginia from the trampling feet of Federal soldiers, giving farmers time to bring in their badly needed crops. Lee also desired to threaten major northern cities in the hopes of convincing the Union government that a continued war was useless. As indicated by a letter he sent to Richmond after the battle, Lee hoped that the invasion of northern soil would have the effect of relieving other parts of the Confederacy then under pressure from Union generals Grant and Rosecrans. While Longstreet had argued for direct relief, Lee seemed to believe that one of these armies would be compelled to move east and assist the Army of the Potomac if the Confederates were able to threaten major northern cities.

Lee's strategy depended on a grand victory, a literal destruction of the Army of the Potomac, and unfortunately for him, that highly sought-after prize was not forthcoming. The Army of the Potomac moved faster than had been expected. Caught unaware with Jeb Stuart and his cavalry away from the main body of the army, Lee was forced to give battle in a location of which he had little knowledge and under circumstances which did not favor his desire to utilize an offensive strategy and employ defensive tactics. Longstreet was adamant throughout the entire battle that the plans being enacted were doomed to failure, and he was proven correct. The disagreements between Lee and Longstreet, then only a footnote to the campaign, provided fuel for the fiery attacks of Early, Pendleton, and fellow Georgian John Gordon after the war. Gettysburg was the spark that ignited the "Lost Cause" mythology that has dominated much of what we have learned of this pivotal event in our nation's history.

Longstreet's performance throughout the battle of Chickamauga was magnificent. On more than one occasion he inspired the men under his command by his personal exertions, his positive words, and his calm and collected nature. After the battle General Deas was moved to report that "Longstreet is the boldest and bravest looking man I ever saw. I don't think he would dodge if a shell were to burst under his chin." At one point, Longstreet nearly proved Deas correct. Meeting Colonel Thomas Claiborne, temporarily attached to General Buckner's staff, a shell came screeching past. Claiborne ducked, to which Longstreet laughingly commented, "I see you salute them," and then, "If there is a shell or bullet over there destined for us, it will find us." Longstreet did not budge.

Shortly before he paused for his now-famous lunch of Nassau bacon and sweet potatoes, taken within range of Federal cannon, Longstreet met with General Benjamin Humphreys who commented, "I never saw him wear so bright and jubilant a countenance." Longstreet directed Humphreys in good humor to "drive them, General. These western men can't stand it any better than the Yankees we left in Virginia. Drive them." Before the end of the day, these soldiers along the Chickamauga had a new nickname for Longstreet: the Bull of the Woods.

The final year and a half of the war was for Longstreet, as for the rest of the Confederacy, filled with disappointment and despair. Accidentally wounded at the

Wilderness by his own men, as Jackson had been in nearly the same area the year before, Longstreet was unable to rejoin Lee and the Army of northern Virginia until they were already holed up in the trenches around Petersburg during the Confederacy's last gasps of life. Still, despite the looming specter of defeat, Longstreet remained forever faithful and loyal to Lee and the army.

Had Longstreet not criticized Robert E. Lee, we could probably more easily evaluate Longstreet's place in history and end with the evaluation that he was one of the war's finest generals who fought the good fight and lost. However, not content to calmly and quietly ride out the remaining years of his life remembering the glories of the past, Longstreet became involved in the quagmire of postwar politics and opened an entirely new chapter to his life that blended the past and the present, which ultimately proved to be his undoing. Like the Shakespearean protagonists, Longstreet's fatal flaw emerged, and he, for the rest of his days, re-fought the war on an almost daily basis, only this time with the pen rather than the sword.

After the war, Longstreet renewed his friendship with Grant and became a Republican. General Grant wrote to President Andrew Johnson on November 7, 1865, requesting a pardon for Longstreet,

> In the late rebellion, I think, not one single charge was ever brought against General Longstreet for persecution of prisoners of war or of persons for their political opinions. If such charges were ever made, I never heard of them. I have no hesitation, therefore, in recommending General Longstreet to your Excellency for pardon. I will further state that my opinion of him is such that I feel it as a personal favor to myself if this pardon is granted.
>
> Very respectfully, your obedient servant,
> U. S. Grant,
> Lieutenant-General[6]

After receiving a pardon from President Johnson, Longstreet settled in New Orleans and began to advocate compliance with Reconstruction. This postwar affiliation was the single most important factor in destroying his reputation in southern history. To confederate veterans he appeared like nothing less than a traitor to the white race.[7] Longstreet wrote letters urging southerners to support the Reconstruction Acts of 1867:

> ...If I appreciate the issues of Democracy at this moment, they are the enfranchisement of the Negro and the rights of Congress in the premises, but the acts have been passed, are parts of the laws of the land, and no power but Congress can remove them.... If everyone will meet the crisis with proper appreciation of our condition and obligations, the sun will rise tomorrow on a happy people. Our fields will again begin to yield their increase, our railways and waters will teem with abundant commerce, our towns and cities will resound with the tumult of trade, and we will be reinvigorated by the blessings of Almighty God.[8]
>
> Very respectfully yours,
> James Longstreet

Criticism of Longstreet spread all over the country. Black Republicans were perceived as the devil incarnate threatening to destroy southern civilization. One historian wrote, "In every ex–Confederate State a new Republican party ... constituted a presence as unsettling to traditional southern life as the Union army or the Freedmen's Bureau."[9]

Longstreet supported Grant in the 1868 presidential election and was rewarded with various federal appointments such as surveyor of the port of New Orleans, levee board commissioner, adjutant general of the state of Louisiana and commander of the Louisiana state militia.[10]

To the people of the South, Longstreet seemed a deserter and a traitor. This evaluation was reinforced when, on September 14, 1874, in an encounter that became known as the "Battle of Liberty Place" took place in downtown New Orleans. The illegal White League routed the Metropolitan Police and the black state militia under General James Longstreet to overthrow the legally elected government of New Orleans. "On September 15, Longstreet abandoned the state house which was immediately occupied by the White League. By the end of the day, the Conservative forces had occupied all the city's police stations and state arsenals, confiscating more than 1,600 rifles, 46,000 rounds of ammunition and four cannon. They controlled all state facilities."[11] Until a few years ago, in the center of a traffic island at the foot of Canal Street, directly in front of the ferry terminal, a white obelisk pointed skyward. Erected in 1891, it commemorated the Battle of Canal Street, renamed the Battle of Liberty Place after Reconstruction. Inscribed on the memorial are the names of the White League captains and their comrades-in-arms who fell in this fight. A more recent plaque assures visitors that the triumph of white supremacy is not the philosophy of modern-day New Orleans. This insurrection was more than the federal government could bear. President Grant sent six regiments of federal troops under Major Lewis "Dog" Merrill, a veteran of the KKK uprising in South Carolina. Later, Grant sent General Philip H. Sheridan to New Orleans to declare the ringleaders of the White Leagues in Louisiana, Arkansas and Mississippi "banditti" and then let the army deal with them under martial law. "Little Phil's" actions created a furor in the South and the North but ultimately restored the legally elected government in New Orleans. A correspondent for the Daily Picayune described him as "a smiling red-faced man, of a short cut Herculean style of architecture, and very ... stout.... He would make a severe trial of any Fairbanks scale in the city."[12] Longstreet's presence on the side of an armed black militia engaged in a bloody battle with white men completed his degradation in the estimate of southerners. He was never forgiven. Later, Longstreet was named supervisor of internal revenue (1878), a postmaster (1879), minister to Turkey (1880) by President Rutherford B. Hayes, and later United States Marshall and other federal offices including commissioner of Pacific Railroads under Presidents McKinley and Roosevelt from 1897 to 1904.

In 1896 at age seventy-five, Longstreet married Helen Dortch, a beautiful woman some forty years his junior. Helen Longstreet survived Longstreet by nearly sixty years and was at the time of her death in 1962 the last surviving wife of a Civil War general. An ardent supporter of her husband, Helen Longstreet published *Lee and Longstreet at*

High Tide in 1905 in rebuttal to the anti–Longstreet campaign of Confederate generals Jubal Anderson Early and William Nelson Pendleton; former Confederate president Jefferson Davis; other Confederate officers John B. Gordon, Braxton Bragg, Wade Hampton, William Preston Johnson and Cadmus M. Wilcox; Fitzburgh Lee (Robert E. Lee's nephew); and J. William Jones, a former chaplain in the 13th Virginia Infantry.

As William Garrett Piston wrote in 1998,

> Early and Pendleton were unmitigated, willful liars who hated Longstreet because of his postwar Republican affiliation. This fact is thoroughly established by frequent comments in their postwar private correspondence (neither man's wartime letters, official or private, held anything but praise for Longstreet). Their churlish fabrications should not have been credited.... But Early and Pendleton hired agents to tour the South and deliver their speeches as a means of raising funds for memorials to Lee. Once Longstreet erased his own credibility with the southern people by his heretical actions on the streets of New Orleans in 1874, the Early-Pendleton version of Gettysburg found ready listeners. By placing the blame on Longstreet, they provided an explanation for the defeat which neither conceded the loss of God's Grace, nor questioned southern manhood. Thus was Longstreet's reputation tarnished at the grass roots level.[13]

Longstreet was therefore unfairly blamed for the loss at Gettysburg and by extension for the loss of the Civil War. He spent the remaining years of his life in vicious battles with Early, Pendleton and Gordon. In 1896, James Longstreet finally published his autobiography, *From Manassas to Appomattox, Memoirs of the Civil War in America*, in a vain attempt to present his side of the story and salvage his reputation. But across the South, Longstreet was a hated man because of the lies spread by the anti–Longstreet cabal.

Whether he is named "the Confederacy's Most Controversial Soldier" by Jeffrey Wert or "Lee's Tarnished Lieutenant" by William Garrett Piston, Longstreet was something else to the men he supervised during those trying years of war. Despite the lies spread by the anti–Longstreet cabal, when Longstreet died on January 2, 1904, he still commanded the respect of thousands of former soldiers, both blue and gray, as a very good general worthy of more respect than he has been given.

Finally, on July 3, 1998, a memorial to Lt. General James Longstreet was dedicated at the Gettysburg National Battlefield Park. The bronze memorial was sculpted by Gar Casteel and made possible by the efforts of Robert C. Thomas, chairman of the Longstreet Memorial Fund. The fund was established by the North Carolina Division of the Sons of Confederate Veterans to overturn more than a century of slander and finally achieve for James Longstreet the status he so richly deserved.

11

John Roy Lynch (1847–1939): An Unusual Man Living in an Unusual Time

During the congressional debate on the 1875 Civil Rights Bill, a twenty-six-year-old black congressman from Mississippi, John Roy Lynch, gave the following answer to those who said the bill would legislate social equality: "I can then assure … my Democratic friends on the other side of the House whom I regard as my social inferiors that if at any time I should meet any one of you at the hotel and occupy a seat at the same table with you, or the same seat in a [railroad] car with you, do not think that I have thereby accepted you as my social equal." He also appealed to the chivalry of the "gentlemen of the House," asking them to imagine how they would feel if their mothers, wives, daughters were constantly being insulted in public places.

John Roy Lynch was an unusual man living in an unusual time. A black man born into slavery on a Louisiana plantation in 1847, Lynch came to manhood and educated himself during the Reconstruction period. He lived a public-spirited life as politician, congressman, lawyer, historian and writer until he died at age ninety-two.

Following John R. Lynch's death on November 2, 1939, the *New York Times* obituary eulogized him as "one of the most fluent and forceful speakers in the politics of the seventies and eighties." The *Chicago Defender* praised Lynch for his accomplishments, crediting them "to the dauntless spirit he possessed, the seemingly unlimited capacity for the entertainment of useful knowledge and the overmastering desire for unselfish service."[1] Who was this fluent and forceful speaker with the dauntless spirit? Who was this black man for whom the City Council of Jackson, Mississippi, named one of its principal thoroughfares in 1973?

John Roy Lynch was only twenty-one years of age when the fifteenth Amendment to the Constitution granted freedmen the right to vote. As an active member of the local Republican Club, Lynch met Governor Adelbert Ames[2] who was so impressed that he appointed Lynch as justice to the peace of Adams County. Since there were no black bondsmen, Lynch had the problem of raising the required bond of $2,000. Finally, Lynch found two black men who owned some real estate and could sign notes for $1,000 each. After he took office in April 1869, a local Democratic newspaper wrote sarcastically, "We are now beginning to reap the ravishing fruits of Reconstruction."[3] In that same year, Lynch was elected to the Mississippi state legislature, where he exhibited a lively interest in the proceedings and served on two standing committees: military affairs and elections. Within three years, he was elected Speaker of the House and he apparently served with great distinction. At the age of twenty-five, Lynch became the first African American from Mississippi to be elected to the U.S. House of Representatives where he served three terms. While congressman-elect, Lynch presided over the 1873 session of the Mississippi state legislature. At the end of the session, the chairman of the committee on public works of the House made a presentation to Lynch which reads in part as follows:

John Roy Lynch (1847–1939). Born a slave, Lynch led a remarkable and varied life of ninety-two years. He was elected Speaker of the Mississippi House of Representatives at twenty-five. Elected to the U.S. Congress, he was the first black to deliver the keynote address at a Republican National Convention. He was admitted to the bar in 1896 and served in the U.S. Army, reaching the post of major. Lynch was the author of *The Facts of Reconstruction*, *Some Historical Errors of James Ford Rhodes* and *Reminiscences of an Active Life*. (Chicago Historical Society, ICHI-03695; photographer: C. M. Bell)

The members of the House, over whom you have presided so long and so well, with so much impartiality ... have confided the agreeable task upon me of presenting to you the gold watch and chain which I now send to your desk by the son of one of Mississippi's deceased speakers. Believe me, sir, it is not for its intrinsic worth, nor for its extrinsic show, but rather as a memento of our high admiration and respect for you as a gentleman, citizen and speaker.

Indeed, if it were possible to weld into one sentiment and to emit by one impulse of the voice the sentiments of all, at this good hour, me thinks it would be "God bless Hon. J.R. Lynch: he is an honest and fair man."[4]

Another member of the House, R. W. Houston of Washington County, commented that the Speaker's decisions on questions of parliamentary law had given "no cause to murmur on account of urbanity or impartiality. And I ask, Mr. Speaker, that you accept my profoundest gratitude for the dignified courtesy and distinguished manliness and marked ability which have characterized your entire conduct as the chief honored officer of this body."[5]

When Lynch took his seat at the opening of the 43rd Congress in December 1873, he was, at twenty-six years of age, the youngest member of Congress. One of the first major issues he dealt with was the Civil Rights Bill in June 1874. Lynch made an impassioned plea for its passage.

> I appeal to the members of the House — republicans and democrats, conservatives, and liberals — to join with us in the passage of this bill which has for its object the protection of human rights. And when every man, woman and child can feel and know that his, her and their rights are fully protected by the strong arm of a generous and grateful Republic, then can all truthfully say that this beautiful land of ours, over which the Star Spangled Banner so triumphantly waves, is in truth and in fact, the "land of the free and home of the brave."[6]

Upon the completion of his first term in Washington, the leading Democratic newspaper on the Mississippi Gulf Coast, a part of Lynch's district, had kind words for him. Regarding the forthcoming congressional election in the district it wrote, "Personally we have a high appreciation of Hon. John R. Lynch but we must say that we prefer to be represented in the National Congress by a white man — providing he is the equal of Lynch in intelligence, moral worth and integrity — which virtues we give the latter credit for possessing."

In the 43rd Congress, Lynch described the indignities he suffered on an official trip to Washington:

> Think of it for a moment; here am I a member of your honorable body, representing one of the largest and wealthiest districts in the state of Mississippi and possibly in the South; a district composed of persons of different races, religions and nationalities; and yet, when I leave my home to come to the capital of the nation, to take part in the deliberations of the House and to participate with you in making laws for the government of this great Republic ... I am treated, not as an American citizen, but as a brute. Forced to occupy a filthy smoking-car both night and day, with drunkards, gamblers and criminals; and for what? Not that I am unable or unwilling to pay my way; not that I am obnoxious in my personal appearance or disrespectful in my conduct, but simply because I happen to be of darker complexion. If this treatment was confined to persons of our own sex, we could possibly afford to endure it. But such is not the case. Our wives and our daughters, our sisters and our mothers are subjected to the same insults and to the same uncivilized treatments. The only moments of my life when I am necessarily compelled to question my loyalty to my Government or my devotion to the flag of my country is when I read of outrages having been committed upon innocent colored people and ... when I leave my home to go traveling. Mr. Speaker, if this unjust discrimination is to be longer tolerated by the American peoples ... then I can only say with sorrow and regret that our boasted civilization is a fraud; our republican institutions a failure; our social system a disgrace; and our religion a complete hypocrisy.[7]

In the fall of 1876, Lynch ran for reelection to Congress and was defeated for the first time in his political career.[8] John Lynch said, when he was counted out of his election:

> You certainly can't expect them [the Negroes] to resort to mob law and brute force, or, to use what may be milder language, inaugurate a revolution. My opinion is that revolution is not the remedy to be applied in such cases. Our system of government is supposed to be one of law and order, resting upon the consent of the governed, as expressed through the peaceful medium of the ballot. In all localities where the local public sentiment is so dishonest, so corrupt, and so demoralized, as to tolerate the commission of election frauds, and shield the perpetrators from justice, such people must be made to understand that there is patriotism enough in this country and sufficient love of justice and fair play in the hearts of the American people to prevent any party from gaining the ascendancy in the government that relies upon a fraudulent ballot and a false return as the chief source of its support.
>
> The impartial historian will record the fact that the colored people of the South have contended for their rights with a bravery and a gallantry that is worthy of the highest commendation. Being, unfortunately, in dependent circumstances with the preponderance of the wealth and intelligence against them in some localities, yet they have bravely refused to surrender their honest convictions, even upon the altar of their personal necessities.[9]

The presidential election of 1876 was fractious and disputed. Through a political deal known as the Compromise of 1877, Rutherford B. Hayes was at last declared the winner in exchange for promises to withdraw federal troops from the South, provide economic assistance to southern railroads and public works, and choose a southern conservative for his cabinet. Thus Hayes' election ended the Reconstruction period.

In 1883, Lynch retired from the House after losing another congressional election. He continued to serve as a chairman of the Republican State Executive Committee until 1892. He was a delegate to the Republican National Convention in 1884, 1888, 1892 and 1894.

At the 1884 convention, he received the highest recognition he would ever receive from the Republican Party. Lynch was elected to the post of temporary chairman of the eighth Republican National Convention. It was the first time that an African American delivered the keynote address before a major political convention. It would not happen again until 1968. In 1889, Lynch's long devotion to the Republican Party was rewarded with his appointment by President Benjamin Harrison as fourth auditor of the United States Treasury.

Early in the 1890s Lynch began to study law, and in 1896 he passed the Mississippi bar examinations. Shortly thereafter he became a partner in the law firm of Robert H. Terrell in Washington, D.C. Terrell had been a clerk in Lynch's office when he was fourth auditor of the Treasury. Lynch practiced in Mississippi and the District of Columbia until he went into the army in 1898. Lynch had no keen interest in the military but when President McKinley asked him to serve during the Spanish-American War, he accepted with personal regard for McKinley and a deep sense of party loyalty. His marriage to Ella Somerville in 1884 produced one daughter and ended in divorce in 1900. In 1901, he was offered the commission as major to travel to many parts of the world including Haiti and the Philippines. It was during these travels that he met Cora Williamson, who became his second wife in 1911, the year he retired from the army.[10]

From 1912 until his death in 1939, Lynch lived in Chicago where he practiced law and engaged in the real estate business. John R. Lynch was a historian and a thorough researcher. He wrote his autobiography called *Reminiscences of an Active Life*, which was not published until 1970. In 1913, he published *The Facts of Reconstruction* to "present the other side" since contemporary interpretation of the Reconstruction era impugned the ability and integrity of blacks during Reconstruction. Lynch's work is the most extensive account of the post–Civil War years written by an actual African American participant.

The publishing of Lynch's *The Facts of Reconstruction* went virtually unnoticed by historians. The reasons are not hard to fathom. In an introduction to the reprinting in 1970, William C. Harris, a professor of history at North Carolina State University in Raleigh, wrote that "the book's sympathetic appraisal of Reconstruction conflicted sharply with the current interpretation of that era — a view that had been in the process of developing since the 1890s and had become a hardened dogma by the 1910s. John W. Burgess, James Ford Rhodes, and most significantly, William A. Dunning and his talented students at Columbia University had advanced an interpretation of Reconstruction which followed southern conservative opinion in considering the period the 'most soul-sickening spectacular that Americans had ever been called upon to behold.'"[11]

This view prevailed for decades, as Harris went on to explain:

> At the turn of the century the American public and the academic community in general, moved by both international and domestic social trends that emphasized the progress of Western Teutonism as opposed to the backwardness of the colored races, had come to believe the extreme theories of black inferiority, and had accepted the disfranchisement and social regimentation of southern Negroes. The allegedly sordid spectacle of black participation in Reconstruction was advanced as public exhibit number one that Negroes were incapable of political sophistication; social scientists and fiction writers presented a formidable array of racist material that convinced a receptive white America of the innate cultural and moral inferiority of blacks. It was against this strong intellectual current that Lynch's *The Facts of Reconstruction* was forced to swim when it was released in 1913. The book failed to ride the first wave.[12]

Built around John R. Lynch's remarkable career in Mississippi, Reconstruction politics, and his association with national leaders of the period, *The Facts of Reconstruction* refuted all of the main contentions of the orthodox version of Reconstruction and advanced an interpretation of the era as one of achievement and hope. By "placing before the public accurate and trustworthy information relative to Reconstruction," Lynch sought to change the contemporary image of "the most important and eventful period in our country's history." Myths that he found especially vulnerable to criticism were that Negro domination existed during Reconstruction, that blacks were anxious to draw the color line in southern politics, that extravagance and corruption characterized the Republican regimes, that southern Republicans represented the scum of the region's society, and that the rule of the so-called Redeemers was better and more honest than that of the Republicans. In retrospect, it is clear that Lynch's book was the first important full-scale challenge to the traditional story of Reconstruction, although it was ignored for more than two decades after its publication.

Lynch said that his primary object was "to bring to public notice those things that were commendable and meritorious." Lynch's first-hand report refuted the heavily slanted Reconstruction histories that claimed that the enfranchisement of black men had been a mistake, that the Reconstruction governments were a failure, and that the Fourteenth and Fifteenth Amendments were premature and unwise. Though an octogenarian, Lynch was still active in 1929 when Oscar De Priest broke the congressional color barrier again to become the first black elected in twenty-eight years.

On November 3, 1939, John R. Lynch died at the age of ninety-two and was buried with military honors in Arlington National Cemetery.[13]

12

Albert Talmon Morgan (1842–1922): Union Officer, Radical Republican Officeholder in Mississippi, a Man Ahead of His Time

Albert T. Morgan grew up in the village of Fox Lake, Wisconsin, where his father was the proprietor of a wheat warehouse and a general store. His parents were pioneers who moved from New Hampshire to northern New York to clear a virgin forest and create a farm. Albert was one of ten children (seven boys and three girls). When the Civil War broke out, Morgan was about to enter Oberlin College. Instead he enlisted as a private in the 2nd Wisconsin Regiment. At the second battle of Bull Run he was captured by the Confederates but was later exchanged. He rejoined his regiment and was promoted to captain. He fought at Gettysburg where he was seriously wounded when a bullet struck him in the left thigh, traveled inside the bone and exited through his buttock. Although the wound healed in a few months, Morgan was permanently lame. Nevertheless, he returned to service and subsequently reenlisted after three years.

He and his older brother Charles, both veterans of the Union Army, determined to relocate to the fertile Delta area of Mississippi to make their fortune. Morgan had served for four years in the Union Army and overcame both malaria and crippling wounds. Albert was a unique human being and a man ahead of his time. In 1884, Albert Morgan "wrote a moving, highly accurate account for his time in Mississippi, leaving us with a burning portrait of how the sweeping events of this era affected the lives of real people in one particular community."[1] His book is an unusual and vastly revealing account of local politics in Mississippi during Reconstruction. It is one of the very few first hand accounts written from an abolitionist point of view by a participant in local state politics.[2]

Morgan and his brother leased for three years a 900-acre farm called Tokiba from Mr. and Mrs. J.J.B. White. Colonel White was a Confederate veteran who, at the time, was under bond by order of the local head of the Freedmen's Bureau to keep the peace after having threatened to kill a crippled black veteran of the Union Army. The Morgans recruited about one hundred men from the many black freedmen looking for work. These men were expecting the federal government to distribute land in keeping with the persistent rumors of "forty acres and a mule." Charles Morgan returned from the North where he made arrangements to finance a sawmill and a crew of skilled workers to harvest a forest of cypress trees on their leased land.[3] Albert and Charles Morgan invested their hard-earned life savings in the lumber and cotton business in Yazoo County. Neither of them had race relations or politics on their agenda. They were interested in going into business, making money and establishing themselves and their families as landed gentry. Morgan wrote in the introduction to his book,

> In these pages the reader will find faithfully set out a simple and truthful narrative of the author during his residence in Yazoo County, Mississippi, together with occasional pictures illustrative of the social conditions of the people of that State. The characters are real persons, whose true names are given only in cases where it was found impossible to disguise their identity. The conversations quoted, of course, are not verbatim. They are, nevertheless, strictly within the line of the truth.[4]

Author T. J. Stiles wrote about Morgan's book,

> First, he is searingly honest, and his accuracy is unusual for most personal memoirs (he wrote the book only eight years after Reconstruction came to an end in Mississippi). Second, his portrait of ten years in Yazoo County brings to life the many grass-roots black leaders — now forgotten by the public — who made this revolution happen.
> Third, and most important, his life epitomized the spirit of Reconstruction at its best — a spirit that transcended racial divisions. It is true that many other whites in the South, including Republicans, thought in terms of white vs. black — but Morgan did not. Nor did the recently freed African Americans who were his allies. Together, they sought to build a movement that would erase racial lines. Morgan broke with fellow white Republicans to run for office on the same ticket with black candidates; he both appointed and willingly served under black officials; and he married a black woman, after securing a change in state law to be able to do so.[5]

Morgan's book provides us with a rare look at Reconstruction from the grassroots level. He wrote about his personal experiences with local whites who were recently members of the Confederate Army and who scorned all blacks and all so-called carpetbaggers. Morgan did not focus on national or global issues. As Joseph Logsdon wrote in 2000 in his Introduction to Morgan's book, "[Morgan] concentrated on events in Yazoo, a black belt county far away from Washington, D.C. isolated even from the state capital and generally unreported in the legislative journals and major daily newspapers of the times." Logsdon continued, "In Yazoo County and Mississippi generally, there had been little corruption, no dramatic rise in taxation, no vengeful violence by former slaves, and virtually no exclusion of native whites from political life and influence. Yet his adopted county and state witnessed some of the most reactionary violence of the era. Indeed, Yazoo was where former slaveholders initiated the outrageous terror of the Mississippi Plan, testing the will of the nation to defend the Constitution and finding it wanting."[6]

By 1867 the Morgans were faced with multiple problems that threatened their various enterprises. The 1866 harvest had been disappointing, producing only sixty-eight bales of cotton worth only $14,000. With their partners, the Morgans had invested $11,000 in their sawmill and the needed horses, mules, oxen, wagons, plows, harnesses and other farm equipment; now the debt loomed, as did the rising Yazoo River, which, if it overflowed its banks, could damage the cotton crop.

But by far the most serious threat faced by Morgan, Ross & Company was the ever-increasing hostility of the native white population, the ex-confederates. These southerners looked with scorn on the carpetbagger Morgans who had the audacity to build a school for black children. When Morgan's sister Mollie and a friend came down from the North to teach the black chil-

Albert Talmon Morgan (1842–1922) was about to enter Oberlin College when the Civil war broke out; instead he became a Union officer. A Yankee entrepreneur and Radical Republican officeholder in Yazoo County, Mississippi, he was also a lawyer and silver miner in Kansas and Colorado. (Angela Morgan Papers, Box 55, Bentley Historical Library, University of Michigan)

dren, they were ostracized by Colonel J. J. B. White and his wife, Rebecca, and other Yazoo white adults. Morgan further angered the white population of Yazoo by adding a schoolroom to the small Negro church in town. Morgan wrote that white youths would often encircle the church and with their "nigger shooters" (slingshots) annoy the children and break church and school windows.[7]

Despite its reputation (furthered by John Fitzgerald Kennedy's badly researched opinion in *Profiles in Courage* about Governor Adelbert Ames), Mississippi was the best-run southern state during Reconstruction. In *Reconstruction in Mississippi*, James W. Garner and Vernon Wharton report that there were no great frauds in Mississippi during this period. Garner wrote, "So far as the conduct of state officials is concerned, it may be said that there were no great embezzlements or other cases of misappropriation during the period of Republican rule." After diligent study, Garner could only find the following three cases: 1) the "carpetbagger" treasurer of a Natchez hospital defaulted to the shortage of $7,281; 2) a black state librarian was accused of stealing books from the library; 3) the Democratic state treasurer embezzled $61,962. After Reconstruction, the white Democratic Party, who claimed to redeem the state from Republican fraud and mismanagement, stole $300,000!

Lerone Bennett, Jr., concluded that black power in Mississippi brought not ruin but hope. By 1874, there were 75,000 students in school in that state; at least 50,000 of them were Negroes. By that time, public buildings had been refurbished, welfare institutions had been established and extensive improvements — new sidewalks, pavements, gutters — had been made in counties and towns. By 1874, in short, Mississippi had entered the modern world because of the vigor of its Reconstruction government. It was clear that it would take only a few more years to make the revolution irreversible. Could the Republicans hold on?[8]

Albert T. Morgan had grave doubts, based on his personal experience in Yazoo County, that the hard-fought gains of the blacks could be maintained. Morgan wrote:

> The marvelous fecundity of that race, their physical strength and powers of endurance, their wonderful progress in the science of politics, and their boundless ambition, as fully recognized by the leading minds among the enemy as by myself, and much more than by the people of the Northland, had completely changed the character of the free negro question from one of doubt and sincere apprehension of his ability to survive, to one of the white man's ability to do so while in the presence of the negro and while the conditions of existence were equal. The greatest minds in the State, on the "superior side of the line," were gravely debating the question, which would be the wiser policy for the white man, emigration and the abandonment of the State to the negro, or a general arming of the white race with the purpose of checking by force the "threatened supremacy" of the negro race. To such persons these were the only alternatives.[9]

The white reactionaries had observed the unbelievable expansion of democracy in Mississippi from 1870 to 1875. Alexander K. Davis, the black lieutenant governor, ran the state during Governor Adelbert Ames's monthlong vacations; Hiram Revels and Blanche Kelso Bruce were the first blacks ever elected to the United States Senate; Robert H. Wood served as mayor of Natchez; black manager Benjamin Montgomery ran Joseph Davis's plantation (the older brother of Confederate President Jefferson Davis), which became the third most successful cotton operation in the entire South.

The common reasons given by white southerners for the failure of Reconstruction was Republican Party radicalism, high taxes and corruption. However, a careful study of the state of Mississippi under Reconstruction governments finds very little corruption, no dramatic rise in taxes, no violence by former slaves and no removal of white confederates and their supporters from economic and political life. Yazoo County was particularly free of these influences. And yet the level of violence by whites against so-called carpetbaggers and blacks was vicious, barbaric and ultimately successful. The former confederates who fought the bloodiest war in history fired on the American flag and killed American soldiers claimed the high ground after the war. They somehow convinced the North that they were patriots who had been badly treated after the Civil War. While they lost the war, they clearly won the peace during the Reconstruction and post–Reconstruction periods. They managed to convince the country that their traitorous rebellion was a "Lost Cause" and a "War between the States." They were able to regain their political power, avoid punitive legal action, gain their voting rights and get elected to public positions, even including to the Congress of the United States. In all of recorded history, there never was such an example of a defeated traitorous army getting off so easily and regaining their political and economic power merely by signing a personal oath of loyalty to the winning side.

They accomplished this by merely signing amnesty oaths, one of which was signed on May 26, 1868, by one Thomas K. Davis in the District of Columbia containing the following words:

> Whereas, Andrew Johnson, President of the United States, did on the 7th day of September, A.D., 1867, issue a Proclamation proclaiming full pardon to certain persons engaged in the late rebellion, conditioned on taking and subscribing a certain oath therein set forth and hereto attached and herein inserted and Whereas this affiant is entitled to all the benefits of said Proclamation set forth and prescribed; NOW THEREFORE, in order that the undersigned may receive the benefit of said Proclamation he makes oath as follows:
>
> "I, Thomas K. Davis do solemnly swear [or affirm] in presence of Almighty God, that I will hereforth faithfully support, protect and defend the Constitution of the United States, and the union of the States thereunder; and that I will, in like manner, abide by and faithfully support all laws and proclamations which have been made during the late rebellion, with reference to the emancipation of slaves. So help me God."

We might ask from the vantage point of 130 plus years, why the glorious experiment of Reconstruction failed. In Yazoo County, Mississippi, at least, Albert T. Morgan found the answer and recorded it in his biography. His book focused on local politics and the answer to the above question. "What Morgan found was an elite (former confederates) single-mindedly motivated by rational self-interest especially in terms of their own power, the maintenance of which, they believed, depended ultimately on supporting 'the superiority of all white men at whatever cost.'"[10]

Before the Civil War, Mississippi was a primitive frontier state with its black slave population concentrated in the Delta, a verdant and fertile area extending from Memphis to New Orleans. Slavery was at its most brutal on the huge Delta plantations, producing illiteracy, broken families and poverty in the Reconstruction era. In 1860, almost 75 percent of the population of Yazoo County were slaves. Given the demand for land (forty acres and a mule) by the freedmen, plantation owners, many recently pardoned by Andrew Johnson's amnesty program, moved quickly to prevent blacks from buying land. These wealthy white planters were politically astute enough to join the Republican Party, to embrace the Fourteenth and Fifteenth amendments with forked tongues and thereby to modify and control the radical direction of the Reconstruction government.

Some of the leaders of the wealthy whites were James L. Alcorn, a former Confederate Army general and slaveholder, R.W. Flournoy, one of the largest planters and shareholders, and Reuben Millsaps, who founded one of Mississippi's liberal arts colleges.

Incredibly, although Albert Morgan lost his farm and sawmill he was exhilarated by the prospects before him. He and Charles had been driven out of business by his white southern landlord and a dedicated combination of former Confederates and local officials. T.J. Stiles writes,

> And yet, Morgan was a changed man. The foray into planting and lumbering had been his brother's idea; the business may not have suited the hotheaded Albert in the first place. Now that they were driven out of it by the most gross injustice, now that he had seen the cruelty visited upon black people, he rediscovered his sense of mission. He had felt it before as a student at Oberlin College (coincidentally, a leading center of abolitionism). It had burned in him during four years of war, sending him back to the front again and again after near-crippling wounds and bouts with malaria. Now, after having lost so much on what he called "the stubble-ground of slavery," he saw a new path in the light of his defeat: politics....
>
> And so the young ex-colonel, the limping outcast of Yazoo County, rocketed into the political heavens, propelled by enthusiastic (and shrewd) black support. He faced vicious opposition from most local whites. Steeped in racism, they could hardly believe that the nation would stand for the Radical plan of letting blacks vote. Undaunted, Albert Morgan launched his dramatic political career with the unforgettable election of 1867.[11]

At the time, Yazoo County had no public courthouse, no free public school buildings, no prisons, no facilities for the aged, insane or handicapped. Its roads and bridges were practically unpassable. By 1875, all this had improved under the integrated Reconstruction government: one hundred free public school buildings had opened for blacks and whites and a new courthouse and jail had been built. Joseph Logsdon says that "by any standard, Yazoo was one of the best run counties in Mississippi and the entire South."[12]

More than three hundred farmers owned real estate ranging from small houses and lots in town to 2,000-acre tracts in corn and cotton. Morgan wrote that "several of the colored planters were in quite independent circumstances. Their wives and daughters no longer worked in the cotton and corn fields. Each one owned a carriage, not always of the best pattern, to be sure, but ample for the family and sufficiently elegant in appointments for country uses.... Many more colored men owned livestock; horses, mules, cows, sheep, hogs and chickens innumerable." The total value of the property of the colored people of Yazoo at that date (1874) was not less than a million and a half dollars. They were in truth rising. Indeed, there was danger that "our nigros" would, before long, "own the whole country." Logsdon writes that "A revolution was underway in Yazoo that was as extensive as could be found anywhere in the rural South during Reconstruction."

After his election as a state senator, Morgan decided to get married. He was in love with Carolyn Highgate, an African American schoolteacher. Brother Charles warned Albert that in most states it was a felony for a white man to marry a woman of African ancestry. Albert replied that "more than a month ago, I introduced into the Senate a bill repealing all laws upon that subject, and five days afterward that bill, having passed both houses, was approved by the Governor." Morgan wrote,

> Shortly afterward the records of the Circuit Court of Hinds, the capital county of Mississippi, bore the fact of my marriage to Miss Carrie V. Highgate, on August 3, 1870. The bond required was about the same as that exacted of my brother, a failure to give which had resulted in his incarceration in a murderer's cell in that Yazoo common jail. But now that Grant, instead of Johnson, was President, and the new constitution had been ratified unanimously, and the black code had been repealed, and the "nigros" had "done riz," I had no trouble at all to give it.
>
> During this season "we all Yankees," "nigros," and "scalawags" in Yazoo gathered the first fruits of all our planting in that county during the Reconstruction period, and with high hopes for the future prepared the ground for other seed, and prayed for the blessed showers of love from on high to quicken them.

Morgan said that people often asked him, "Would you have me marry my daughter to a Negro?" Morgan replied,

> I have never denied nor been ashamed of the fact that my wife and my children have in their veins negro blood; "nigro taint" is the enemy's phrase. The only thing about it which grieves me is the fact that so many of our good boys and girls can see no difference between miscegenation, as practiced in the South, and amalgamation through honorable marriage, or, seeing the true distinction, nevertheless prefer and honor the miscegenationist above the amalgamationist.
>
> Wife and I have been married fourteen years; we have six children. During all the dreary years that have passed since the enemy, by force and murder, took possession of my new field, stole our grand flag from us, and occupied our temples, this woman and these children have been my refuge.

Albert T. Morgan was asked by a delegation of black voters in Yazoo County, Mississippi, to run for the state's constitutional convention on a ticket with an African American blacksmith. He agreed and thus launched a political career that took him into the Mississippi state legislature.

The changes Morgan and his supporters were able to achieve in Yazoo County are best described by Morgan himself:

> The smallest political subdivision in Mississippi is the county government. "Town meetings" are unknown there. There are township territorial subdivisions, but no township governments. For this reason the county officers and the county "rings" are the most powerful factors in State politics.... By the old constitution, during the slave regime, the county board was styled the Board of County Police; by our new constitution the county board was styled the Board of County Supervisors....
>
> Thus the board of supervisors would be the most important position in our new government. I resolved to guard that position myself, and having asked for it, I was appointed supervisor for Beat No. 3 — the Yazoo City beat — by General Ames, and was made president of the board by the voice of my colleagues. This was 1869....

I think the reader will agree with me that I have not had very much to say of myself as leader and "dictator" in Yazoo. But we have now reached a point where I must give some account of my stewardship, and tell the reader what I, backed by the loyal true of our brave crew, did in Yazoo during the period of my trust. I shall be brief, and I shall begin with our party's management of the county finances.

At the beginning of our term of office, the board discovered that not only was there no money in the treasury, but that the total indebtedness of the county could not be ascertained for lack of proper records. We were able to know, beyond a doubt, that it amounted to quite $10,000. It might be 30,000. The county poor house was a hovel.... The courts were being held in a little, old hall. The only protection for the valuable county records were the brick walls of this hall, and a watchman. The highways had been neglected; some of them were impassable. The bridges were nearly all old, and sadly in need of repair. Populous settlements were deprived of access to the county seat for several months in the year for want of bridges, unless men could spare from their business the time requisite for a tedious, circuitous, and expensive journey, partly by private teams, and partly by irregular river packets. The county jail was a rickety old brick contrivance, with a board fence, half rotted down, and toppling over in places....

There was not a free public school-house in the county. Mississippi was an old State when Nebraska was peopled only by Indians and hunters, but in 1869 there was hardly an organized county in what is now the State of Nebraska that had not a better free school building than any house used for school purposes in Yazoo County in 1869, a center of population, of wealth, and of commerce. The only school-houses in use were such as had been erected for private schools, and some that had been erected with so much of the proceeds of the sixteenth-section school lands as had not been stolen by Yazoo slave-lords....

Carolyn Highgate Morgan, an African American schoolteacher, married Albert Morgan, a white Radical Republican officeholder in Yazoo County, Mississippi. (Angela Morgan Papers, Box 55, Bentley Historical Library, University of Michigan)

The truth is, that while the assessed value of the property of the county, from 1865 to 1869, was in round numbers four and a half millions, it could not have been purchased of its owners for less than twenty millions. By way of illustration, Tokeba, for which we paid seven dollars per acre rent in 1866 and 1867, and would have continued to pay the same sum through 1868, but for the determination of Colonel Black and the enemy to "get rid a' them damned Yankee sons of bitches now," was assessed at one dollar per acre for some, and none at a higher rate than eight dollars per acre.... My recollection is that there was not an acre assessed at so high a figure as twelve dollars. Yet the northerners who rented them [the county's plantations] in 1866 and 1867 paid ten dollars per annual rent for the cultivated lands.... Therefore, I proposed that we revise and correct the inequalities in the present assessment rolls and make a slight increase in the total valuation while doing so.

This was done. Plantations like Tokeba were increased in value upon the roll to two, eight, and twelve dollars per acre; those like the Paynes' to two, ten, and fifteen dollars per acre, according to the land

and improvements; while those that had been assessed at too high a rate, correspondingly, were reduced in value upon the assessment roll. The result was an increase of the total valuation of the real and personal property of the county in round numbers to five millions....

The enemy employed legal counsel and fought these innovations, as they were termed, step by step, but in vain. I had anticipated this opposition and, in the selection of members for this vital point in our loyal government, had procured the appointment of two colored men, who, with myself, constituted a majority of the board. It may be regarded as a little singular that I should have been willing to entrust so sacred an interest to the chance of an alliance between two "ignorant nigros," as they were called by the enemy, and the old ex-slaveholder on the board. A little reflection, however, will satisfy the reader that I acted from correct principles.

It is true that, as a rule, southern men, whether Unionists, Conservatives, or irreconcilables, have always maintained that the Negro is unreliable when placed in charge of an important trust. Most of such people maintain, even to this day, that he is not only unreliable, but incapable. But here were two freedmen — men who had been slaves until the war freed them — one of whom could barely read, who could not sign his name, the other of whom could write only about as well as he could read, and that was very poorly, and yet I trusted them implicitly. In the first place, I knew that the freed people were in truth craving an opportunity to educate their children. I believed that these men, in such a position, would represent faithfully the known wishes of their "own color."

I also believed that the great mass of freed people did in truth appreciate their freedom, and would be as prompt to condemn wastefulness or extravagance on the part of their representatives as the whites, if not more so. And, although the color of one was "light," and his eyes gray, the color of the other black, with black eyes, I felt that I could trust them. They both had worked hard since the war, and saved their money, and upon the very first opportunity had purchased land.

The result proved the wisdom of my choice, for while the northerner on the board "wavered" several times during the contest, and while the ex-slaveholder often got very hot, indignant, and "outraged," the voices of the two colored men were always on the side of right.

First "the enemy" attempted to coax, then to bribe, and then to drive them from me, but, without a particle of coaxing, or of "convincing," or of bulldozing from me, or any of my friends, these men stood firm as a rock upon the naked line of duty, swerving neither to the right nor the left, and I here testify that they discharged their duties faithfully, ably, and most creditably to themselves and the county. The fact is, they were men, with the instincts common to good, well-meaning men. They were citizens and they appreciated the fact that they were public officers in charge of a sacred trust. They were representatives, and they understood that fact, and they bowed loyally to the known will of their constituents.[13]

Albert Morgan published his book in 1884 while supporting his family on a $1,600 annual salary as a U.S. government clerk and a $13 per month veterans' pension. He had hoped that his book *Yazoo; or On the Picket Line of Freedom in the South* would have been published by the Republican National Committee. Instead, he had to publish and pay for it himself, a cost he could ill afford. At the time, Morgan was suffering chronically from the injuries and ailments he contracted in the Civil War. In 1879, his application for an invalid pension says, "his elocution has been impaired, and every effort at continued, clear and loud speech ... has resulted in great exhaustion;... he has suffered great loss of his ... vigor of body, of energy and will ... he is totally disabled from performing continuous manual labor or successfully prosecuting his profession."[14]

Morgan lost his job when President Cleveland appointed former Confederate General L. Q. C. Lamar to head the Department of the Interior. In 1866, Morgan moved to Lawrence, Kansas, with his wife and their daughters and two sons where he started and failed several business ventures. After five years in Kansas, Morgan moved to Colorado in 1890 to try his luck at silver mining, leaving Carrie and the girls in Topeka. He spent the remaining thirty-two years of his life in Colorado prospecting for gold and silver and working as a lawyer. He campaigned for William Jennings Bryan and the "free silver" cause in 1896 and 1900. Morgan wrote and published *Real Money Magazine* and books called *The Passing of Gold* (1908), *On Our Way to the Orient* (1909) and *The Bank of the Beast* (1910).

Carrie Morgan and her beautiful daughters remained in Kansas until 1896 when they began to sing nationally as a professional quartet known as "The Morgan Sisters" and "The Angela Sisters." Brother Albert sang baritone and was the business manager and booking agent for the musical troupe, who were so light in complexion that they passed for white. The group apparently performed until 1898 when the death of one of the sisters and the marriage of the others ended the collaboration. Carrie Morgan became a Christian Science practitioner and was, according to the oldest of her girls, Carolyn Victoria, "wonderfully equipped in all phases of literature, art and religion."[15] Some years later Carrie Morgan went to live in London with another daughter Nina Lillian, who wrote poetry under the name Angela Morgan.

T. J. Stiles summarized Morgan's achievements: "After long years of persecution and failure, Morgan at last found success. He found it all the sweeter because he achieved more than a political victory — by any measure, the movement he led had made Yazoo County a better place to live. He set a personal example in his marriage to Carrie Highgate. For centuries, white men had mated with black women, taking them as unacknowledged concubines; Morgan was disgusted by the practice, and when he fell in love, he changed state law to make his union an open and honorable one."[16]

Morgan wrote what can be considered his own epitaph,

> Let the incredulous reader withhold his smile or scorn until in the course of this history, we shall have dug down to Elisha's bones. Then, if he be a lover of his country, of justice and of liberty, let him accompany the spirit of the immortal Lincoln from the dedication ceremonies at Gettysburg to that Yazoo grave-yard, and there again resolve, "that government of people, by the people and for the people shall not perish from the earth."[17]

Albert T. Morgan died in Denver on April 15, 1922, at the age of eighty-six and was buried in Indianapolis.

13

Albert R. Parsons (1848–1887): Confederate Soldier, Republican, Haymarket Martyr

On November 11, 1887, thirty-nine-year-old Albert R. Parsons was one of the four Haymarket martyrs sent to the gallows and hanged for a crime he did not commit. This, in spite of the protest of the entire United States labor movement and intellectuals on two continents. Anarchism and socialism in the United States has always been considered a foreign doctrine, imported by European immigrants. But there was nothing foreign about Albert R. Parsons, who was a descendant of *Mayflower* pilgrims from Massachusetts. Five Parsons brothers, refugees from religious persecution, were passengers on the second voyage of the *Mayflower*, which landed in 1632 on the shores of Narragansett Bay. Over the next 150 years, Albert Parsons proudly noted, they and their descendants took "an active and useful part in all the social, religious, political and revolutionary movements in America."[1] Parsons had been labeled a "scalawag," a southern-born white Republican. To Democrats a scalawag was "the local leper of the community"—even more reprehensible than the hated carpetbaggers. Called "white negroes" by their opponents, scalawags dominated the Reconstruction governments of Alabama, Georgia, Mississippi, North Carolina, Tennessee and Texas. Parsons published a newspaper in Waco, Texas, advocating black rights and promoting Republican candidates in central Texas.

The first Parsons to attain reknown was "Uncle Jonathan," as he was reverently, and affectionately, called. He was an old Puritan, strong-minded and passionate, second only to his friend, George Whitefield, among the revivalist ministers of the day. Like Albert Parsons, old Jonathan was something of a traveling agitator: his preaching tour, on which he delivered open-air sermons to eager audiences, horrified the conservative-minded clergymen of New England.

Liberty-loving Jonathan could not endure British tyranny. According to one story, he denounced the English oppressors from his pulpit and, in the very aisles of his

111

church, mustered a company that marched to Bunker Hill — where another Parsons lost his arm in the famous battle of the Revolution.[2]

Jonathan's son was Major-General Samuel Parsons, a Harvard graduate, one of the first members of the Patriot party and the revolutionary Committee of Correspondence in Connecticut. As early as 1773, the general dispatched a letter to Samuel Adams, urging that a continental congress be held. "The idea of inalienable allegiance to any prince or state," he wrote, "is an idea to me inadmissible; and I cannot but see that our ancestors, when they first landed in America, were as independent of crown or king of Great Britain, as if they never had been its subjects."

General Parsons fought in a number of Revolutionary battles. He helped plan the expedition that led to the capture of Fort Ticonderoga by Ethan Allen and the Green Mountain boys. He saw heavy fighting at Long Island, and then at Harlem Heights and White Plains. He served under General George Washington in New Jersey. Later the commander-in-chief placed him in charge of the entire Connecticut front, depending upon him for the defense of the state. He gave battle to the British at Norwalk, forcing them to retire in confusion. After the war, General Parsons was appointed first judge of the Northwest Territory. Although he was past fifty, he became a frontiersman, traveling back and forth. One day his canoe overturned in the rapids of the Big Beaver River and he was drowned.[3]

Samuel Parsons, a namesake of the Revolutionary general, left New England early in 1830. He married Elizabeth Tompkins, and together they trekked down the coast to Alabama. They set up a shoe and leather factory in Montgomery. Here Albert R. Parsons was born June 20, 1848, the youngest of ten children. His father was one of the outstanding figures in the community and was highly respected as a public-spirited citizen who led the temperance movement in the state.[4]

Albert's mother also came of pioneer stock. One of her ancestors had been a trooper in General Washington's bodyguard, serving under him at Trenton and Brandywine, weathering the privations of Valley Forge, and helping to defeat the Hessians at Trenton. Like her husband, she was a devoutly religious person, loved by her neighbors as well as by her children.[5] At least this was the picture that Albert's eldest brother, William, gave Albert of his parents. Albert retained only the flicker of an impression of his mother, who died when he was still a baby. And before Albert was five his father followed.

Albert went to live with his eldest brother, William Henry Parsons (twenty years his senior), whose home was on the Texas frontier.[6] In later years, he treasured the remembrances of his boyhood, spent near the border. Life on the Texas range during the eighteen fifties was an adventurous affair. Indian raids and outlaw attacks were things of the present. Buffalo and antelope ran over the plains. While still a boy, Albert became an expert rifle-shot; he always remembered the praise he had won for his marksmanship and hunting, as well as his skill in riding the fiery Mexican mustangs. He thought often, too, of days spent on his brother's farm in the valley of the Brazos River, so far away from the next house that he couldn't hear the barking of their neighbor's dog.

When he was twelve, Albert was sent to Waco to live with his sister's family and to get some schooling. He was soon apprenticed to the *Galveston Daily News*. It was an honor to be employed by the biggest and most influential paper in the state, when it was edited by Mr. Willard Richardson. His brother, who had run a small paper of his own in Tyler City, always spoke with reverence of Richardson, the leading Texan editor of the time. Albert worked on the paper as a printer's devil and as a news carrier. Running through the streets of the town, making new friends and acquaintances every day, he soon changed from a frontier boy into a city youngster.[7]

A few years later the Civil War broke out. Albert and the people he knew were greatly agitated. The city whirled with excitement. Meetings were held, speeches were made. Civic spokesmen called for action. Albert's employer, old "Whitey" Richardson — who looked like a conventional portrait of a typical southern gentleman — was a leader of the secession movement. He carried on a vigorous campaign against his political enemy, Sam Houston — conqueror of Santa Ana and father of the Texas Republic. Houston hoped the civil conflict could be averted and the Union preserved; but when Texas joined the Confederacy, he was deposed as governor of the state.

All of Albert's friends were rabid Confederates. Carried away by the war fever, the young Texans immediately organized a local volunteer company, which they named the Lone Star Grays. Albert was only thirteen and was very short compared to the rangy natives, but he wiggled his way into the infantry squad. Of course, the whole thing was nothing more than an exciting adventure to him. He was too young to wonder about the real reasons behind secession and, besides, if he did have any ideas about it they were merely carbon copies of Richardson's opinions. Everyone Albert knew was a hot partisan of the Confederacy; his circle of acquaintances did not include any of the followers of Sam Houston, nor did he know any of

Albert R. Parsons (1848–1887) was born in Texas and joined the Confederate Army at fourteen. During Reconstruction, he supported the 13th, 14th, and 15th amendments. He married a woman of mixed race and relocated to Chicago and became a labor organizer. He was framed in the Haymarket bombing and hanged at age thirty-nine for a crime he did not commit. (Chicago Historical Society, ICHI-38278; photographer unknown)

the numerous German abolitionists who populated the state and who valiantly opposed the slaveowners.[8]

Texas, however, was far removed from the center of hostilities. Many of the young men thought they would never get into the fight if they stayed at home; so they formed independent companies and proceeded eastward to the battle zone. Albert decided he would join the Rebel army, too; he made up his mind to leave for Virginia and serve under Lee. But when he asked his guardian's permission, old Whitey ordered him to remain at home. Looming over young Albert, Richardson lectured his apprentice. "It's all bluster, anyway," he told him. "The war will be ended in the next sixty days, and I will be able to hold in my hat all the blood that's shed in this war."[9]

Albert just had to get into action before it was all over. He had no way of traveling to Virginia, but he took "French" leave (that is, went AWOL) and joined his brother, Richard, who captained an infantry company at Sabine Pass on the Texas coast. Albert drilled with the soldiers and served as a powder monkey for the artillery. When the Union Army invaded Texas, it was under the command of General Banks, who made for the mouth of the Rio Grande. He landed on the coast and hoisted the Union flag on Texas soil. Meanwhile, Albert had joined a cavalry detachment known as McIngley Scouts stationed on the west bank of Mississippi. It was led by his eldest brother, known to his soldiers as "Wild Bill" Parsons. They fought a number of battles with the Federal troops along the Mississippi. He was with his brother's brigade when General Banks's forces, retreating down the Red River, were attacked by Parsons's dismounted cavalrymen who, armed only with rifles, charged the ironclad gunboats of the Union fleet at Lane's Landing. By the time he was seventeen, after serving four years in the military, Albert took part in the last skirmish of the Civil War, occurring just before news reached the state of Lee's surrender at Appomattox.

At the close of the war, Albert returned to his home in Waco. All he owned was a good mule — but it proved to be quite a valuable possession. He ran into a man who had to get out of the state in a hurry; the man had forty acres of corn in his field standing ready for harvest, so Parsons traded the mule for the corn. Then he rounded up a number of former Negro slaves and offered them regular farmhands' wages if they would help him reap the harvest. They jumped at the opportunity, for it was the first salary they had ever received. He made enough out of the sale of the corn to pay for half a year's tuition at Waco (now Baylor) University, which he had long dreamed of attending. There he studied philosophy and political economy. His instructors, and everybody else who knew him, liked Albert. To his neighbors he was a clean-cut, gritty, pleasant and — considering everything — a well-mannered young man.[10]

By the time he was twenty, however, something happened that suddenly ended his popularity. He had begun to think for himself, and he found it impossible to accept many southern conventions that he had formerly taken for granted. Working as a typesetter didn't give him much of a chance to tell people about his new convictions — but it did increase his desire to do so. Since these new beliefs were decidedly unorthodox, there was no place where he could put them into print; so at nineteen he started a small weekly paper of his own, calling it the *Spectator*. Parsons wrote,

In it I advocated, with General Longstreet, the acceptance, in good faith, of the terms of surrender and supported the thirteenth, fourteenth and fifteenth constitutional amendments, and the reconstruction measures, securing the political rights of the colored people. (I was strongly influenced in taking this step out of respect and love for the memory of dear old "Aunt Ester," then dead, and formerly a slave and house servant of my brother's family, she having been my constant associate, and practically raised me, with great kindness and a mother's love.)[11]

In the main, however, his new humanitarian convictions had grown out of his reading and independent thinking, based on what he saw and heard during the years after his return from the war. He had found that in spite of the defeat of the Confederacy, the old slaveowners — thanks to President Andrew Johnson's proclamation of amnesty and pardon — were back in power. Things hadn't changed very much. Many of the blacks continued to work for their former masters; most of the landowners even believed that slavery would be perpetuated. During this period, Negro suffrage was shelved. At first Parsons had more or less accepted the situation, but he was shocked by several incidents in which Negroes, demanding their freedom, were hounded by his neighbors.

When the Radical Republicans were victorious in the congressional elections of 1866, drastic changes took place. As in other rebel states, the conservative government of Texas was swept away. General Sheridan, appointed commander of the "Fifth Military District" which included Texas and Louisiana, set up Radical-Military rule. Carpetbaggers as well as native loyalists organized the Negroes into Union Leagues. Radical Republican papers, usually edited by southerners who were sneeringly called scalawags, sprang up in the state and called for Negro rights.

This was the wave that caught Parsons. His paper was started in Waco for this purpose. The *Spectator* appeared in 1868, during the tensest moment of the Reconstruction struggle in Texas, after Sheridan had been forced out by President Johnson and succeeded by General Hancock, a Democrat whose sympathies were with the southern planters. The latter organized guerrilla gangs to terrorize the new freedmen and intimidate the Republicans. Out of these early groups rose the specter of the Ku Klux Klan. Bands of horsemen, shrouded in white, raided Negro settlements, whipped and even murdered their victims.[12]

It was during this critical time that Parsons first tried his talents as an editor. He became a Republican and went into politics. He took to the stump, upholding the right of Negro suffrage. The Reconstruction Acts and the Fifteenth Amendment had been passed and the Negroes had their first chance to vote in Texas. The enfranchised slaves came to know and idolize Parsons as their friend and champion. Naturally these new activities cut Parsons off from most of his former friends. His army comrades cursed and threatened him. He was branded a heretic, a traitor, a renegade. His life was endangered. Since his arch enemies made up most of his reading audience in Waco, there was no chance of continuing with the *Spectator*, and it soon expired.

Nevertheless, he continued his newspaper work. He became a traveling correspondent and agent for the *Houston Daily Telegraph*, which had been a conservative paper before the Republicans carried the state. This new job took him on a long trip on horseback through northwestern Texas. While he was in Johnson County, where he had once lived with his brother's family, he met an attractive young girl of Black-Spanish-Indian descent. She lived in a beautiful section of the country near Buffalo creek with her uncle, a Mexican ranchero. Parsons lingered in the neighborhood as long as he could. Three years later he returned to marry Lucy Eldine Gonzalez.

Shortly before his marriage, he was appointed as assistant assessor of U.S. Internal Revenues under President U.S. Grant's administration. He served as reading secretary of the Texas State Senate, of which his brother William was a member, and later as chief deputy collector of the U.S. Internal Revenue at Austin. In 1873, when the Republicans were defeated in the state elections, he resigned and joined a group of Texan editors in a tour that took him through Texas, Missouri, Iowa, Illinois, Ohio and Pennsylvania. In the course of the trip he decided to settle in Chicago. He wrote to his wife, who joined him at Philadelphia, and together they reached the Windy City late in the summer of 1873.

Just as Parsons and his wife reached Chicago, the economic crisis of 1873 struck the nation. Ever since the war, huge factories had been changing the urban skyline. Armies of workers streamed into manufacturing centers. Mass production became the order of the day. Trade unions expanded. Profits skyrocketed. Prosperity soared. Then came the crash. Early in the fall of '73 — financial panic. The price of securities, which had risen to new highs during the boom years, suddenly collapsed. The wave of feverish speculating and inflation was over.

Old-line financial houses folded up. In September, the firm of Jay Cooke, monetary pillar of the states, shut its doors. There was consternation on Wall Street. After several wild days, the Stock Exchange closed down. Meeting with financiers, President Grant urged a moratorium to stem widespread disaster. Banks were besieged by frenzied depositors. In Chicago, on a "black Friday," five big banking institutions — beginning with the Union National, the largest financial concern outside of New York — were suspended. Life savings were swept away. Economic distress spread through the land. Bewildered workers straggled out of factory gates. They hung disconsolately around public squares. The specter of unemployment drifted along the streets of American cities. Layoffs. Wagecuts. Strikes. Evictions. Breadlines. Starvation. Street demonstrations against poverty were met with clubs and bullets.

Parsons, however, was lucky enough to land a job as soon as he got to Chicago. After subbing for a while on the Chicago Weekly Inter Ocean newspaper, he became a regular typesetter for the *Times*. He joined Typographical Union No. 16. In Chicago, tens of thousands who had helped rebuild the city after the great Chicago fire, were thrown out of work. Along the wide avenues, swept by freezing winds of the lake, children cried for bread, for shelter. Meetings of unemployed workers formed spontaneously. They paraded through the streets holding ragged banners, with "Bread or Blood" scrawled on them in big black letters. Public attention was directed toward the needs of the poor. A procession marched on the Relief and Aid Society to appeal for help, but a committee elected by the demonstrators was refused an audience. Several years before, over a million dollars had been contributed to the Society for the Victims of the Chicago Fire of 1871[13]; labor organizations now began to agitate for an accounting of the large sums collected. They charged the Society with speculation and misuse of funds.

Parsons followed the case in the newspapers. He was puzzled by the campaign of abuse directed against the protesting labor groups; they were denounced in the daily press as "Communists," "loafers," "thieves" and "cut-throats." He wondered what was behind the whole thing. He decided to look into the matter; what he found convinced him that the complaints made by the labor groups were justified. Then why did the press and pulpit vilify the labor bodies that made the charges of corruption? He was quick to see the parallel between the Chicago situation and the actions of the later southern slaveholders in Texas toward the newly enfranchised slaves whom they accused of wanting to force their former masters into giving them "forty acres and a mule."[14] It was the rulers against the slaves, whether wage or chattel. In his own way, through his own experience, he was beginning to glimpse the shape of the modern class struggle.

Soon Parsons was making use of the experience he had gained on the stump in Texas. His resonant voice and his good presence quickly made him one of the very best agitators in the city. He was well dressed and distinguished looking. With his long black hair brushed back, his waistcoat buttoned high, his body slim and wiry, the long curve of his mustache neatly trimmed, Parsons commanded attention. He spoke whenever and wherever he could: in parks, in vacant lots, on street corners, in halls and private houses. But the crowds were rather small. Often, after putting up posters and handing out leaflets and speaking, he had to give his last nickel to pay for the hall rent and, late at night, walk all the way home — and to work early the next morning. In July 1877, the great depression nosed downward and hit rock bottom. Even employed workers got barely enough for food. The Pennsylvania railroad companies posted a notice of a new 10 percent wagecut. Accumulated resentment rose and brimmed over. Spontaneous protests broke out; a "striking mania" sped along the railway lines of the nation and the great railway strike occurred. The strike was the largest in number of persons involved of any strike in the nineteenth century. It was not confined to railroad workers; it was joined by miners, millhands, and other unemployed workers. A running battle took place in Baltimore. With fixed bayonets, troops marched to the depot. Beleaguered by an indignant crowd, a soldier fired volleys into the throng indiscriminately.

In Pittsburgh, factory hands turned out to help the railroad men. They took over the switches; the trains couldn't move. Almost the entire city supported the strikers. "Butcher" Hartranft, governor of the state, sent "hussars" from Philadelphia. They attacked the protesters; scores were killed and wounded. The enraged citizens drove the troops into a roundhouse, seized arms and ammunition and counterattacked. The besieged soldiers had to shoot their way out of the city.

A regiment in Reading, made up almost wholly of Irishmen, fraternized with the strikers. "The only one we'd like to pour our bullets into is that damned Blood-hound

Gowen," they said, referring to the notorious coal and rail magnate, who had smashed the miners' union.

U.S. regulars swept through strike-ridden Pennsylvania. Marines were landed. Troop trains with Gatling guns — mounted on gondola cars in front of locomotives — pushed through the state. "Give the strikers a rifle diet for a few days and see how they like that kind of bread," were the instructions of "King" Scott, railroad president. The press howled, raved and ranted; the pulpit ran a close second with its abuse. Only after weeks was the strike smashed.

Traffic was almost wholly paralyzed from the Atlantic to the Mississippi, from the Canadian border to the Virginia line and the Ohio River. In St. Louis the situation developed into a general strike. It was led by the Workingmen's Party. Mass meetings raised the demand for the eight-hour day. Steamers on the Mississippi were halted until the captains agreed to increase wages. Business houses closed down. The city was in the hands of the workers for almost a week. Finally the rich St. Louis merchants, recovering from their panic, raised an army, equipped it with muskets and raided labor centers, putting down the strike by force. The Socialist leaders were seized and charged with conspiracy against the government.

Chicago was ignited too. On Sunday morning, July 22, Parsons learned that Pittsburgh was in the hands of the strikers. An emergency conference was called and a mass meeting arranged for the following day. They issued a leaflet, which began: "Workingmen of Chicago?... Will you still remain disunited, while your masters rob you of all your rights as well as all the fruits of your labor? A movement is now inaugurated by the Money Lords of America to allow only property-holders to vote! This is the first step toward Monarchy! Was it in vain that our forefathers fought and died for Liberty?"

About 20,000 spectators gathered at the Workingmen's Party demonstration, held on Market Square near Madison Street. Workers marched from various sections of the city, converging at the meeting place with torchlight processions, carrying slogans reading "We Want Work Not Charity," "Why Does Over-Production Cause Starvation?" and "Life By Work Or Death By Fight."

Parsons was developing into a remarkable public speaker, learning how to hold the attention of multitudes. He looked over the seething square. It was the largest assembly he had ever addressed. The listeners seemed tense, rigid, straining toward him. He mounted to new peaks of oratory; his gestures and his inflections were flawless.

"Fellow workers, let us remember that in this great republic that has been handed down to us by our forefathers from 1776 — that while we have the republic, we still have hope. A mighty spirit is animating the hearts of the American people today.... When I say the American people I mean the backbone of the country [loud cheers], the men who till the soil, who guide the machines, who weave the fabrics and cover the backs of civilized men. We are part of that people [from the crowd — 'We are!'], and we demand that we be permitted to live, that we shall not be turned upon the earth as vagrants and tramps."

By this time the Board of Trade had mobilized a formidable army. Infantry regiments patrolled various districts, firing on the slightest pretext. Thousands of special "citizens' patrols" and bands of uniformed vigilantes like the Boys in Blue and Ellsworth Zouaves, smashed down on parades of the strikers, marching with set faces. Troops of cavalry clattered through the streets at a sharp trot, their bridles jingling, the horses' hooves kicking against the cobblestones. The Board of Trade dispatched couriers to General Sheridan, who was campaigning in Sioux country. Soon, several companies of veteran Indian fighters, bronzed and covered with dust, rode into the city, their repeating rifles slung over their shoulders. They were quartered in the Exposition building and sent patrols through the murky streets to end any sign of protest. With the frenzy of a holy crusade, the Chicago strike was suppressed.

After the strike, Parsons couldn't find work. He tried every newspaper in Chicago, but it was no use: he couldn't get anywhere near a composing room. He was blacklisted. Parsons turned with added determination to the economic side of his activities. At this time the Eight-Hour League was established in Chicago and he was elected recording secretary. Parsons maintained that winning the eight-hour day would give the workers more leisure in which to train for the greater task of emancipating themselves from capitalism. Moreover, he tried to show by statistics — he was fascinated by such data and quoted figures in almost every address he made — that in the past a reduction of the workday had always been followed by an increase in wages and a rising of the cultural level of the masses.

On July 4, a giant workers' demonstration and picnic was organized that lasted three days. It began with a lavish parade that assembled at the Randolph Street marketplace. Early that morning the sky was gloomy and leaden but before the procession was ready to move, the threatening clouds rolled back and the sun broke through. The grand marshal and his aides, mounted on spirited horses, assigned the organizations with their floats to places in the line, and by ten o'clock they started off, each division led by a blaring band. One of the features was the large number of old, worn American flags displayed by the marchers.

First came a brigade of Socialist Amazons, in bright costumes, splashed with vermilion bonnets, armbands, sashes, scarves. Then followed a tableau vivant, made up of a group of men around a leather cannon and gun-carriage heaped with leather cannonballs. It was a neat burlesque on the press, which had spread rumors of a Communist uprising, and was also directed against the proposed military law forbidding the display of arms by unlicensed companies. The gunners who marched with the battery were arrayed in mock military uniforms of blue blouses, red scarves and tall, conical red hats. They were armed to the teeth with enormous fake revolvers and long daggers of painted wood.

Next came the Eight-Hour Car of the Furniture Union. Drawn by six white horses, the wagon contained a hidden bell, which pealed out in deep tones. Above the wagon rolled a large transparency wreathed in evergreens: Eight Hours Are Coming. And on the sides and back of the wagon were inscribed these words: It Will Stop Overproduction — It Will Take Away Tramps — It Will Give the Idle Brothers Work.

The Workingwomen's Union also had a float of its own. It was decked in pink and white fabric and ribbons and its leading banner read, "In a Union of Strength We Seek the Strength of Union." And on the side: "When Woman Is Admitted into the Council of Nations War Will Come to an End, For Woman, More Than Man, Knows the Value of Human Life." Later came the Printers' Union float, with a press in full operation, producing copies of the *Eight-Hour Agitator*, which were distributed along the route.

The weekend was made up chiefly of wheelbarrow and sack races, vaulting and feats of strength; in spite of a rainstorm, the three-day festival came to an inspiring conclusion on Sunday, when Albert and Lucy Parsons and others listened to a speech by Peter McGuire, who had won them to Socialism years ago, and who told them now that the "eight-hour movement was but the Lexington of the coming revolution in labor."

On May 1, 1886, Albert Parsons, head of the Chicago Knights of Labor, led 80,000 people through the city's streets in support of the eight-hour day. In the next few days they were joined nationwide by 350,000 workers who went on strike at 1,200 factories, including 70,000 in Chicago. On May 3, August Spies, editor of the *Arbeiter-Zeitung* (Workers Newspaper), spoke at a meeting of 6,000 workers, and afterwards many of them moved down the street to harass scabs at the McCormick plant. The police arrived, opened fire, and killed four people, wounding many more. On May 4, Spies, Parsons, and Samuel Fielden were speaking at a rally of 2,500 people held to protest the police massacre when 180 police officers arrived, led by the Chicago police chief. While he was calling for the meeting to disperse, a bomb exploded, killing one policeman. The police retaliated, killing seven of their own in the crossfire, plus four others; almost two hundred were wounded. The identity of the bomb thrower remains unknown to this day. Parsons wrote, "My own belief, based upon careful examination of all the conditions surrounding this Haymarket affair, is that the bomb was thrown by a man in the employ of certain monopolists, who was sent from New York City to Chicago for that purpose, to break up the eight-hour movement, thrust the active men into prison, and scare and terrify the workingmen into submission. Such a course was advocated by all the leaking mouth-pieces (newspapers) of monopoly in America just prior to May 1. They carried out their program and obtained the results they desired."[15]

On June 21, 1886, eight labor leaders, including Spies, Fielden, and Parsons went on trial, charged with responsibility for the bombing. The trial was rife with lies and contradictions, and the state prosecutor appealed to the jury to "convict these men, make an example of them; hang them, and you save our institutions."

Although the bomb thrower was unknown, the prosecutors held that the eight defendants were guilty of conspiracy on the grounds that their speeches and writings might have inspired someone to throw the bomb. Of the eight men who stood trial, all were convicted, and seven, including Parsons, were sentenced to death. The defendants appealed to the Illinois Supreme Court, which upheld the verdict of the lower court. On November 2, 1887, the United States Supreme Court refused to hear the case. Parsons refused to appeal to the governor for clemency, declaring himself innocent and demanding his freedom. Governor Richard Oglesby commuted sentences of two defendants to life imprisonment who had appealed for mercy, and the consensus of historians is that the governor would have spared Parsons's life had he appealed. On November 11, 1887, Parsons was hanged with three comrades whom he refused to desert. Six years later, Illinois Governor John Peter Altgeld pardoned the three defendants who remained in prison and condemned the convictions as a miscarriage of justice. Altgeld said that the men had been the victims of hysteria, packed juries and a biased judge. He noted that the defendants were not proven guilty because the state "had never discovered who it was that threw the bomb which killed the policemen and the evidence does not show any connection whatsoever between the defendants and the man who threw it."[16]

In a letter to his wife, written August 20, 1886, from the Cook County "Bastille," Parsons admitted that the verdict would cheer "the hearts of tyrants," but still optimistically predicted "the downfall of hate."

> Cook County Bastille, Cell No. 29,
> Chicago, August 20, 1886.
> My Darling Wife:
>
> Our verdict this morning cheers the hearts of tyrants throughout the world, and the result will be celebrated by King Capital in its drunken feast of flowing wine from Chicago to St. Petersburg. Nevertheless, our doom to death is the handwriting on the wall, foretelling the downfall of hate, malice, hypocrisy, judicial murder, oppressed of earth are writhing in their legal chains. The giant Labor is awakening. The masses, aroused from their stupor, will snap their petty chains like reeds in the whirlwind.
>
> We are all creatures of circumstance; we are what we have been made to be. This truth is becoming clearer day by day.
>
> There was no evidence that any one of the eight doomed men knew of, or advised, or abetted the Haymarket tragedy. But what does that matter? The privileged class demands a victim, and we are offered [as] a sacrifice to appease the hungry yells of an infuriated mob of millionaires who will be contented with nothing less than our lives. Monopoly triumphs! Labor in chains ascends the scaffold for having dared to cry out for liberty and right!
>
> Well, my poor, dear wife, I personally, feel sorry for you and the helpless little babes of our loins.
>
> You I bequeath to the people, a woman of the people. I have one request to make of you: Commit no rash act to yourself when I am gone, but take up the great cause of Socialism where I am compelled to lay it down.
>
> My children — well, their father had better die in the endeavor to secure their liberty and happiness than live contented in a society which condemns nine-tenths of its children to a life of wage-slavery and poverty. Bless them; I love them unspeakably, my poor helpless little ones.
>
> Ah, wife, living or dead, we are as one. For you my affection is everlasting. For the people. Humanity. I cry out again and again in the doomed victim's cell: Liberty! Justice! Equality!

When Albert Parsons was sentenced to death, Lucy headed a nationwide campaign for clemency. She toured the country distributing information about the unjust trial and gathering funds. Everywhere she went, Lucy was greeted by armed police who often barred her entrance into meeting halls.

In her attempts to save the lives of the convicted men, Lucy confronted another battle, this one within the labor movement's own ranks. The leadership of the Knights of Labor, the group to which Parsons belonged for over ten years, took a strong stand against the Haymarket activists. Terence Powderly, the leader of the Knights, took a passive approach to the labor struggle of the time. He opposed strikes, often discouraging members of his group from using those means of obtaining their demands. In addition, he was strongly opposed to the growing trends toward radicalism. Powderly stood against the Haymarket defendants with the belief that the government should make an example of them. Although she found herself without support from the Knights, Lucy continued her speaking tour, gaining more and more people's interest in the Haymarket case and making a name for herself.

Lucy's efforts, however, did not sway the courts or the governor of Illinois who was under political pressure to execute the men although all evidence against them had been circumstantial. Four men were executed on November 11, 1887. Lucy brought her two children to see their father one last time, but she was arrested, along with her kids, taken to jail, forced to strip, and left naked with her children in a cold cell until the hanging of her husband was over. In tears upon her release, she vowed to continue to fight injustice even though her husband had been killed and she feared the same fate for herself. After the execution, Lucy lived in poverty, receiving eight dollars a week from the Pioneer Aid and Support Association, a group formed to support the families of the Haymarket martyrs and others deprived of support because of working for labor interests.

In October 1888 Lucy went to London to address the Socialist League of England. On her return, the struggle for free speech consumed her as she compared the freedom she found in England with the repression at home in the United States. She felt that the free speech struggle was of primary importance and harbored frustration toward others who did not fight with as much dedication. Even after Judge Tuley's 1889 ruling that anarchists also have the right to free speech, she continued to fight for this right throughout her life in constant conflict with forces wanting to silence her. After a major shift toward industrial unionism, in 1905 Lucy began editing *The Liberator*, a paper published by the IWW and based in Chicago. Through this medium, she took her stand on other women's issues, supporting a woman's right to divorce, remarry, and have access to birth control. She also wrote a column about famous women and a history of the working class.

From 1907–1908, a period encompassing huge economic crashes, Lucy organized against hunger and unemployment. In San Francisco Lucy and the IWW took over the Unemployment Committee, pressuring the state to begin a public works project. The San Francisco government's refusal to acknowledge the committee gave rise to a march of 10,000 people. At the front were unemployed women. The success of Lucy's Chicago Hunger Demonstrations in January 1915 pushed the American Federation of Labor, the Socialist Party, and Jane Addams' Hull House to participate in a huge demonstration.

A biography available from the website of the Lucy Parsons Center in Boston, Massachusetts, summarizes the last decades of Lucy's life:

> In 1925, Lucy began working with the newly formed Communist Party. Though she didn't officially join until 1939, she held an affinity with the party, seeing them work toward revolution from a perspective of class consciousness. At this point, after major conflicts with the new directions of the anarchist movement and watching its momentum slow, Lucy felt that the anarchist movement had no future as it no longer actively moved the people toward revolution.
>
> During this period, Lucy mainly worked with the coalition for International Labor Defense, a Communist Party group, aiding with the Scottsboro Eight and Angelo Hearndon cases.... This was Lucy's first return to the South and her first work on issues involving race.... Though controversy exists over the Communist Party's involvement in both of these cases, especially its indictment of the NAACP and its party propaganda during the Scottsboro Boys' Trial, they extended the Communist Party's influence in African American communities, where Communist Party members helped organize unions.
>
> Even with her eyesight failing, Lucy Parsons was active in the fight against oppression until her death. An accidental fire killed her on March 7, 1942, at the age of 89.[17]

Lucy was buried a few days later next to the Haymarket Monument. Her life, observed one newspaper, had been "one long battle with established order of society."[18]

Only a short time before her death, Lucy had mounted a soapbox and delivered an impassioned speech to the striking workers of the International Harvester Company, the old McCormick Company, where Haymarket had all begun. She had served the cause of labor to the last. Along with Albert Parsons, Lucy deserves to be remembered and appreciated.

14

Pinckney Benton Stewart Pinchback (1837–1921): Riverboat Gambler, Governor of Louisiana, Lawyer, Congressman and U.S. Senator-Elect

In 1871, P.B.S. Pinchback, the charismatic black lieutenant-governor of Louisiana, characterized blacks as sandwiched "between the hawk of Republican demogogism and the buzzard of Democratic prejudices."[1] Pinchback was the son of an aristocratic white plantation owner and mulatto slave whose freewheeling gambling and love life involved him in several gun fights and six formal duels. Pinckney was a newspaper publisher, civil rights leader, university founder and lawyer. He served as a delegate to the Louisiana Constitutional Convention of 1867–1868 and the Republican National Conventions of 1868 and 1892. He was the only politician to contend simultaneously for seats in the House of Representatives and the U.S. Senate. He previously was elected to the Louisiana State Senate and served as president of that body. He served as the first black governor ever in the United States and accomplished more in his eighty-four years than most men.

P. B. S. Pinchback was the eighth of ten children of William Pinchback, a white planter of Holmes County, Mississippi, and his mulatto slave Eliza Stewart, whose ancestry was African, American Indian and Caucasian. Major Pinchback had taken the mother of his children to Philadelphia to free her. The couple was returning home when Pinckney Benton Stewart Pinchback was born in Macon, Georgia, on May 10, 1837.

In 1846 young Pinckney and his elder brother Napoleon, who was seven years his senior, were sent to Cincinnati to Gilmore High School. After their father's death in the late 1840s, Pinchback's mother fled to Cincinnati with her children to escape their father's heirs. Administrators of the estate feared that Pinchback's white relatives, having already robbed his black children of their inheritance, would ruthlessly sell their Negro kinsmen into slavery.

After his brother Napoleon had a nervous breakdown, twelve-year-old Pinckney went to work on a riverboat as a cabin boy at eight dollars a month running from Cincinnati to Toledo, Ohio. From 1854 to 1861, he followed steamboating on the Red, Missouri and the Mississippi Rivers, eventually reaching a steward's position, the highest attainable by a black man. He also learned to gamble. In *Forty Years a Gambler on the Mississippi*, George H. Devol recalled, "He was my boy. I raised him and trained him. I took him out of a steamboat barber shop. I instructed him in the mysteries of card-playing, and he was an apt pupil."[2] In particular, the gambler remembered the lucky streak that began the night "we sent Pinch to open a game of Chuck-a-luck with the niggers on deck, while we opened 3-card monte in the cabin." One concludes that Pinchback was more than a casual acquaintance of such gamblers as Devol and Canada Bill Jones.

Pinckney Benton Stewart Pinchback (1837–1921) served as the first black governor in the United States. A newspaper publisher, civil rights leader, and university founder and lawyer, he was the only politician to contend simultaneously for seats in the U.S. House of Representatives and the U.S. Senate. (©Corbis)

After the start of the Civil War, Pinchback abandoned the steamer *Alonzo Childs* on May 10, 1862, in Yazoo City, Mississippi, ran the Confederate blockade and made his way to occupied New Orleans. There, in a family dispute he had a serious difficulty with his brother-in-law, John Keppard, who was wounded in the encounter. Tried for assault and attempted murder by a military court, he was sentenced to two years in the workhouse, where he served only a month. Light-skinned enough to pass for white, he joined the Federal Army after his release. When General Benjamin Butler began to recruit free men of color with his celebrated order No. 62, Pinchback left his white unit and raised a company of Native Guards and was put in command of Company A. In 1863, General N. P. Banks refused to commission Captain Pinchback based upon the fact that no authority existed then for the employment of colored persons in any other capacity than that of privates, citizens and noncommissioned officers. This great injustice caused the resignation of black officers including Captain Pinchback. The slender, smartly groomed captain would not tolerate discriminatory treatment of his soldiers. When the army proposed giving second-class pay and assignments to his men, he resigned from the army. Though

Pinchback later recruited a company of Negro cavalrymen, Banks refused to recommission him.[3] In 1865, Pinchback went to Washington with the hope of obtaining from President Abraham Lincoln authority to raise a black regiment in Ohio and Indiana but the end of the war and Lincoln's assassination rendered his trip useless.

At last the war was over — the bloodiest war in history with Americans killing Americans for four long years. The Confederate Army, in tatters, dragged home, exhausted, to face farms gone fallow, plantation houses deserted and gardens overrun with weeds.

The 200,000 black men who had fought so valiantly in the Union Army returned to the land that had enslaved them for 250 years. What did freedom mean? After the initial euphoria, they returned to the slave quarters where the harsh and cruel whip of the overseer was an ever-present memory. After the reunion with wives and children, at least those who hadn't been sold to distant owners and locations before the war, these veterans of the Civil War were free but at a loss to know what to make of it. They were almost universally illiterate. It was against the law to teach any slave to read or write, at pain of death. Remember that for 250 years, the slaves were treated like beasts of burden. Remember that slave children were bred like cattle by white masters and overseers raping black slave women. They were finally free but without any safety nets: no jobs, no land, no political power, no wealth, no education.

Pinchback saw his duty and opportunity and embarked on a speaking trip to Montgomery, Selma and Mobile, to assemblies of black people, denouncing the unjust treatment they were receiving from the lawless and vicious in Alabama. Soon after Congress enacted the Reconstruction Acts, he returned to New Orleans to organize the Fourth Ward Republican Club, his first move in politics. Pinchback served as a delegate to the Republican state convention where he made his first major speech to the Republican Party:

> One thing more gives me uneasiness. There is a sense of security displayed by our people that is really alarming. They seem to think that all is done, the Great Battle has been fought and the victory won. Gentlemen, this is a fallacy. The Great Contest has just begun.... The fact that we are all free and have the ballot does not prove that we must necessarily carry the election. Our enemies are strong in wealth, strong in political trickery, and in many places they have official influence on their side which makes them no mean adversary. They are vigilant, energetic and persevering, and unless we use all the discipline in our party, we will be defeated.[4]

Later he was elected to the state senate where he was the author of several important legislative measures. In 1868, he introduced and succeeded in securing the adoption of the thirteenth article of the Constitution that guaranteed civil rights to all the people of Louisiana. In 1869 he declined an appointment by President Grant as register of the land office in New Orleans in order to remain a state senator. Also late in 1869, he established a cotton factorage business in partnership with a remarkable free black man named Caius Cesar Antoine who later was elected lieutenant-governor of Louisiana. "So great was the enthusiasm manifested at [Antoine's] nomination that he was carried bodily to the rostrum, when, in his usual unaffected manner, he delivered a telling address…. In his capacity as second officer of the State of Louisiana, Lieutenant-Governor Antoine secured the admiration and confidence of his race and the respect of the whites, and his good qualities are acknowledged even by his political opponents. A man of the strictest integrity, his private character is unblemished." [5]

The following advertisement appeared in the *New Orleans Republican* from October 10 to November 5, 1869:

Pinchback and Antoine
(P. B. S. Pinchback, New Orleans–C.C. Antoine, Shreveport, Louisiana)
Commission Merchants
114 Carondelet Street, New Orleans
Liberal Advances Made on Consignments.
Prompt attention given to buying, selling and leasing of farms, paying of taxes,
collecting rents, etc.[6]

In 1870, Pinchback began the publication of the *New Orleans Louisianan*, a semi-weekly and then a weekly newspaper, which he published for eleven years.

On November 22, 1871, when Lieutenant-Governor Oscar James Dunn died suddenly, Governor Henry Clay Warmouth called the senate into special session to elect a president pro tem who would serve as lieutenant-governor. The *New Orleans Republican* reported the next morning that "the community was startled yesterday afternoon by the report that Lieutenant-Governor Dunn was so seriously ill with an attack of pneumonia that it was doubtful that he could recover. As hour after hour passed the situation became more discouraging, and the last reports were that the attending physicians declared that his recovery was impossible, and it was not probable that he could survive the night."[7] By the morning of Wednesday, November 22, Oscar J. Dunn was dead and rumors filled the air that he had been poisoned. Pinchback and Dunn were political enemies and therefore Pinchback did not visit the Dunn household for fear of being called a hypocrite. He apparently was sorry that the black people of Louisiana had lost one of their heroes. Governor Warmouth reluctantly supported Pinchback to replace Dunn as lieutenant-governor. Pinchback was named to this position after a black senator broke a 17–17 tie in Pinchback's favor. It was alleged that the man was promised $15,000 by the governor but when, by court order, the locked box supposedly containing this money was opened, it was empty. Pinchback's opponent was also accused of buying votes. As lieutenant-governor, Pinchback was ex-officio president of the Board of Metropolitan Police, practically the head of the police force in the city of New Orleans.

P. B. S. Pinchback was, according to the *New York Commercial Advertiser*, "the best-dressed southern man we have had in Congress from the South since the days when gentlemen were Democrats…. Were he to walk into Delmonico's café he would be mistaken by even so experienced an eye as Admiral Wenberg's for a wealthy Creole planter educated abroad." The reporter remarked that his good breeding and polite manners was in sharp contrast to the "Texan and Louisiana Yahoos who shout 'nigger, nigger,

nigger' in default of common sense or logic." The reporter described Pinchback as "about thirty-seven years of age, not darker than an Arab, less so than the Kanaka. Like Lord Tomnoddy, his hair is straight but his whiskers curl. His features are regular, just perceptibly African, his eyes intensely black and brilliant, with a keen restless glance. His most repellent point is a sardonic smile, which hovering continuously over his lips, gives him an evil look, undeniably handsome as the man is. It seems as though the scorn which must rage within him, at the sight of the dirty ignorant men from the South who affect to look down upon him on account of his color, finds play imperceptibly about his lips."[8]

On August 25, 1872, he was nominated by the Republican state convention for governor of the state of Louisiana. But the federal officials placed another state ticket in the field, headed by William Pitt Kellogg. The Democrats had their own slate whose election seemed imminent unless a compromise could be reached between the two Republican slates. The resultant compromise resulted in one Republican ticket composed of four nominees of the custom-house faction and three nominees of the Pinchback ticket headed by William Pitt Kellogg for governor, C. C. Antoine as lieutenant-governor, and Pinchback as congressman-at-large from Louisiana. The ticket supported President Grant's bid for a second term.

Because of his role as ex-officio lieutenant-governor, Pinchback served as acting governor from December 9, 1872, to January 13, 1873, when Henry Warmouth was debarred from his office during impeachment proceedings. The next day the legislature elected Pinchback to the United States Senate for a six-year term. This election gave him the extraordinary distinction of being a member-elect of both houses of Congress. Since the Senate's first duty was the second inauguration of President Grant, leading Republican senators advised the senators-elect from Alabama and Louisiana to refrain from presenting themselves to be sworn in until the inaugural ceremonies were over.

Two days of deliberation were sufficient to admit the white candidate George Spencer of Alabama. Pinchback, on the other hand, was kept waiting for two years before he was accorded any serious attention, even though the Louisiana legislature reaffirmed his election. On March 5, 1875, Senator Oliver P. Morton of Indiana introduced two resolutions, the first to recognize the Kellogg government, the second in these words: "Resolved, that P. B. S. Pinchback be admitted as a Senator from the State of Louisiana to the term of six years, beginning March 8, 1873." Senator Edmunds, the "iceberg" of Vermont, moved to amend by inserting the word "not" before "be admitted." It took another year for the revised amendment and resolution to be adopted by a vote of thirty-two to twenty-nine, which ruled that Pinchback's election was illegal. He was paid $16,666 by the Senate to cover salary and travel expenses up to that time. The congressional seat was also stolen from Pinchback and given to his opponent in the last hours of the session. Pinchback's intelligence, his extraordinary ability and political acumen were unable to overcome the race-based conspiracy that existed to keep him out of both houses of Congress. Subsequently, Governor Kellogg appointed him as commissioner to the Vienna Exposition from the state of Louisiana. He visited France, Italy, Austria, Switzerland and England over a three-month period.

Then in 1875, the Louisiana state legislature tried to cure the objections raised in 1873 and reelected Pinchback as senator in case of a vacancy. At the Republican state convention, held in 1875, Pinchback was elected president of the convention and the following resolution was adopted:

> Resolved, that we reaffirm our unalterable allegiance to, and confidence in the Honorable P. B. S. Pinchback, United States Senator-elect from Louisiana, and while we regret that he has not been seated we have every faith that the Senate of the United States will, in due time, honor his credentials as one of the representatives of the sovereign state of Louisiana. But in case it should be deemed necessary for the General Assembly of Louisiana at its next session to ratify his credentials as United States Senator, we hereby nominate and reendorse the Honorable P. B. S. Pinchback as our unanimous choice and only candidate for United States Senator from this State, and direct all the Republicans, members of the General Assembly, to put in force and to execute this declaration of the deliberate wisdom of the Republican party in convention assembled.[9]

In 1885, at the age of forty-eight, Pinchback decided to become a lawyer and enrolled at Straight University, "the University for the education of persons of color." He had helped to create this university and served on its board of trustees. Given his knowledge of the general principles of Louisiana and United States law, it took him only one year of study to pass the Louisiana bar examination. He was admitted to the bar in April 10, 1886.

But the racist anti-democratic forces in Louisiana were too entrenched and too politically powerful to allow a black man to take his seat in the United States Senate. No matter that he was democratically elected, no matter that he overcame appalling election fraud, no matter that his supporters had to risk their lives to cast their vote. After 250 years of brutal treatment and castigation of blacks as beasts of burden and chattel property, the popular American culture could not accept a talented, well-educated black man as an equal. Any ignorant, uneducated white man had more access to the fruits of American democracy than P. B. S. Pinchback and what's worse, some of the organizations created by the white society could engage in vicious, murderous behavior without recourse and without punishment. Blacks could be lynched and killed, their daughters and wives raped, their houses burned and their property stolen, all without indictment or conviction of the perpetrators. The white-controlled legal infrastructure perverted the "justice is blind" doctrine and rationalized its horrendous behavior against all blacks.

After President Rutherford B. Hayes withdrew the federal troops in 1877, most white Republicans left the party and, for the most part, blacks constituted the bulk of the membership. Even an optimist like Pinchback could not maintain his hope for equal rights for blacks in the South. In 1890, he helped to organize the American Citizen's Equal Rights Association at the National Convention of Colored Men. Their purposes were "securing the free and full exercise of every political and civil right guaranteed the American citizen by the Constitution and laws of the country, and the improvement of the moral, intellectual and material interests of all."[10] Pinchback was married in 1860 to Nina Emily Hawthorne who bore him six children. A *New Orleans Times* reporter, visiting for an interview in 1872, described the Pinchback home at 13 Derbigny Street as a "very nice two-story house" with a "neatly but not gaudily furnished parlor. A fine brussels carpet covered the floor.... The windows were draped with handsome curtains. An upright piano on one side gave evidence of musical capacity in the household.... In a rear room, divided by folding doors, was a library and sideboard."[11] Although two children would die at a young age, three sons and a daughter lived to adulthood. Pinckney Napoleon graduated from the College of Pharmacy, Philadelphia, in 1887. Walter A. graduated from Andover Academy and Howard University Law School and served as a lieutenant in the Spanish-American War.[12]

P.B.S. Pinchback had a remarkable political career for twenty years during which time he was elected to more public offices than any other black man in the United States. In business, too, he was very successful, and he was deeply involved in lotteries and racetrack gambling. By 1900, it was estimated that he had an annual income of $10,000.

Since 1891, a monumental white obelisk has stood on a traffic island at the foot of Canal Street in downtown New Orleans. It commemorates the Battle of Canal Street (renamed the Battle of Liberty Place after Reconstruction), an armed insurrection in 1874. It was inscribed with the names of sixteen White Leaguers killed in the original battle and the date, September 14, 1874. No additional text appeared.

> Antoine Bozonier, Jr.
> Michal Betz
> Charles Brulard
> James Considine
> James Crossin
> Adrien Feuillan
> Albert M. Gautier
> John Graval
> Robert G. Lindsey
> F.M. Mohrmann
> Samuel B. Newman, Jr.
> William C. Robbins
> John M. West

This monument memorialized a violent overthrow of a duly elected state government. Nowhere in the former Confederate states had such a lawless insurrection ever been attempted. The White League also succeeded in overturning the democratically elected Republican governments of at least eight parishes. Emboldened by President Grant's unwillingness to send in Federal troops, the White League planned the overthrow of Governor Kellogg's administration in a military coup. In the afternoon of September 14, 1874, the well-equipped White League army demanded Kellogg's resignation. Three hours later, a 9,500-man White League army fought some 3,000 black militiamen and 500 Metropolitan policemen led by General James Longstreet, a former

Confederate general. Longstreet had been Robert E. Lee's senior commander at Gettysburg. After the war, Longstreet believed that the Fourteenth and Fifteenth amendments should have been enforced to provide blacks with full citizenship rights (see chapter 10). The White League army routed the defenders, overthrew the elected state government and ruled supreme in Louisiana in a victory of white supremacy over democracy.[13]

President Grant finally sent six regiments of Federal troops to New Orleans under the command of Major Lewis "Dog" Merrill, who had put down a Ku Klux Klan uprising in South Carolina in 1871. Major Merrill reported, "the whole community is practically an armed mob" who recognize "no such thing as the existence of law, or any authority save individual will." The entire region bordered on anarchy, which caused terrified blacks to sleep in the woods at night.[14]

In 1876–1877, white Democrats used violence to end Reconstruction and gain control of the local government. In 1891, after nineteen Italian immigrants were acquitted of murdering the New Orleans police chief, the White League again took the law into their own hands. The mob shot nine of the prisoners and hung two others. That same year, the White League installed an obelisk supported by a shaft and four columns inscribed with the names of sixteen White Leaguers killed in the original battle dated September 14, 1874. In 1932, fearful of Senator Huey Long's coalition of white and black workers, a commission of white citizens posted the following inscription to the monument:

> [Democrats] McEnery and Penn having been elected governor and lieutenant-governor by the white people, were duly installed by this overthrow of carpetbag government, ousting the usurpers, Governor Kellogg [white] and Lieutenant-Governor Antoine [colored].
>
> United States troops took over the state government and reinstated the usurpers but the national election of November 1876 recognized white supremacy in the South and gave us our state.

In 1974, with more blacks voting in New Orleans, thanks to the 1965 Voting Rights Act, the city government added another marker next to the original, which read, "Although the 'Battle of Liberty Place' and this monument are important parts of New Orleans history, the sentiments in favor of white supremacy expressed thereon are contrary to the philosophy and beliefs of present-day New Orleans."

Although the New Orleans city council voted to move the monument to a museum, it still remains at the foot of Iberville Street "and the second battle of Liberty Place, the battle of the monument, is still far from over."[15]

When evaluating the performance of blacks in public office during Reconstruction, there were essentially two conclusions:

1. Representative Robbins of North Carolina said in the floor of Congress: "Sir, the Negro is a clinging parasite. He looks up to others as his superiors.... Even here on this floor (and I mean no disrespect to any fellow member by this remark) he does

nothing, he says nothing except as he is prompted by his managers; even here he obeys the bidding of his new white masters, who move him like a puppet on the chess board.... He is the world's merry Andrew.... But when you come to grand tragic and heroic parts ... the Negro fails."[16]

2. Senator Pugh in 1890 observed the following on the floor of the Senate: "I have read some of their various subjects and they struck me as being characterized by intelligence and ability. I think that the colored Representatives from the South, as a rule, so far as my knowledge extends, have been men of fair ability and intelligence.... The Negro is an imitative being and absorbs knowledge mostly by observation and association.... I do not know of a single one ... elected to the House of Representatives who was not educated, raised, trained, and made what he was by white association and white influence, by white training."[17]

These conclusions reveal stereotypic racism at its most basic: The Negro is incapable of independent thought and if he expresses himself well, it is because a white person taught him! These conclusions are expressed in a quintessential format in the following closing paragraph of Professor Samuel Denny Smith's book *The Negro in Congress, 1870–1901*:

> This study has attempted to prove that the Negroes who served in Congress from 1870 to 1901 were as a whole superior to those of their race who, with unfortunate results, took a contemporary part in local, county and state government. It has been demonstrated ... that the Negroes in Congress ... were rather well equipped by education, previous political experience, and health, and that most of them had considerable white blood in their veins and were frequently aided by white friends.
>
> Therefore, much was expected of them as they had advantages most of their race did not have. Their lack of accomplishment was an argument that the Negro would do well, for a time at least, to forego political ambition in this realm and to confine his efforts to other vocations where he had a better chance of success.[18]

A publication of the Louisiana State Museum, New Orleans, issued in September 1938, was entitled "Carpet-Bag Misrule in Louisiana — the Tragedy of the Reconstruction Era." Its foreword, written by James J. A. Fortier seventy-three years after the end of the Civil War, describes the persistently pro-white supremacy attitude that ruled the South for much of the history of the United States.

> A Radical Congress, using all of the resources and strength of twenty-two million people declared the policy [of Reconstruction] and undertook to enforce it that the Negro must have political equality with the whites, although in any number of localities in the South the negroes largely outnumbered the whites, causing an intolerable dislocation of southern society politically, socially, morally and financially. It was absolutely necessary, in order to prevent anarchy, for the South to resist this policy and itself solve the negro question.
>
> This booklet is dedicated to the patriotic Louisianans who in the aftermath of the War Between The States so soundly, valiantly, and heroically gave their all to maintain White Supremacy as a cardinal principle of a wise, stable, and practical government.

Pinchback died on December 21, 1921, at the age of eighty-four. He was one of the last Reconstruction politicians to die. His life encompassed slavery through the glorious brief moment of Reconstruction to the tragic Jim Crow brutality and terrorism at the end of the 19th century and first half of the 20th century. He was a rare and unusual black man of enormous talent.

15

Robert Smalls (1839–1915): Military Hero, Political Activist, United States Congressman

In the coastal town of Beaufort, South Carolina, the map of important sites lists the Henry McKee house, a pre–Civil War home, which, like many others in Beaufort, was spared destruction when the Union Navy captured the Sea Islands along the South Carolina coast in 1862. What is fascinating about the McKee house is that it became the home of Robert Smalls — war hero, political activist and five-term U.S. congressman — who was raised there as the slave of Henry McKee.

Robert Smalls was born on April 5, 1839, in Beaufort, South Carolina, the son of Robert and Lydia Smalls, slaves of the Henry McKee family. Smalls was allowed a limited education. At the age of twelve, Robert was taken from Beaufort to Charleston where he was hired out. His mother was pleased with this turn of events because Robert did not have the "proper attitude" for plantation work. Robert was the fourth American generation of his mother's family, which was taken from the Guinea coast of West Africa. Smalls worked on the Charleston wharves, first as a lamplighter and then as a wagon-driver. At fifteen he became the foreman of a crew of stevedores and in the years that followed he learned sailmaking, rigging and seamanship. Smalls lived in the Charleston home of Mrs. McKee's sister and had to give most of his wages to the McKees. At eighteen, Smalls fell in love and married Hannah Jones, a hotel maid whose regular earnings as a slave went to her owners. After the birth of their daughter, Elizabeth Lydia, on February 12, 1858, Smalls bought freedom for his wife and baby for eight hundred dollars.

When the Civil War began, Smalls was pressed into service by the Confederate Navy on the cotton steamer *Planter*, first as a deckhand and then as a helmsman. Fifteen dollars of his sixteen-dollar monthly salary was paid to owner Henry McKee. On May 12, 1862, in the second year of the Civil War, the 140-foot *Planter* was docked at Charleston, South Carolina. The ship had been transporting military supplies for the

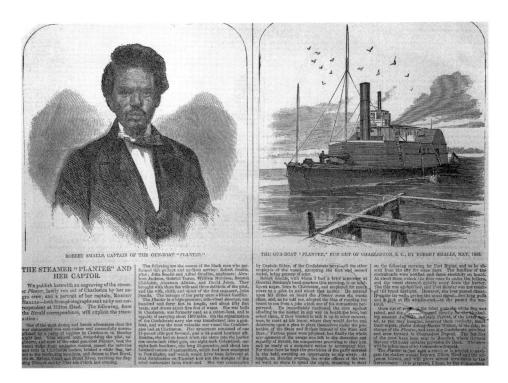

ROBERT SMALLS, CAPTAIN OF THE GUN-BOAT "PLANTER."   THE GUN-BOAT "PLANTER," RUN OUT OF CHARLESTON, S. C., BY ROBERT SMALLS, MAY, 1862.

Robert Smalls (1839–1915). Born in slavery, Smalls became a war hero when he and his black crew commandeered a Confederate side-wheeler and delivered it to the Union Navy in 1862. Smalls entered politics and was elected to five terms in the U.S. House of Representatives after serving in the South Carolina Senate and House. He remained a political power into the 20th century and was one of six black delegates to the 1895 Constitutional Convention, where he spoke against the disenfranchisement of black voters. (©Corbis)

rebel army between Charleston and the outer islands. It was loaded with ammunition and guns to be delivered to the Confederate forts of Sumter and Riley.

In the evening, when the white officers went ashore, Smalls and seven other black seamen who had families living in Charleston rowed their families out to the ship. In the party, along with Mrs. Robert Smalls and their two small children, were her sister-in-law, Mrs. John Smalls, the wife of the ship's engineer, three other women, a man and another child.

Ever since he heard that Union General David Hunter was welcoming slaves into their lines, Smalls had been waiting for this opportunity. He knew it would be dangerous to make the run past the Confederate harbor forts and guns. The *Planter*, a 300-ton side-wheeler, could carry 1,400 bales of cotton or 1,000 soldiers and, therefore, could not easily pass unnoticed by Fort Sumter's guns.

At daybreak, Smalls broke into the captain's wardrobe, put on his dress uniform, (including the captain's familiar floppy straw hat), and strutted back and forth on the bridge, imitating the captain's walk. As they passed under Fort Sumter's guns, Smalls gave the proper Confederate salute on the ship's whistle. After receiving an answering signal, the *Planter* picked up speed as it headed to Beaufort via the inland waterway. Once past the rebel batteries, Smalls faced the Union blockade.

Inside St. Helena Sound and in sight of the Union fleet, Smalls worried that the Union ship *Onward* would think the *Planter* was attempting to ram her. At sunrise that day, acting Lieutenant J. F. Nickels, commanding the *Onward* off Charleston, was startled to see "a steamer coming from the direction of Fort Sumter and steering directly for" his ship. He "immediately beat to the quarters," swung his ship around so as to bring her broadsides to bear, and was preparing to fire when he observed "that the steamer, now rapidly approaching, had a white flag set at the fore."[1] Smalls shouted that they were surrendering the *Planter* to the Union Navy. Soon thereafter, Smalls gave up command to Lieutenant J.F. Nickels.

This bold deed made Robert Smalls a national celebrity overnight, especially when the Confederates offered a $4,000 reward for his capture. A southern newspaper, the Charleston *Mercury*, referred to Smalls' betrayal of trust in stealing the *Planter* as an exploit, which led to "great notoriety for Robert and much caress by his new allies." Robert Smalls' delivery of the *Planter* into Union hands was a sensation at the time. *Harper's Weekly* printed pictures of Smalls and the *Planter* with a prominent article on the "plucky Africans."[2]

The *New York Commercial Advertiser* wrote:

> We suppose few events that have taken place during the war have produced a heartier chuckle of satisfaction than the capture of the rebel armed steamer *Planter*.... It is a remarkable instance, even in these times, of riches taking themselves to wing and flying away. Here were eight "contrabands" made out of the commonest clay imaginable ... yet they actually emancipated not only themselves, but as many others bringing a highly valuable present to Uncle Sam. The fellow who managed this affair proves that, in spite of his name, he is no "small" man.[3]

Admiral Samuel F. Du Pont wrote to Secretary of the Navy Gideon Welles recommending that the *Planter's* crew be given a substantial reward. "This man, Robert Smalls," he wrote, "is superior to any [of the Negroes] who has yet come into the lines, intelligent as many of them have been. His information has been most interesting, and portions of it of utmost importance.... I do not know, whether in the view of the government, the vessel will be considered a prize; but if so, I respectfully submit to the Department, the claims of this man Robert and his associates."[4]

Just six days after the *Planter* was surrendered to the blockading fleet, a bill (S. 317, "An act for the benefit of Robert Smalls and others") was introduced on the Senate floor. On that day, skipping debate and consideration of this bill by any committee, the Senate passed it without a recorded vote. On May 27, 1862, the House also approved the legislation without amendment, and it was signed by President Lincoln on May 30th.[5] Half the prize money of over $9,000 was assigned by Congressional Act to the "Negroes responsible for rescuing [the vessel] from the enemies of the government." Smalls himself received $1,500 as leader of the party.

By direction of Du Pont, Smalls was employed as helmsman of the *Planter* during the four months it remained under Navy supervision and he took part with it in attacks on Confederate positions. Smalls served thereafter as a pilot aboard other vessels including the *Crusader, Huron, Paul Jones* and *Keokuk.*[6]

Smalls proved of great service to the Department of the South in obtaining Washington's approval for the use of black troops, some of whom General David Hunter had already organized without authorization. The commander of the Department of the South hoped that by sending the witty, self-possessed Smalls to Washington as an example of the kind of courageous men he wanted to put into the military, he would convince President Lincoln and Secretary of War Edwin Stanton that black freedmen should be given a chance to fight for their country. In 1864, while in Philadelphia for repairs on the *Planter,* Smalls became involved in a cause célèbre when he was evicted from a streetcar. A resulting mass protest meeting led to the racial integration of the city's public transportation.

Quite fittingly and dramatically, Robert Smalls piloted the *Planter* into Charleston when that city fell in February 1865, and he guided the ship into the city along with Henry Ward Beecher, William Lloyd Garrison and George Thompson when the flag of the United States was hoisted above Fort Sumter on April 15, 1865: the day Lincoln was assassinated.

The *Planter's* last wartime assignment was to help ferry General William Tecumseh Sherman's men into South Carolina. Smalls piloted the *Planter* carrying more than 2,000 passengers to the gala victory celebration at Fort Sumter. In the fall of 1866 with Captain Robert Smalls in command for the last time, the *Planter* sailed to Baltimore where it was put out of commission and sold into commercial service. A decade later the ship was lost in a storm off Cape Romain in 1876 while assisting a stranded ship. A *Savannah News* correspondent wrote that Smalls said "he felt when he learned of the wreck of the steamer *Planter* as though he [had] lost a member of his family."[7]

Smalls returned to Beaufort where he purchased at government auction a home at 501 Prince Street, the same house where he was born, and which was once owned by his former master Henry McKee. The building and grounds were appraised at $700 and Smalls's successful bid was $600.

For a while, Smalls operated a retail store in Beaufort in partnership with black political leader Richard H. Gleaves. The McKee family had lost everything during the war and the ex-slave gave his former owners a home and some tillable land where they lived out their days. The gift was to repay the "many kindnesses shown him and his mother," according to the notes made by his son William.

In Beaufort, Smalls hired a teacher — a northerner who had come to the South to teach in the public schools — to come to his house to give private instruction, taking up where he had left off in Philadelphia. He charted himself a concentrated course of learning. For three months he arose everyday at five in the morning and studied until seven to prepare for his two or three hours of instruction.[8] Smalls's heroic wartime record, his ability to speak the Gullah dialect of Sea Islanders, and the solidly Republican electorate around Beaufort opened the way for his postwar career in politics.[9] He was active in founding the Republican Party in South Carolina and in initiating freedmen into politics. In a district with the highest ratio of blacks in the state, Smalls was elected to the state House of Representatives and the Senate where he worked for the interest of white constituents as well as blacks. In 1874 he was elected to the U.S. Congress.

Smalls took his seat in the 44th Congress on March 4, 1875, and served on the Agriculture Committee. He fought against the transfer of federal troops from the South to the Texas frontier, warning that their removal would encourage private militia groups to take the law into their own hands and declare open warfare on citizens loyal to the Reconstruction governments. He also opposed racial discrimination in the armed services.

Smalls won reelection in 1876 over Democrat George D. Tillman. In February 1877, Smalls delivered a major address calling for an "honest ballot," praising the Republican state government of South Carolina and decrying efforts to deprive blacks of their political and economic rights. After regaining control of the state, Democrats seeking Smalls's resignation from Congress gained his conviction on false charges of having received a $5,000 bribe while in the state Senate. Smalls was jailed briefly but pardoned by Democratic Governor William D. Simpson, who acted on assurances from the United States district attorney that South Carolinians accused of violating election law would be prosecuted.

The abolition of voting precincts in counties with a Republican majority and the presence of armed whites who harassed the largely black audiences at his election meetings doomed Smalls's bid for reelection in 1878. Although he was beaten by Tillman, he stood for election to the seat again in 1880. Narrowly defeated, he successfully contested the result and was finally seated in the 47th Congress on July 19, 1882.

In 1884 Smalls was elected to fill the vacancy created by the death of Edmund W. M. Mackey and took his seat in the 48th Congress on March 18, 1884. Later that year he won reelection to a full term over William Elliott and in December was nominated for the United States Senate by black legislators. He lost the Senate nomination to Wade Hampton by a vote of 31 to 3. He supported an amendment to interstate commerce legislation sponsored by black Representative James E. O'Hara of North Carolina, requiring equal accommodations for all railroad passengers regardless of their color. He sought legislation guaranteeing the integration of eating places in the District of Columbia. Smalls asked the House to defy President Cleveland and approve a fifty-dollar monthly pension for the widow of General David Hunter, who in 1862 had issued an order freeing slaves in Florida, Georgia and South Carolina and had authorized the raising of one of the earliest black regiments, the First South Carolina. He also advised South Carolina blacks against joining the "Exodusters" emigrating to Kansas and opposed the 1877–1878 Liberia exodus. In 1889 President Harrison appointed Smalls as collector to the town of Beaufort. He held this position almost continuously (with the exception of four years in the 1890s) until the opposition of South Carolina senators Benjamin Tillman and Ellison D. Smith forced him to step down to in June 1913.[10]

Smalls remained a political figure into the twentieth century. He was one of six black delegates to the 1895 Constitutional Convention where he spoke out against the disenfranchisement of black voters. Smalls turned down an offer to become the colonel of a Negro regiment during the Spanish-American War. He also declined the post of minister to Liberia, probably because he suffered from diabetes. In 1900 he took to the campaign trail again, touring the Midwest to work for McKinley's reelection.

His final test as a community leader came in the spring of 1913. Two Negroes, suspected of murdering a white man, were threatened by a lynch mob marching on Beaufort. Smalls quickly dispatched blacks to key points throughout the city and spread the word that the torch would be set to Beaufort if the sheriff did not protect his prisoners. The message got through. The sheriff posted special guards at strategic places and the white lynching mob was turned back. Two years later, on February 22, Robert Smalls died quietly in his sleep at the age of seventy-six in the home where he and his mother had once worked as slaves.[11]

Smalls's death had little impact on South Carolina politics because he had outlived the majority of his enemies, rivals and political partners. He and his Sea Island constituents, by the accident of geography, continued to live in isolation, and "they were spared contacts (with whites) at a time when race relations in America reached their most disgraceful depths."[12]

Following his heroic wartime service to the Union, he was a major participant in every important event from the beginning of black political participation in South Carolina. He rose above his beginnings and, with a vigorous and generous spirit, reached as high in public accomplishment as has any black citizen of his state.[13] His remarkable life's story was the embodiment of the proverbial American success story. If he had been a white man, the citizens of South Carolina would have erected a statue and designated a holiday in his name instead of merely a junior high school in Beaufort. He was the longest serving and possibly the foremost ethnic leader in the history of the state.[14] The body of his life's work is, however, impressive. He overcame the disadvantages that his lack of formal education, his life in slavery and his color imposed on his advancement. Although not a revolutionary, he never failed to protest injustice and sought constantly throughout his life to improve social, political, and economic conditions for black South Carolinians.

Smalls is buried at the Tabernacle Baptist Church in Beaufort, S.C. The grave includes a bust of Smalls and a quote that reads:

> My people need no special defense, for the past history of them in this country proves them to be the equal of any people anywhere. All they need is an equal chance in the battle of life.

In February 2004, the U.S. Army announced that a new transport would be christened the *Major General Robert Smalls*, making it the first Army ship named for an African American. The vessel is a 313-foot Army logistic support transport designed to carry more than 2,000 tons of deck cargo. It was to be christened on April 21, 2004, in Pascagoula, Mississippi.[15]

At about the same time, the South Carolina House of Representatives was considering a bill to put into motion a private and public effort to erect a monument to Robert Smalls on the State House grounds in Columbia — nearly 150 years after his act of heroism.[16]

16

Albion Winegar Tourgee (1838–1905): Politician, Clear-eyed Analyst, Best-selling Novelist

In 1879, 117 years before *Primary Colors* was published anonymously, another political novel, *A Fool's Errand*, became a best-seller in the 1880s without an author's name on it. Within a year of the release of *A Fool's Errand*, its author, Albion Winegar Tourgee, published *The Invisible Empire*, a nonfiction account of his fourteen years in the South after the Civil War. Tourgee reported that it was a society dominated by the Ku Klux Klan and riddled with racism, ignorance, violence and corrupt politics. The announcement of the publishing of *The Invisible Empire* finally solved the mystery of the author of *A Fool's Errand*. The following three 19th-century book reviews will show what rave notices *A Fool's Errand* received:

> A tale of life at the South since the late war, full of the racy humor of the country people, the rich and laughter-provoking characteristics of Negro fun, and the pathos of Negro prayer meetings, the dashing excitement of the hunt, the oddities of up-country mass meetings, the social lives of caste, the hot passions of politics, the darker and bloody doings of an enraged people, and their startling logic of self-justification.... It is full of sunshine as well as shadow; and interwoven in the narrative is the old yet even new romance of youth and love. — *Indianapolis Journal*

> The newspapers are trying their wits at tracking the author. One reasonable guess is that the writer is Edmund Kirbe, well known for a picture of the South in "Among the Pines." But since the book has been compared to "Uncle Tom's Cabin," why not make the parallel complete by attributing it to the same author. — *Chicago Tribune*

> The story throughout is intensely interesting and profoundly thoughtful. In point of originality it will rank with the best productions of American writers of fiction; and it may be well to inquire, in view of the power here displayed, whether the long-looked-for native American novelist who is to rival Dickens and equal Thackeray, and yet imitate neither, has not been found. A romanticist, sage, publicist, politician, and philosopher in one, is a rare combination. — *Concord* (N.H.) *Monitor*

Albion W. Tourgee (he pronounced the name Toor-zhay) was born on a farm in Northeast Ohio. He was the descendant of Huguenot refugees from France, successive generations of whom had migrated from Rhode Island to the Massachusetts Berkshires, then to New York's Hudson Valley, and finally to Ohio's Western Reserve. At the age of fourteen, Tourgee lost the sight of his right eye when a playmate exploded a percussion cap too close to Tourgee's face.

Tourgee enlisted in the Union Army at the outbreak of the Civil War. He was seriously injured in the first Battle of Bull Run when the wheel of a speeding gun carriage struck him in the back. After a three-day coma, he woke in a Washington hospital to find himself paralyzed from the waist down. It was almost a year before he could walk without crutches. While recovering, he received his B.A. degree from Rochester (getting academic credit for his military service), studied law in Ashtabula, Ohio, and made recruiting speeches in the vicinity. Then, returning to the war as lieutenant of an Ohio company, he got a piece of shrapnel in his hip at Perryville and, after being captured at Murfreesboro, spent four months in Confederate prisons. When he was released, he met and married Emma in Columbus, Ohio. In a few weeks he was again in the army. He fought at Chickamauga, but at Chattanooga he reinjured his back in the fall. His disability kept him from promotion, and he protested by resigning from the army at the end of 1863 when he returned to Ohio to practice law.[1]

During his Union Army experiences, Tourgee displayed a devotion to the antislavery cause. He took a sympathetic interest in the Negro "contrabands" who were entering the northern lines and subscribed increasingly to the view that the North was fighting not merely for the Union, but, more importantly, for racial equality.[2] After the war, he left Ohio to settle in North Carolina in 1865, largely because the South seemed to offer economic opportunities to a man with initiative. As he recalled later, he shared the hope of other Yankee settlers that the South would be quickly transformed into a duplicate of the North "by the power of commerce, manufactures, and the incursion of northern life, thought, capital, industry, enterprise." During the first year as a carpetbagger, he devoted himself almost exclusively to developing a nursery business.[3]

By 1866, however, Tourgee found himself concerned with the course of political events in North Carolina. Under Andrew Johnson's conciliatory Reconstruction program, ex–Confederates were harassing native Unionists who had given aid and comfort to the northern cause during the war. Tourgee was also disturbed by the unfair treatment of the freedmen. Tourgee saw North Carolina as a society in which wealth and privilege held sway over the poor and landless of both races. What North Carolina needed was a democratic revolution of the kind that had swept the North in the three decades before the war. He wished to eradicate caste and class prerogatives by abolishing property qualifications for voting and holding office. He wanted to improve public education and to provide for a system of taxation that would make the wealthy pay their fair share while extending democratic procedures to include direct election of judges and local officials. Tourgee was a century ahead of his time when he combined two prewar reform traditions: the opposition to "privilege" of the Jacksonians and the racial egalitarianism of the abolitionists. The North Carolina Union Party of 1866, composed primarily of whites who had endorsed peace during the Civil War, shared some of his objectives. But to Tourgee's way of thinking, the Union Party was not sufficiently reformist and all too reluctant to include the Negro in its plans. Soon he emerged as the leader of a small faction known as "the straightest sect," supported primarily by northerners, local whites who had been openly disloyal to the Confederacy, and Negroes interested in gaining suffrage.[4]

The onset of congressional Reconstruction and the rise of a Republican Party based on black suffrage gave Tourgee an opportunity to put some of his ideas into practice. As a delegate to the North Carolina state constitutional convention of 1868, he emerged as a strong proponent of democratic reform. He led the successful fight for local self-government, a homestead law and the abolition of the bigoted dual system of legal procedure. Tourgee was as much concerned with lower-class whites as with blacks when he supported the traditional demands of the class that had never held slaves and had objected to the dominance of the large planters.[5]

In the elections that followed the convention, Tourgee was elected a superior court judge. In his six years on the bench, Tourgee gradually gained a reputation for honesty, consistency and courage. Even his bitterest enemies came to respect his judicial behavior. He became especially noted for his fearless attempts to bring the leaders of the Ku Klux Klan to justice. Although he remained an active Republican politician during his tenure as a judge, his record was remarkably fair in adjudication, as demonstrated by the fact that he made a strenuous effort to avoid giving special consideration to Negro offenders.[6] Tourgee was fundamentally a man of principle who was detested because his principles were unacceptable to the white leadership of North Carolina. In 1879, after Radical Reconstruction had been overthrown, Tourgee gave up his apparently hopeless struggle

Albion Winegar Tourgee (1838–1905) was born in Ohio and educated at Rochester. He was badly wounded in the Civil War; later he relocated to North Carolina where he served as judge and became known for his fearless attempts to bring the leaders of the Ku Klux Klan to justice. A writer, editor, lawyer and advocate of equal rights for blacks, he served as chief counsel for Homer Adolph Plessy before the Supreme Court in the famous *Plessy v. Ferguson* trial of 1896. (Library of Congress) to make North Carolina into a more democratic society and returned to the North.

A Fool's Errand was published in 1879 shortly after Tourgee's departure from North Carolina. Presented in the form of a novel, this thinly veiled account of Tourgee's own experience became a national best-seller. It deserves attention because of its accurate picture of Reconstruction and its presentation of why black freedom did not lead to black equality. With cogency and clarity Tourgee defends a viewpoint that has been given less than its due by students of the post–Reconstruction era.

Much of *A Fool's Errand* is devoted to dramatizing the brutal behavior of the Ku Klux Klan. Tourgee wrote *The Invisible Empire* to document Klan atrocities that were targeted at derailing the federal government's efforts to transform the South. Subsequently this view was challenged by early 20th-century historians of Reconstruction, who rationalized Klan terrorism as a justifiable effort to suppress the crime allegedly spawned by the Union Leagues (the semi-secret political organizations of blacks).

Later historic investigations showed that the belief that the Klan characteristically directed its terror against lawbreakers was fraudulent. Authenticated examples of vigilante action against crime and immorality are hard to find. In most cases, blacks and their white allies were beaten, mutilated, or murdered, either because of their politics or because they had violated antebellum racial mores. There is substance to Tourgee's claim that the Klan was led, initially at least, by respectable and socially prominent whites. Thus Tourgee's account of the Klan as a revolutionary movement dedicated to the restoration of white supremacy at any price turns out to be accurate. *A Fool's Errand*, therefore, is more than an exposé of the Klan. It is also a critical evaluation of the national Reconstruction policy. Tourgee also found fault with the congressional Reconstruction plan promulgated by the Radical Republicans.

The congressional plan provided for quick readmission of the southern states into the Union under constitutions providing for Negro suffrage and the disenfranchisement of prominent ex–Confederates. In a letter to *The National Anti-Slavery Standard* in October 1867, Tourgee stated, "No law, no constitution, no matter how cunningly framed, can shield the poor man of the South from the domination of that very aristocracy from which rebellion sprang, when once states are established here. Anarchy or oligarchy are the inevitable results of Reconstruction. Serfdom or bloodshed must necessarily follow. The 'Plan of Congress,' so called, if adopted, would deliver the free men of the South, bound hand and foot, to their old-time, natural enemies."[7]

It was not that he opposed Negro suffrage in principle; he had advocated it himself the previous year. His point was that full Negro suffrage, imposed by the North and followed by almost immediate readmission to the Union, would create an explosive situation from which Negros could scarcely hope to benefit.

Between 1867 and the writing of *A Fool's Errand* he came to realize that more than a defense of class privilege was involved in the die-hard opposition of most southern whites to the Reconstruction measures; in the novel he put a somewhat greater emphasis on racism as an explanation. His mature judgment as to why Reconstruction failed is set forth in the passage in *A Fool's Errand* that describes what the "wise" statesmen of the North had done in 1868.

> After having forced a proud people to yield what they had for more than two centuries considered a right, — the right to hold the African race in bondage, they proceeded to outrage a feeling as deep and fervent as the zeal of Islam or the exclusiveness of the Hindoo caste, by giving the ignorant, the unskilled, and dependent race — a race which could not have lived a week without the support or the charity of the dominant one — equality of political right! Not content with this, they went farther, and by erecting the rebellious territory into self-regulating and sovereign state, they abandoned these parties like cocks in a pit, to fight out the question of predominance without the possibility of national interference. They said to the colored man ... "Root, hog, or die!"

As the rest of the novel makes clear, the Negro never had a chance in this struggle. His lack of education and poverty made him no match for the wealth, political experience, and ruthlessness of the white "conservative" forces.

If Tourgee had predicted the inevitable failure of Radical Reconstruction and had only joined in its implementation because no other course was left open for him, what program of Reconstruction had he himself advocated in 1867? It is sometimes forgotten that the nation did not have to choose between the presidential scheme and the congressional plan, as it finally emerged. There was another alternative, described in *A Fool's Errand* as "the Third Plan." This approach, defended by Tourgee in 1867 as "Regeneration Before Reconstruction," would have divided the South into territories under federal control. This "territorial tutelage" would have lasted for an indeterminate period, possibly as long as twenty or thirty years — long enough, in any case, to give the federal government time to prepare the freedmen for citizenship through extensive programs of education and guidance, including some form of continuing economic assistance.

The main federal activity under Tourgee's territorial plan would undoubtedly have been in education. When he wrote *A Fool's Errand*, he was fully aware that it was impossible to reconstruct the South for a third time, but he clung to a belief that a large-scale program of federal aid to education might still achieve some of the ends of Radical Reconstruction. In a subsequent novel, *Bricks Without Straw*, and in the nonfictional tract *An Appeal to Caesar*, Tourgee advocated direct federal aid to the school districts of the South — bypassing the conservative state governments — as the best method to combat the racial prejudice that fed on the ignorance of poor whites and to eliminate Negro illiteracy, which was regarded as a barrier to equal rights.

When Tourgee's old friend James Garfield was elected president in 1880, he immediately asked the ex-carpetbagger for his views on the situation in the South, and Tourgee managed to arouse Garfield's interest in his national education plan. Tourgee promised the president to write a book setting forth these proposals in greater detail. But by the time *An Appeal to Caesar* came out in 1884, Garfield had been dead for three years and the Republican Party had lost interest in the proposal. In his career as a novelist and journalist, Tourgee continued to call attention to the plight of the southern Negro, who was sinking deeper and deeper into peonage and segregation, but the nation preferred to ignore the problem. Tourgee's lonely voice was heard by an ever-narrowing circle. Northern intellectuals, concerned with the immigrants of supposedly inferior stock who were flooding into northern cities, tended increasingly to endorse southern racial views, and the egalitarianism of *A Fool's Errand* was regarded by a new generation as old-fashioned and unscientific.

Tourgee was not easily discouraged, however, and in the 1890s he was at the center of a brief flurry of civil rights activity. As the prime mover in an organization called the National Citizens' Rights Association, he declared war on the new segregation laws that were being passed by one southern state after another. Believing these laws unconstitutional, he advocated testing them in the federal courts, and he helped bring the famous case of *Plessy v. Ferguson* before the Supreme Court. As one of the attorneys for Plessy, the Negro litigant, Tourgee argued that segregation constituted discrimination and was therefore forbidden by the Fourteenth Amendment. This view was echoed in Justice Harlan's classic dissent, but the majority of the Court, in its epoch-making decision of 1896, endorsed the segregationist doctrine of "separate but equal."

Tourgee's belief that segregation could be effectively challenged in the courts was of course vindicated by the later work of the National Association for the Advancement of Colored People, culminating in the school desegregation decision of 1954 (*Brown v. Board of Education*). Tourgee, however, was no naïve believer that the appeal to law was, in and of itself, sufficient to reverse the tide of racism. He was also a prophet of the other main emphasis of the 20th-century civil rights movement: the appeal to Negro militancy and self-assertion. He fought the accommodationist philosophy of Booker T. Washington and argued that American Negroes would never be granted equal rights until they organized themselves in vigorous protest against racial justice.

Two months after Tourgee's death in 1905, a group of militant Negro leaders met at Niagara Falls, Ontario, and launched the modern civil rights movement with an uncompromising demand for racial equality. One of the first actions of the Niagara Movement (which was later to evolve into the NAACP) was to sponsor memorial services for three "Friends of Freedom": William Lloyd Garrison, Frederick Douglass, and Albion Tourgee.[8]

17

George Henry White (1852–1918): Educator, Lawyer, Real Estate Developer, Member of Congress

George Henry White, a tall, broad-shouldered, ebony man, was the only black member left when the 55th Congress began its work on March 14, 1897. In a floor speech, White enlivened the routine by suggesting that he, as the undisputed black leader, was ready to get together with the members "on the other side" to organize the House to legislate for the entire country. He was a gifted humorist, but as a southerner with manners, he was not at all amused by some of his southern colleagues who sprinkled their House speeches with plantation dialect stories about their favorite "darkies."[1]

Acutely aware of being the sole representative of his race in Congress, White frequently departed from the issue under discussion to call the country's attention to the plight of its black citizens. On January 26, 1899, he charged that Negroes were still being denied a chance to compete fairly in American life. Flaying the Mississippians for their talk of racial supremacy based on intimidation and carnage, he continued: "Yes, by force of circumstances, we are your inferiors. Give us 240 years the start of you, give us your labor for 240 years without compensation, give the wealth that the brawny arm of the black man made for you, give us the education that his unpaid labor gave your boys and girls, and we will not be begging, we will not be in a position to be sneered at as aliens or members of an inferior race...."[2]

Expressing his disgust at having to sit in the House and hear blacks vilified as savages and brutes, he again reminded the southerners that their states were overrepresented in Congress to the extent by which Negroes were deprived of the franchise.

"Our ratio of representation is poor," White continued. "We are taunted with being uppish; we are told to keep still; to keep quiet. How long must we keep quiet? We have kept quiet while numerically and justly we are entitled to fifty-one members of this House; and I am the only one left. We kept quiet when numerically we are entitled to a member of the Supreme Court. We have never had a member, and probably never will; but we have kept quiet.... We should have the recognition of a place in the President's Cabinet.... We are entitled to thirteen United States Senators, according to justice and our numerical strength, but we have not one and possibly never will get another; and yet we keep quiet."

The House and the gallery listened intently as he moved to the climax: "We have kept quiet while hundred and thousands of our race have been strung up by the neck unjustly by mobs of murderers. If a man commits a crime he will never find an apologist in me because his face is black. He ought to be punished, but he ought to be punished according to the law as administered in a court of justice. But we keep quiet; do not say it, do not talk about it. How long must we keep quiet, constantly sitting down and seeing our rights one by one taken away from us?"

White was determined that the historical record would show what he had put up with, not only in Congress, but outside of it where he was considerably abused by the press. On February 5, 1900, during the first session of the 56th Congress, he asked the clerk to read an insulting editorial about him from the *Raleigh News and Observer*. "It is bad enough that North Carolina should have the only nigger Congressman," the article began. The paper sympathized with the "humiliated" white people of the Second District whose representative had said: "I have investigated the lynchings in the South and find less than fifteen percent of them are due to the crime of rape. And I desire to announce here that if it were not for the assaults of the white men upon the black women, there would be less of the other class." The paper termed White beneath contempt, but indicative of the race problem since he was an educated man. His behavior was cited as proof of the absolute necessity for permanent white rule in the state.

George H. White, whose lineage was a mixture of Negro, Irish, and Indian, was the last former slave to serve in Congress. Born in Rosindale, North Carolina, on December 18, 1852, he was ten years of age when slavery ended, and he had started his education with a Caucasian teacher. After emancipation, he attended public school when he could be spared from work in the family farming and cask-making businesses.

At twenty-one, George Henry White pocketed his savings of $1,000 and went to Washington to enroll at Howard University. He began by taking a medical course but did not like it and switched to liberal arts and the law. He financed four years at the university by teaching school during the summers in North Carolina.

Following his graduation in 1877, he taught school in New Bern and Raleigh while reading law with a superior court judge. Within two years he had passed the bar examination and opened a law office in New Bern. He mixed teaching and law practice, but borrowed time from both to take an increasingly active role in Republican Party affairs.

In 1880, the voters sent White to the state House of Representatives, where he put through several bills of local interest to his constituents, including one to protect Craven County crops from roving cattle and pigs. He worked to get a budgetary appropriation for four Negro normal schools to train teachers, and he was named principal of the New Bern school. His crusade to upgrade the state's school system continued in

1885 in the state Senate where he pressed for compulsory attendance regulations, better facilities for black children, reduced administration expenses, and federal aid for education.

The lawyer-teacher edged further up the political ladder in July 1885 by winning the Republican endorsement for solicitor and prosecuting attorney for the Second Judicial District. He carried the general election by 2,000 votes over John Collins, the black incumbent, who also ran as a Republican. During two terms as an energetic prosecutor, White maintained residences in both New Bern and Tarboro to cover the territory assigned to him. The *Raleigh Sentinel* said he was a "terror to evildoers" in court. Another Republican newspaper, the *Raleigh Gazette*, rated him as one of the top criminal lawyers in the state when he practiced privately.

The nomination was his for the asking for a third term in 1894, but White, a dynamic speaker, was convinced he had built a sufficient following to send him to Washington. He turned down another four years as prosecutor to vie for his district's seat in the House of Representatives. The principal obstacle in his path was his brother-in-law, former congressman Henry Cheatham. These would-be candidates were married to sisters — the daughters of State Assemblyman Henry Cherry.

There was a brouhaha over the seating of delegates at the nominating convention at Weldon. Seven men who had been instructed by their counties to vote for White were ejected. After a noisy floor battle, both candidates emerged from the convention claiming to be the nominee. Named to arbitrate this dispute, the Republican congressional committee gave the nod to Cheatham, who lost the election.

Two years later the brothers-in-law clashed again. Strategy as well as personal ambition split these two. Aggressive and demanding, White would tolerate no temporizing on constitutional rights. Diplomatic and conciliatory, Cheatham tried to bring conservatives around to his way of thinking. Again it was a hard-fought contest, but this time White was the nominee. In the November election, he out-polled the combined total of the Democratic and Populist candidates to win this 50 percent white district by more than 3,900 votes.

George Henry White (1852–1918) was the last black congressman of the post–Reconstruction era. Born a slave in North Carolina, he later attended law school at Howard University. Besides practicing law, he had an extraordinary second career as a real estate developer and banker in southern New Jersey where he created a black residential community called Whitesboro. The town still exists today. (©Corbis)

White had gained stature during the summer by taking part in the Republican national convention, which chose William McKinley as its nominee for president. The congressman-elect had not been enthusiastic about the party's choice, because of McKinley's endorsement of the gold monetary standard, but he was happy to see the Republicans back in control of the presidency.

White decided not to run in 1900. He had made this decision months before the nominating convention, and he stuck to it. He was convinced he could not win a third term with the white supremacists in control of his state. They had already rammed through a state constitutional amendment designed to keep blacks from voting. Still, White was very much on the minds of the district Democrats, who went out of their way to lambast him. They vowed to make it forever impossible for another black to represent North Carolina's Second District, which had sent more Negroes to Congress than any other in history.

On January 29, 1901, George Henry White stood in the House of Representatives for the last time. It was not until twenty-eight years later that Congress was to greet its next Negro member. In his farewell speech, the last African American in Congress summarized the Negro's accomplishments in the first thirty-five years of freedom and predicted that the occasion was "perhaps the Negro's temporary farewell to the American Congress."

The *Washington Star* carried White's speech and introduced it as follows: "With the close of this session, Mr. White of North Carolina, the only colored man in the House of Representatives, goes out of Congress, January 29th, in the House. Mr. White pronounced 'the Negro's temporary farewell to the American Congress' in an impassioned speech, which brought forth applause on the floor and in the galleries."

White delivered one of the most poignant and moving speeches ever heard in the halls of Congress before or since. The speech presented here has been excerpted from the original in the Congressional Record.[3]

> I want to enter a plea for the colored man, the colored woman, the colored boy, and the colored girl of this country. I would not thus digress from the question at issue and detain the House in a discussion of the interests of this particular people at this time but for the constant and the persistent efforts of certain gentlemen upon this floor to mold and rivet public sentiment against us as a people and to lose no opportunity to hold up the unfortunate few who commit crimes and depredations and lead lives of infamy and shame, as other races do, as fair specimens of representatives of the entire colored race.[4] And at no time, perhaps, during the Fifty-sixth Congress were these charges and countercharges, containing, as they do, slanderous statements, more persistently magnified and pressed upon the attention of the nation than during the consideration of the recent reapportionment bill, which is now a law.[5] As stated some days ago on this floor by me, I then sought diligently to obtain and opportunity to answer some of the statements made by gentlemen from different States, but the privilege was denied me; and I therefore must embrace this opportunity to say, out of season, perhaps, that which I was not permitted to say in season.
>
> I would like to advance the statement that the musty records of 1868, filed away in the archives of southern capitols, as to what the Negro was thirty-two years ago, is

not a proper standard by which the Negro living on the threshold of the twentieth century should be measured. Since that time we have reduced the illiteracy of the race at least 45 percent. We have written and published nearly 500 books. We have nearly 800 newspapers, three of which are dailies. We have now in practice over 2,000 lawyers and a corresponding number of doctors. We have accumulated over $12,000,000 worth of school property and about $40,000,000 worth of church property. We have about 140,000 farms and homes, valued at the neighborhood of $750,000,000, and personal property valued at about $170,000,000. We have raised about $11,000,000 for educational purposes, and the property per capita for every colored man, woman, and child in the United States is estimated at $75.

We are operating successfully several banks, commercial enterprises among our people in the Southland, including one silk mill and one cotton factory. We have 32,000 teachers in the schools of the country; we have built, with the aid of our friends, about 20,000 churches, and support seven colleges, seventeen academies, fifty high schools, five law schools, five medical schools, and twenty-five theological seminaries. We have over 600,000 acres of land in the South alone. The cotton produced, mainly by black labor, has increased from 4,669,770 bales in 1860 to 11,235,000 in 1899. All this we have done under the most adverse circumstances. We have done it in the face of lynching, burning at the stake, with the humiliation of "Jim Crow" cars, the disenfranchisement of our male citizens, slander and degradation of women, with the factories closed against us, no Negro permitted to be conductor on the railway cars, whether run through the streets of our cities or across the prairies of our great country, no Negro permitted to run as engineer on a locomotive, most of the mines closed against us.

Labor unions — carpenters, painters, brick masons, machinists, hackmen, and those supplying nearly every conceivable avocation for livelihood have banded themselves together to better their condition, but, with few exceptions, the black man has been left out. The Negroes are seldom employed in our mercantile stores. At this we do not wonder. Some day we hope to have them employed in our own stores. With all these odds against us, we are forging our way ahead, slowly, perhaps, but surely. You may tie us and then taunt us for a lack of bravery, but some day we will break the bonds. You may use our labor for two and a half centuries and then taunt us for our poverty, but let me remind you we will not always remain poor. You may withhold even the knowledge of how to read God's word and learn the way from earth to glory and then taunt us for our ignorance, but we would remind you that there is plenty of room at the top, and we are climbing.

After enforced debauchery, with the many kindred horrors incident to slavery, it comes with ill grace from the perpetrators of these deeds to hold up the shortcomings of some of our race to ridicule and scorn.

The new man, the slave who has grown out of the ashes of thirty-five years ago, is inducted into the political and social system, cast into the arena of manhood, where he constitutes a new element and becomes a competitor for all its emoluments. He is put upon trial to test his ability to be counted worthy of freedom, worthy of the elective franchise; and after thirty-five years of struggling against almost insurmountable odds, under conditions but little removed from slavery itself, he asks a fair and just judgment, not of those whose prejudice has endeavored to forestall, to frustrate his every forward movement, rather those who have lent a helping hand, that he might demonstrate the truth of "the fatherhood of God and the brotherhood of man."

Now, Mr. Chairman, before concluding my remarks I want to submit a brief recipe for the solution of the so-called American Negro problem. He asks no special favors, but simply demands that he be given the same chance for existence, for earning a livelihood, for raising himself in the scales of manhood and womanhood that are accorded to kindred nationalities. Treat him as a man; go into his home and learn of his social conditions; learn of his cares, his troubles, and his hopes for the future; gain his confidence; open the doors of industry to him; let the word "Negro," "colored," and "black" be stricken from all the organizations enumerated in the federation of labor.

Help him to overcome his weaknesses, punish the crime-committing class by the courts of land, measure the standard of the race by its best material, cease to mold prejudicial and unjust public sentiment against him, and take my word for it, he will learn to support, hold up the hands of, and join in what that political party, that institution, whether secular or religious, in every community where he lives, which is destined to do the greatest good for the greatest number. Obliterate race hatred, party prejudice, and help us to achieve nobler ends, greater results, and become more satisfactory citizens to our brothers in white.

This, Mr. Chairman, is perhaps the Negroes' temporary farewell to the American Congress; but let me say, Phoenix-like he will rise up some day and come again. These parting words are on behalf of an outraged, heart-broken, bruised and bleeding, but God-fearing people, faithful, industrious, loyal people, rising people, full of potential force.

Mr. Chairman, in the trial of Lord Bacon, when the court disturbed the counsel for the defendant, Sir Walter Raleigh raised himself up to his full height and, addressing the court, said:

Sir, I am pleading for the life of a human being.

The only apology that I have to make for the earnestness with which I have spoken is that I am pleading for the life, the liberty, the future happiness, and manhood suffrage for one-eighth of the entire population of the United States. [Loud applause]

After George White left Congress in 1901, twenty-eight years passed before the African American Oscar DePriest of Illinois fulfilled White's prediction and desegregated Congress again.

The Raleigh News and Observer ran a cartoon depicting White as a creature with a human head, dragon's spine, and elephant trunk dipping into a container of water. "He doesn't like to let go," ran the caption, "but most people think our Negro congressman has had it [his salary of $5,000] long enough."[6]

After leaving Congress, White moved from North Carolina and embarked on a remarkable second career. White practiced law in Washington and Philadelphia, carried on real estate business in both cities, established the only black bank in Philadelphia between 1907 and 1918, and founded an all-black town in Whitesboro, New Jersey. In addition, his correspondence with Booker T. Washington contains interesting information. Thus, his famous valedictory on January 29, 1901, did not bring an end to his career.

The establishment of a black residential community in Cape May, N.J., was not without strong resistance by the white establishment. In a history of Whitesboro, published in 1998 by local resident Shirley Green, the following background is reported:

In March 1901, Joseph G. Vance, a prosperous store owner, William L. Selvy, a hotel porter and James W. Fishburn, pastor of the Cape May City African Methodist Episcopal Church, organized the Colored Equitable Industrial Association. This organization sought to establish institutions for the care and welfare of African Americans and to purchase land for a town. The desire to build an African American town somewhere in Cape May county derived, at least partly, from a growing pattern of discrimination in Cape May City, such as:

R. J. Gresswell, City Councilman, refused to allow any blacks on a city-sponsored trip to Wilmington in June 1901 to watch the launching of the City of Cape May, a ferryboat.

A few months later, the city administration excluded African American students from the new City High School. The "Apartment for the colored annex," the county superintendent of the schools explained, had not been completed. Black students had to attend the dilapidated Franklin Street School until the construction of the segregated wing of the Cape May City High School.

In 1901, the Cape May Herald campaigned to remove African Americans residents from Cape May City. Marcus Scull, the newspaper's editor, who owned property along an African American section of Lafayette Street, printed lurid accounts of the Cape May City's "colored population" who allegedly loitered about Lafayette Street drinking heavily and insulting white vacationers as they passed by in their fine carriages.

Reverend James W. Fishburn, a South Carolina clergyman who moved to Cape May City [in 1900] led the movement to build an African American town not representing Cape May City's black community [alone] but a syndicate of wealthy southern investors.

This real estate group included Paul Lawrence Dunbar, the preeminent turn-of-the-century African American poet and novelist; Harriet Aletha Gibbs of Washington, D.C.; Wiley H. Bates of Annapolis, Maryland; and [postmaster and educator] Samuel Vick of North Carolina. The syndicate' s largest investor was George Henry White, a former North Carolina educator and state legislator, prominent Washington, D.C. lawyer and the last post–Reconstruction Era African American to hold a seat in the U.S. House of Representatives [1896–1901].

White's most important preoccupation while in the District of Columbia was the buying and selling of land in Cape May County in the southern part of New Jersey. White's firm, the George H. White Land Improvement Company, was located in Cape May County. His stationery, which advertised for his land improvement business and also his law business, indicated this. The letterhead read:

George H. White,
Attorney and Counselor at Law
Office 609 F. St. N.W., Room 4 Phone, East 183M.
Practices in all the Courts of the District of Columbia,
Including the Supreme Court of the United States.
Conveying and Handling of Real Estate a Specialty Residence:
1814 Eighteenth Street, Northwest.
Secretary and Treasurer of the
George H. White Land and Improvement Company,
Of Cape May County, New Jersey.

Choice Lots from $50 Up.
Initial Payment, $5, and Subsequent Monthly
Payments Two to Five Dollars.

According to *Who's Who in Colored Philadelphia*, White was in real estate before 1902:

> In 1901, he bought a tract of 2,000 acres of fertile land in Cape May County, New Jersey and founded the town of Whitesboro, with 1,000 acre of lots and 1,000 of small farms.
>
> These are being sold to colored people who constituted the entire population of the place, and already the town has nearly 300 inhabitants, a good school, two churches, a railway station, a hotel owned by White, a post office and telephone. It is located eight miles from Cape May City and four miles from Cape May Court House, with the markets of numerous seashore resorts within a few miles of it for the sale of its produce, and is ... only two and a half miles from the Ocean.[7]

Geographically, on the east Whitesboro is bordered by the Atlantic Ocean, to the west, the Delaware Bay, to the north and south it is bordered by the sizable towns of Ocean City and Wildwood, respectively.

The Cape May County Planning Board revealed that the first inhabitants in Whitesboro, New Jersey, were Henry and Hattie Spaulding. Henry Spaulding became the postmaster and superintendent to handle and develop the town. Deed Book 166 revealed that the first land sold in the town was in 1902, to Ernest A. Cherry, White's father-in-law.

In an explanation of how blacks were attracted to Whitesboro, R. R. Wright stated:

> Several years ago, just after the Wilmington, N.C. riot, hundreds of Negroes left that state going to New York, Philadelphia and other life ... a movement was headed by ex–Congressman George H. White of North Carolina, which resulted in securing about eighteen hundreds of acres of land in Cape May County, New Jersey. It was proposed to begin a rural settlement of Negroes.[8]

Wright also said that Whitesboro was just one of four all–Negro communities in southern New Jersey. By 1903, Negroes had begun to emigrate from many places into Whitesboro in efforts to find jobs and a "good place to live." On January 1, 1903, the Atlantic Railroad Company bought land from White and started railroad construction, thus supplying many of the unemployed with jobs. When the first two railroad lines were complete, Whitesboro was connected to both Philadelphia, Pennsylvania, and Wildwood, New Jersey.

By April 30, 1906, the First Baptist Church of Whitesboro had been built. More than 300 families (some 800 people) lived in the town, so the need for the church was very pressing. The lot for the church (50 feet wide and 150 feet deep) was purchased from White for the philanthropic sum of one dollar. Grace Methodist Episcopal Church, built in 1907, was the second such establishment erected in the town. The land for this church was also purchased from White at a very "reasonable" rate. The actual date of completion for the Grace Church was December 16, 1907. By 1906, approximately 95 percent of all the inhabitants of Whitesboro owned their homes.

In 1908, a sawmill was built, which provided Whitesboro its second major source of income. Farming was also practiced rather extensively while the Endicott mill made fish boxes for use by fishermen.

By 1908, there was also a real need in Whitesboro for a larger school. On October 1, 1908, the Middle Township Board of Education purchased land for the school from White. The land cost $120. White's company built the school, and on July 14, 1909, it sold the building to the Middle Township Board of Education.[9]

White was very active in Philadelphia where he served on the board of editors for the publication *Who's Who in Philadelphia.* That directory was housed in the same building as his real estate and banking businesses. White was also a member of the NAACP and on the board of directors for the Frederick Douglass Hospital, the Home for the Protection of Colored Women and the Berean School.[10]

White created the People's Savings Bank for the purpose of helping black home-buyers secure mortgages denied to them by white-owned banks. A historic marker on the site reads as follows: "The first Negro-managed bank in Philadelphia was organized here in September of 1907 by the last Negro of post–Civil War days to serve in Congress. The bank was the People's Savings, founded by former Congressman George H. White of North Carolina.... Until the founding of People's Savings, Philadelphia Negroes deposited their fund in savings and loan associations. People's Savings remained solvent a number of years."[11]

Declining health forced White to close his bank before his death in Philadelphia on December 28, 1918, at the age of sixty-six.[12]

18

The End of Reconstruction

Congressional Reconstruction was in trouble from the beginning. It was one thing for the Congress to sit in Washington and map out plans for Reconstruction. It was much harder to secure the peace needed in the South if the plans were to work. At first, the Democrats had been sure under presidential Reconstruction that they could rebuild their party and regain control of the blacks. But when the Radical Republicans in Congress put troops in the South to protect the freedmen, the path seemed blocked.

Unable to win power by legal means, the whites tried to take it by a campaign of terrorism, force and violence. Secret terrorist societies — called Knights of the White Camellia, Pale Faces, White Leagues, Rifle Clubs, the Ku Klux Klan — were soon operating everywhere. Their goal was to drive the blacks and their white allies from power. They wanted a "lily-white" South restored.

Boasting it had half a million members, the KKK rode through the South with lash, torch and gun. They hid under robes and masks and had support from the so-called respectable people of the white community. The Klan used business pressure, bribery, beatings and murder to regain white supremacy. Blacks who would not vote their way were kept from the polls or had their ballots destroyed and discarded. Black militants were whipped, lynched and driven out. Their crops, barns and homes were burned.

As W. E. B. Du Bois wrote:

> The South was impelled to brute force and deliberate deception in dealing with the Negro because it had been astonished and disappointed not by the Negro's failure but by his success and promise of greater success.... There was one thing that the white South feared more than Negro dishonesty, ignorance and incompetency and that was Negro honesty, knowledge and efficiency.[1]

Open terror on such a vast scale could not be ignored. In 1871, Congress passed laws to crush the Klan and the other secret societies. But these laws did not end the terror. The ex–Confederates would not quit. They behaved as though the Civil War

155

were still on. Only now it had gone underground with secret armies carrying on the battle.

The blacks saw their power slipping away. Their white allies had been willing to work with them in Reconstruction — not as equals — only on the condition that the blacks accept white leadership. When blacks asked for leadership positions in relation to their numbers, many white Republicans broke away from the alliance. Thousands who once voted Republican deserted the party to vote with Democrats. The southern whites, back again in one party, were strong enough to win.

With the freedmen isolated, the Democrats returned to power in one southern state after another. The backing that the North had once given the blacks disappeared rapidly, for the severe depression that had begun in 1873 put millions out of work, and in the North the problems of Reconstruction were largely forgotten in the wake of economic crisis. Crusaders like Congressman Thaddeus Stevens and Senator Charles Sumner were gone, and the new Republican chiefs focused on business rather than civil rights. Made into a great industrial power by the war, the North wanted nothing to disturb its growth. Its political leaders were ready for peace at any price. That price was paid by black people who lost their political and civil rights.

The secret warfare against Reconstruction that had been going on for years came into the open. In 1875, the Mississippi Democrats organized rifle companies to take control of the state elections and force the Republicans out of power. It was a pattern other southern states were quick to copy.

During the presidential campaign of 1876, the Democrats promised the voters that they would end Reconstruction. Many Republicans also let it be understood that they would no longer fight to keep it going. The election results were very close. Force or fraud were charged at many polling places, and each side claimed victory. To settle whether Rutherford B. Hayes (Republican) or Samuel Tilden (Democrat) would be president — an issue that threatened to cause another civil war — a political bargain was worked out at secret meetings between the two parties.

The Republicans pledged to take federal troops out of the South, letting the whites do what they wanted with the blacks. The Republicans also assured southern leaders of the economic help they wanted to rebuild the region. On their side of the bargain, the Democrats agreed to accept Rutherford B. Hayes, the Republican candidate, as the winner. Hayes took office in March 1877 and ordered the troops to withdraw from the South. The Democrats were back in power, and Reconstruction was over. The South was once more "the solid South." The black people were gradually forced back into a kind of semi-slavery. The glorious experiment of Radical Reconstruction had not lasted very long. In no state did it survive more than seven years.

Perhaps no one described Reconstruction better than W. E. B. Du Bois in 1910[2]:

> Those who see in Negro suffrage the cause of the main evils of Reconstruction must remember that if there had not been a single freedman left in the South after the war the problems of Reconstruction would still have been grave. Property in slaves to the extent of perhaps two thousand million dollars had suddenly disappeared. 1,500 more millions, representing the Confederate war debt, had largely disappeared. Large

amounts of real estate and other property had been destroyed, industry had been dis-
organized, 750,000 men had been killed and many more maimed.... Add to all this
the presence of four million freedmen and the situation is further complicated....

How to train and treat these ex-slaves easily became a central problem of Reconstruction, although by no means the only problem. Three agencies undertook the
solution of this problem at first and their influence is apt to be forgotten. Without
them the problems of Reconstruction would have been far graver than they were.
These agencies were: [a] the Negro church, [b] the Negro school, and [c] the Freedmen's Bureau. After the war the white churches of the South got rid of their Negro
members and the Negro church organizations of the North invaded the South. The
20,000 members of the African Methodist Episcopal Church in 1856 leaped to
75,000 in 1866 and 200,000 in 1876, while their property increased sevenfold. The
Negro Baptists with 150,000 members in 1850 had fully a half million in 1870. There
were, before the end of Reconstruction, perhaps 10,000 local bodies touching the
majority of the freed population, centering almost the whole of their social life, and
teaching them organization and autonomy. They were primitive, ill-governed, at
times fantastic groups of human beings, and yet it is difficult to exaggerate the
influence of this new responsibility — the first social institution fully controlled by
black men in America, with traditions that rooted back to Africa and with possibilities which make the 35,000 Negro American churches today, with their three and
one-half million members, the most powerful Negro institutions in the world.

With the Negro church, but separate from it, arose the school as the first expression of the missionary activity of northern religious bodies. Seldom in the history of
the world has an almost totally illiterate population been given the means of self-
education in so short a time. The movement started with the Negroes themselves and
they continued to form the dynamic force behind it. "This great multitude rose up
simultaneously and asked for intelligence." The education of this mass had to begin
at the top with the training of teachers, and within a few years a dozen colleges and
normal schools started; by 1877, 571,506 Negro children were in school. There can
be no doubt that these schools were a great conservative steadying force to which the
South owes much. It must not be forgotten that among the agents of the Freedmen's
Bureau were not only soldiers and politicians but school-teachers and educational
leaders.

Du Bois then went on to describe the Freedmen's Bureau.

The Freedmen's Bureau was an attempt to establish a government guardianship over
the Negroes and insure their economic and civil rights. Its establishment was a herculean task both physically and socially, and it not only met the solid opposition of
the white South, but even the North looked at the new thing as socialistic and over-
paternal. It accomplished a great task but it was repudiated. Carl Schurz in 1865, felt
warranted in saying "that not half of the labor that has been done in the south this
year, or will be done there next year, would have been or would be done but for the
exertions of the Freedmen's Bureau.... No other agency, except one placed there by
the national government, could have wielded that moral power whose interposition
was so necessary to prevent the southern society from falling at once into the chaos
of a general collision between its different elements."[3]

Notwithstanding this the Bureau was temporary, was regarded as a makeshift and
soon abandoned.... What could prevent this? A Freedmen's Bureau, established for

ten, twenty or forty years with a careful distribution of land and capital and a system of education for the children, might have prevented such an extension of slavery. But the country would not listen to such a comprehensive plan. A restricted grant of the suffrage voluntarily made by the states would have been a reassuring proof of a desire to treat the freedmen fairly, and would have balanced, in part at least, the increased political power of the South. There was no such disposition evident. On the other hand, there was ground for the conclusion in the Reconstruction report of June 18, 1866, that so far as slavery was concerned "the language of all the provisions and ordinances of these States on the subject amounts to nothing more than an unwilling admission of an unwelcome truth." This was of course natural, but was it unnatural that the North should feel that better guarantees were needed to abolish slavery? Carl Schurz wrote:

"I deem it proper, however, to offer a few remarks on the assertion frequently put forth, that the franchise is likely to be extended to the colored man by the voluntary action of the southern whites themselves. My observation leads me to a contrary opinion. Aside from a very few enlightened men, I found but one class of people in favor of the enfranchisement of the blacks: it was the class of Unionists who found themselves politically ostracized and looked upon the enfranchisement of the loyal Negroes as the salvation of the whole loyal element.... The masses are strongly opposed to colored suffrage; anybody that dares to advocate it is stigmatized as a dangerous fanatic.

The only manner in which, in my opinion, the southern people can be induced to grant to the freedman some measure of self-protecting power in the form of suffrage, is to make it a condition precedent to readmission."[4]

Du Bois then enumerates the all-too-often forgotten benefits of the reconstructed state legislatures.

In the midst of all these difficulties the Negro governments in the South accomplished much of positive good. We may recognize three things which Negro rule gave to the South:

1. Democratic government.
2. Free public schools.
3. New social legislation.

Two states will illustrate conditions of government in the South before and after Negro rule. In South Carolina there was before the war a property qualification for office-holders and, in part, for voters. The Constitution of 1868, on the other hand, was a modern democratic document starting [in marked contrast to the old constitutions] with a declaration that "We, the People," framed it, and preceded by a broad Declaration of Rights which did away with property qualifications and based representation directly on population instead of property. It especially took up new subjects of social legislation, declaring navigable rivers free public highways, instituting homestead exemptions, establishing boards of county commissioners, providing for a new penal code of laws, establishing universal manhood suffrage "without distinction of race or color," devoting six sections to charitable and penal institutions and six to corporations, providing separate property for married women, etc. Above all, eleven sections of the Tenth Article were devoted to the establishment of a complete public-school system.

So satisfactory was the constitution thus adopted by negro suffrage and by a convention composed of a majority of blacks that the state lived twenty-seven years under it without essential change and when the constitution was revised in 1895, the revision was practically nothing more than an amplification of the Constitution of 1868. No essential advance step of the former document was changed except the suffrage article.

In Mississippi the Constitution of 1868 was, compared with that before the war, more democratic. It not only forbade distinctions on account of color but abolished all property qualifications for suffrage; it required less rigorous qualifications for office; it prohibited the lending of the credit of the state for private corporations — an abuse dating back as far as 1830. It increased the powers of the governor, raised the low state salaries, and increased the number of state officials. New ideas like the public-school system and the immigration bureau were introduced and in general the activity of the state greatly and necessarily enlarged. Finally, that was the only constitution ever submitted to popular approval at the polls. The constitution remained in force twenty-two years.

In general the words of Judge Albion W. Tourgee, a "carpetbagger," are true when he says of the negro governments:

"They obeyed the Constitution of the United States, and annulled the bonds of states, cities, and cities which had been issued to carry on the war of rebellion and maintain armies in the field against the Union. They instituted a public school system in a realm where public schools had been unknown. They opened the ballot box and jury box to thousands of white men who had been debarred from them by a lack of earthly possessions. They introduced home rule into the South. They abolished the whipping post, the branding iron, the stocks and other barbarous forms of punishment which had up to that time prevailed. They reduced capital felonies from about twenty to two or three. In an age of extravagance they were extravagant in the sums appropriated for public works. In all of that time no man's rights of person were invaded under the forms of law. Every Democrat's life, home, fireside and business were safe. No man obstructed any white man's way to the ballot box, interfered with his freedom of speech, or boycotted him on account of his political faith."[5]

Finally, in legislation covering property, the wider functions of the state, the punishment of crime and the like, it is sufficient to say that the laws on these points established by Reconstruction legislatures were not only different from and even revolutionary to the laws in the older South, but they were so wise and so well suited to the needs of the new South that in spite of a retrogressive movement following the overthrow of the negro governments the mass of this legislation, with elaboration and development, still stands on the statute books of the South.

Reconstruction constitutions, practically unaltered, were kept in:

Florida, 1868–1885	17 years.
Virginia, 1870–1902	32 years.
South Carolina, 1868–1895	27 years.
Mississippi, 1868–1890	22 years.

Even in the case of states like Alabama, Georgia, North Carolina, and Louisiana, which adopted new constitutions to signify the overthrow of negro rule, the new constitutions are nearer the model of the Reconstruction document than they are to the previous constitutions. They differ from the negro constitutions in minor details but very little in general conception.

In summary, W. E. B. Du Bois rates the accomplishments of the integrated southern state governments:

> Besides this there stands on the statute books of the South to-day law after law passed between 1868 and 1876, and which has been found wise, effective, and worthy of preservation.
>
> Paint the "carpet-bag" governments and negro rules as black as may be, the fact remains that the essence of the revolution which the overturning of the negro governments made was to put these black men and their friends out of power. Outside the curtailing of expenses and stopping of extravagance, not only did their successors make few changes in the work which these legislatures and conventions had done, but they largely carried out their plans, followed their suggestions, and strengthened their institutions. Practically the whole new growth of the South has been accomplished under laws which black men helped to frame thirty years ago. I know of no greater compliment to negro suffrage.

Abolitionists like Frederick Douglass, Thaddeus Stevens and Charles Sumner had urged Congress to confiscate land owned by rebellious Confederate planters and to distribute it to landless farmers, black and white alike. Based on federal policies during the war on the Sea Islands off the coast of South Carolina where freedmen had been allowed to buy land cheaply, a legend spread throughout the South that "forty acres and a mule" would be given to all freedmen. But opposition to such a land distribution was too great and instead, freedmen became sharecroppers and tenant farmers. How different the course of American history would have been if land had been widely distributed to the recently freed slaves. A black landed gentry would have been created with the economic and political power that goes with extensive land ownership.

Many colleges were created during Reconstruction by the Freedmen's Bureau that are still in existence today, such as Howard University (named after Gen. Oliver Otis Howard, head of the Freedmen's Bureau), Shaw University (1865), Fisk University (1866), Talladega and Morehouse College (1867), Clark College (1869), Virginia University (1867), Hampton Institute (1868), and Atlanta University (1867). The Bureau distributed food and medicine to both blacks and poor whites; it resettled freedmen in rural areas; it found them jobs, negotiated work contracts, represented them in court or set up courts of its own; it started hospitals and taught sanitary measures.

Under the federal military occupation of the South, 700,000 African Americans and 660,000 whites were added to the voting rolls. In five southern states there were black majorities (Alabama, Louisiana, South Carolina, Florida and Mississippi) where many state offices were filled by blacks. For example, fifty out of sixty-three members of the reconstructed South Carolina state legislature were black; twenty-nine black legislators served in the reconstructed Louisiana Assembly in 1868 under Lt. Gov. O.J. Dunn, also a black man. In Little Rock, Arkansas, Mifflin W. Gibbs was elected the first black municipal judge in the United States. In 1873, Pinckney Benton Stewart Pinchback became acting governor of Louisiana after the removal of the white incumbent. Pinchback was later elected to the United States Senate but was never seated. Alonzo J. Ransier and Richard H. Cleaves served as lieutenant-governor of South

Carolina. A Dartmouth graduate, Jonathan Gibbs was secretary of state in Florida and later superintendent of public instruction. Mississippi elected a black Speaker of the House in 1872 (John R. Lynch), a black lieutenant-governor in 1873 (A. K. Davis), a black tax collector (J. J. Evans), a black Secretary of State (James Hill), and a black postmaster (William Carey).

Reconstruction failed because the nation left basic problems unsolved. Land reform was the first and most important problem. If the freedmen could not become independent farmers, owning their own land, they could not enjoy or maintain full political rights. They were free in a legal sense, but without economic power they had to rely on the old master class for survival. Unfortunately the mud slung at the Reconstruction governments clung to the pages of history books, and for many generations the era was labeled as "The Dreadful Decade"[6] and "The Tragic Era."[7] The failure of Reconstruction was America's failure as a nation. Democracy was crippled in the South for 130 years to come. It set back the cause of freedom and democracy for the whole country.

Dr. Paul H. Buck, writing in 1937, recognized the difficulties of the reconciliation between North and South in the generation following the Civil War:

> The discipline the South elaborated in the years following Reconstruction rested frankly upon the premise of the Negro's inferiority. Much was said about the South acting defensively to erect bulwarks against the threat of Negro domination. But actually the south moved aggressively to reduce the Negro's status to something comparable to serfdom. The intention openly averred was to give an inferior people an inferior role and to efface them as positive factors in the section's life. To this end, the new discipline excluded the colored man from politics by disenfranchising him, rendered him economically impotent by making him a peon, and isolated him socially by an extensive practice of segregation. The net result was to deprive the Negro of more privileges than was necessary to keep him from becoming a menace and to make the South a "white man's country."
>
> The methods of suppressing the Negro vote softened after the whites gained control of the machinery of state and local government, but they continued to be a mixture of fraud, trickery, intimidation and violence. Polling places were set up at points remote from colored communities. Ferries between the black districts and the voting booths went "out of repair" on election day. Grim-visaged white men carrying arms sauntered through the streets or stood near the polling booths. In districts where the blacks greatly outnumbered the whites, election officials permitted members of the superior race to "stuff the ballot box," and manipulated the count without fear of censure. Fantastic gerrymanders were devised to nullify Negro strength. The payment of poll taxes, striking at the Negro's poverty and carelessness in preserving receipts, was made a requirement for voting. Some states confused the ignorant by enacting multiple ballot box laws which required the voter to place correctly his votes for various candidates in eight or more separate boxes. The bolder members of the colored race met threats of violence and, in a diminishing number of instances, physical punishment. When the black man succeeded in passing through this maze of restrictions and cast his vote there was no assurance that it would be counted. Highly centralized election codes vested arbitrary powers in the election boards, and these powers were used to complete the elimination of the Negro vote.[8]

Reconstruction lasted from 1865 until 1877, when millions of people became citizens and were given the right to vote; integrated facilities were created throughout the South; the Thirteenth, Fourteenth and Fifteenth amendments were passed; the first Negro daily, the *New Orleans Tribune*, was published; former slaves served in reconstructed state legislatures; twenty-two black men served in the United States Congress; new state constitutions were written granting universal suffrage and free education without property-holding qualifications. Reconstruction was a time of unparalleled hope, filled with possibility, but the hoped-for changes proved to be inaccessible. Hardworking black tenant farmers were overcharged for seed and supplies and were unable to buy land, black colleges were segregated and underfunded, successful blacks were targeted for white violence and brutal harassment. Faced with evidence of black successes and independence, white southerners inflicted a campaign of terror and oppression on African Americans.

The white South reinforced rigid patterns of segregation, manipulated the election and judicial systems and inflicted unprecedented levels of violence, brutality and intimidation. As Leon Litwack wrote, whites "owned the land, the law, the police, the courts, the government, the armed forces and the press." The political system "denied blacks a voice; the educational system denied them equal access and adequate resources; popular culture mocked their lives and aspirations; the economic system left them little room for ambition or hope; and the law and the courts functioned effectively at every level to protect, reinforce and deepen their political powerlessness, economic dependence and social degradation." Litwack goes on to write,

> Whites employed terror, intimidation and violence to doom Reconstruction, not because blacks had demonstrated incompetence but because they were rapidly learning the uses of political power, not because of evidence of black failure but the far more alarming evidence of black success. This was clearly unacceptable to a people who deemed themselves racially superior and who resisted any evidence to the contrary.[9]

The Reconstruction period remains among the most momentous and terrible in American history, when terrorism and violence pervaded the South, brutalizing and killing African Americans, their families and their allies. This homegrown terror was rationalized as necessary to preserve white supremacy in the United States. However, the democratic promise of Reconstruction deserves to be remembered, studied and memorialized for its uniquely American accomplishments and failures.

Notes

Preface

1. W. E. B. Du Bois, *Black Reconstruction in America*, p. 3.
2. F.B. Simkins, *The Everlasting South*, p. 65.
3. *Ibid.*, p. 74.
4. Howard O. Lindsey, *A History of Black America*, Chartwell Books (Connecticut) 1994, pp. 89–90.

1. Background of Reconstruction

1. Eric Foner, *Freedom's Lawmakers*, p. xi.
2. *Ibid.*, p. 2.
3. Howard O. Lindsey, *A History of Black America*, p. 81.
4. *Report of the Joint Committee on Reconstruction First Session, 39th Congress.* Washington, D.C.: Government Printing Office, 1866.
5. Memphis Riots and Massacres, H.R. No. 101, 1866; New Orleans Riots, H.R. No. 16, 1867.
6. *Ibid.*, p. xvii.
7. This remarkable achievement was accomplished despite the more than 200 year ban (and threat of death) on teaching slaves to read and write.
8. James G. Blaine, *Twenty Years in Congress*, Vol, II, p. 515.

9. A. S. Taylor, "Negro Congressmen a Generation After"; see also John R. Lynch, *The Facts of Reconstruction*; John M. Langston, *From the Virginia Plantation to the National Capitol.*
10. Claude G. Bowers, *The Tragic Era.*
11. *Charleston News*, June 12 and 15, 1868, cited by F. B. Simkins and R. H. Woody in *South Carolina During Reconstruction*, p. 110.
12. W.C. Elam, "A Scalawag," p. 456; Josephus Daniels, *Tar Heel Editor*, p. 129.

2. Adelbert Ames

1. Blanche A. Ames, *Adelbert Ames: Broken Oaths and Reconstruction in Mississippi.*
2. Captain Charles Griffin, official report, July 23, 1861. *Official Records: Union and Confederate Armies*, Series I, Vol. II, p. 394.
3. John J. Pullen, *The Twentieth Maine: A Volunteer Regiment in the Civil War*, p. 2.
4. *Ibid.*, pp. 1–3, 36.
5. Ames to his parents, February 9, 1865; August 15, 1865; February 11, 1866.
6. Richard N. Current, *Those Terrible Carpetbaggers*, p. 113.
7. James W. Garner, *Reconstruction in Mississippi*, pp. 213–216.
8. Ames to James W. Garner, January 17, 1900, in J. W. Garner papers, Mississippi Department of Archives and History.
9. Ames to General Sherman, August 17, 1869, in William T. Sherman papers.

10. Blaine, *Twenty Years of Congress*, pp. 24–26.

11. Ames, *Adelbert Ames*, p. xxii.

12. Current, *Carpetbaggers*, p. 324.

13. Ames to Charles Colton, March 7, 1876, quoted in Garner, p. 402.

14. *Ibid.*, p. 402.

15. John F. Kennedy, *Profiles in Courage*, p. 161.

16. Ames, *Adelbert Ames*.

17. Kennedy, *Profiles in Courage*, p. 161.

18. Not including the several book club editions, foreign translations, nor the paperback edition which has had at least sixteen printings.

19. Allan Nevins (Columbia University in the City of New York, July 6, 1956), to Blanche A. Ames.

20. Wirt A. Cate, *Q. C. Lamar, Statesman of Secession and Reunion*, pp. viii–ix.

21. Ames, pp. 549–555.

22. *Ibid.*, p. 495.

3. Samuel Chapman Armstrong

1. Report 1871, Superintendent of Public Instruction, p. 205; Freedmen's Record, December 1868, pp. 187–188; *Richmond Dispatch*, April 18, 1871.

2. John W. Alvord, *Reports on Schools and Finances of Freedmen*, p. 14.

3. *Norfolk Journal* as quoted in *ibid.*, 9 (1867), p. 151.

4. Edith Armstrong Talbot, *Samuel Chapman Armstrong: A Biographical Study*, p. 217

5. *Ibid.*, p. 186.

6. Report 1880, Superintendent of Public Instruction, p. 8.

7. George Campbell, *White and Black, The Outcome of a Visit to the United States*, pp. 275–276, 131.

8. Robert Francis Engs, *Freedom's First Generation: Black Hampton, Virginia, 1861–1890*, p. 20.

9. My knowledge of Samuel Armstrong's early life comes essentially from the biography written by his wife Edith Armstrong Talbot in 1904.

10. Talbot, p. 6.

11. *Ibid.*, p. 8.

12. *Ibid.*, p. 25.

13. George S. Merriam, *The Negro and the Nation*, pp. 356–357.

14. J. H. Denison in *Atlantic Monthly*, February 1894.

15. Merriam, pp. 70–71.

16. Ms. Helen W. Ludlow, p. 351.

17. Merriam, pp. 71–73.

18. Ludlow, p. 349.

19. Talbot, p. 76.

20. *Ibid.*, pp. 103–104.

21. Booker T. Washington, *The Story of the Negro*, p. 321.

22. *Complete Works of Abraham Lincoln*, Nicolay and Hay, eds., p. 248.

23. Francis G. Peabody, *Education for Life*, p. 19.

24. Op. cit., II, p. 398.

25. Merriam, pp. 79–80.

26. Address delivered by General Oliver Otis Howard at Hampton Institute, 1889; Talbot, p. 135.

27. Talbot, pp. 139–142.

28. *Ibid.*, p. 147.

29. *Ibid.*, pp. 154–155.

30. Peabody, p. 99.

31. Merriam, pp. 363–364.

32. Booker T. Washington, *Up from Slavery*, p. 54.

33. The Hampton Album, *The Museum of Modern Art*, p.7.

34. *Ibid.*, p. 8.

35. Peabody, p. 134.

36. *Ibid.*, pp. 137–138.

37. Talbot, p. 299.

4. Blanche Kelso Bruce

1. *Congressional Record*, 44th Congress, 1st Session.

2. William J. Simmons, *Men of Mark*, pp. 699–703.

3. *Congressional Record*, 44th Congress, 1st Session, pp. 2100–2105.

4. Lynch, *The Facts of Reconstruction*, pp. 78–79.

5. *Congressional Record*, 44th Congress, 1st Session, pp. 1444, 1445.

6. *Ibid.*, pp. 2100–2105.

7. *Ibid.*

8. *Ibid.,* p. 2104.

9. *Ibid.,* p. 2105.

10. *Ibid.,* pp. 2195–2196.

11. *Ibid.,* pp. 45, 71, 435, 1679, 2415; 3d Session, pp. 632, 668.

12. *Congressional Record,* 46th Congress, 2d Session, pp. 45, 273, 538.

13. *Ibid.,* pp. 1619, 1953, 2053, 2384, 4563.

5. Cassisus Marcellus Clay

1. H. Edward Richardson, *Cassius Marcellus Clay,* pp. 12–13.

2. *Ibid.,* p. 24.

3. W. H. Townsend, *Lincoln and His Wife's Home Town,* pp. 129–135.

4. Richardson, p. 34.

5. *Ibid.,* p. 36.

6. Albert A. Woldman, *Lincoln and the Russians,* p. 105.

6. Robert Brown Elliott

1. Maurine Christopher, *Black Americans in Congress,* p. 73.

2. Lerone Bennett, Jr., *Before the Mayflower,* p. 244.

3. *Congressional Record,* 43rd Congress, 1st Session, January 1874.

4. Christopher, p. 74.

5. *Ibid.,* p. 69.

6. Leon Litwack and August Meier, eds., *Black Leaders of the Nineteenth Century,* p. 203

7. Bruce A. Ragsdale and John D. Treese, *Black Americans in Congress,* p. 46.

8. Christopher, p. 76.

9. Ragsdale and Treese, p. 46.

10. Litwack, p. 204.

11. *Ibid.,* p. 206.

12. Simmons, *Men of Mark,* p. 314.

7. Charlotte Forten Grimké

1. Lydia Maria Child, *The Freedmen's Book,* pp. 100–101.

2. Ray Allen Billington, ed., *The Journal of Charlotte L. Forten,* pp. 13–20.

3. James Forten, *Letters from a Man of Colour, On a Late Bill before the Senate of Pennsylvania* (Philadelphia, 1813), pp. 3–4, 7. This letter is reprinted in Carter G. Woodson, *Negro Orators and their Orations,* pp. 42–51.

4. Billington, p. 14.

5. Child, p. 103.

6. *The Liberator,* March 21, 1835.

7. John Greenleaf Whittier, "The Anti-Slavery Convention of 1833," p. 169.

8. William Still, *The Underground Railroad,* p. 612.

9. Richard L. Green, ed., *A Salute to Historic Black Abolitionists.*

10. Willie Lee Rose, *Rehearsal for Reconstruction.*

11. Tonya Bolden, *And Not Afraid to Dare,* p. 39.

12. Lerone Bennett, Jr., *Before the Mayflower,* p. 212.

13. *Ibid.,* p. 42.

14. One of the black uncommissioned officers of the First South Carolina Volunteers, Rivers was an intelligent young man who had spent much time in the North. Col. Higginson described Sutton as "the Wisest man in the ranks." Thomas Wentworth Higginson, *Army Life in a Black Regiment,* p. 62.

Two other descriptions of the New Year's Day celebration agree with Charlotte Forten's account: Harriett Ware in Elizabeth Pearson, *Letters from Port Royal,* pp. 128–134 and in Higginson, *Army Life in a Black Regiment,* p. 55–56.

15. New England Freedmen's Aid Society, Annual Report (Boston 1864).

16. Bolden, p. 44–45.

17. *Ibid.,* p. 46.

18. Billington, p. 39.

8. Thomas Wentworth Higginson

1. Higginson, *Army Life in a Black Regiment,* p. 23.

2. Mary Thatcher Higginson, *Thomas Wentworth Higginson,* p. 15.

3. Higginson, p. 12.

4. James W. Tuttleton, *Thomas Wentworth Higginson*, p. 33.

5. Anna Mary Wells, *Dear Preceptor*, pp. 83–84.

6. Tilden G. Edelstein, *Strange Enthusiasm*, p. 54.

7. Mary T. Higginson, p. 144.

8. Edelstein, p. 159.

9. Tuttleton, p. 36.

10. *Ibid.*, p. 37.

11. *Ibid.*, p. 190.

12. *Ibid.*

13. J. C. Furnas, *The Road to Harpers Ferry*, p. 6.

14. Edelstein, p. 233.

15. Higginson, *Army Life in a Black Regiment*, p. 16.

16. *Ibid.*, p. 28.

17. Rose, *Rehearsal for Reconstruction*, p. xv.

19. Higginson, *Army Life in a Black Regiment*, p. 17.

20. Rose, p. 193.

21. Higginson, *Army Life in a Black Regiment*, pp. 18–19.

22. Saxton to Stanton, November 12, 1862, Official Records, I, XIV pp. 189–191.

23. Rose, p. 195.

24. Descriptions of the Emancipation Day ceremonies are reported in Higginson, *Army Life in a Black Regiment*, pp. 51–57.

25. Tuttleton, p. 39; Howard N. Meyer, *Colonel of the Black Regiment*, p. 244.

26. Higginson, *Army Life in a Black Regiment*, pp. xvi–xvii.

27. Meyer, pp. 244–245.

28. Higginson, *Army Life in a Black Regiment*, p. 22.

29. T. W. Higginson, *Cheerful Yesterdays*, pp. 363–364.

9. John Mercer Langston

1. Simmons, *Men of Mark*, p. 352.

2. *Ibid.*, p. 346.

3. Langston, pp. 138–139.

4. William Cheek and Aimee Lee Cheek, *John Mercer Langston*, preface, p. 2.

5. Frederick Douglass's paper, April 20, 1855.

6. Caroline M. Wall, alumni records, Oberlin College Archives, *Oberlin Alumni Magazine* 11 (May 1915).

7. Langston, pp. 141–142.

8. John W. Cromwell, *The Negro in American History*, p. 159.

9. *National Anti-Slavery Standard,* April 28, 1855; *National Era*, May 3, 1855.

10. *New York Times*, May 10, 1855; *New York Tribune*, May 10, 1855; *National Anti-Slavery Standard*, May 12 and 19, 1855.

11. Simmons, pp. 347–352.

12. Langston, p. 147.

13. Named for General Oliver Otis Howard.

14. The first Negro to be so designated was John A. Rock of Massachusetts.

15. Cromwell, pp. 160–161.

16. William F. Cheek, "A Negro Runs for Congress."

17. *New York Freeman*, September 26, 1885; *Cleveland Gazette*, July 3, 1886; *Anti-Slavery Bugle*, April 28, 1855.

18. *The City of Petersburg, Virginia—The Book of its Chamber of Commerce* (Petersburg, 1894) pp. 16–17.

19. Luther P. Jackson, "Free Negroes of Petersburg, Virginia," pp. 366 and 388.

20. *Virginia Lancet*, October 20, 1883.

21. John Sherman to William Mahone, January 10 and January 16, 1888, in Mahone papers.

22. Langston, p. 473.

23. "Douglass to City of Petersburg, Virginia, and Voters of the Fourth Congressional District," August 15, 1888, in Frederick Douglass papers (Frederick Douglass Home, Anacostia).

24. *Washington Bee*, August 25, 1888; *People's Advocate*, September 1, 1888; *Star of Zion*, September 1, 1888, in Langston Scrapbooks.

25. *Richmond Whig*, September 20, 1888.

26. "Confidential Printed Letter from Langston," October 10, 1888, in Mahone Scrapbook 37.

27. *Richmond State*, November 1, 1888.

28. Jackson, "Negro Office-Holders," Contested Election Case pp. 154–155; *Washington Bee*, May 26, 1888.

29. Petersburg *Index Appeal*, October 5, 1888.

30. *New York Times*, November 4, 1888.

31. William F. Cheek, "A Negro Runs for

Congress," *Journal of Negro History*, Volume 52, January 1967.

32. House Miscellaneous Documents, 2nd Session, 51st Congress, 1890–91, Vol. 16, Digest of Contested Election Cases, 440–444, 464–465.

33. Stanley P. Hirschson, *Farewell to the Bloody Shirt*, pp. 187–188; Petersburg *Index Appeal*.

34. Cheek, "A Negro Runs for Congress," p. 14.

10. James Longstreet

1. William Miller Owen, *In Camp and Battle with the Washington Artillery of New Orleans*, p. 157.

2. Gilbert Moxley Sorrel, *Recollections of a Confederate Staff Officer*, p. 26.

3. Edward Porter Alexander, *Military Memoirs of a Confederate*, p. 609.

4. James Longstreet, *From Manassas to Appomattox*, p. 17.

5. This section and the following narratives are taken from Brian Hampton's monologue, "James Longstreet, A North Georgia Notable."

6. Longstreet, *From Manassas*, p. 634.

7. R. L. DiNardo and Albert Nofi, eds., *James Longstreet: The Man, the Soldier, the Controversy*, p. 197.

8. Longstreet, *From Manassas*, p. 637.

9. Morton Keller, *Affairs of State: Public Life in Late Nineteenth Century*, p. 209.

10. Donald B. Sanger and Thomas R. Hay, *James Longstreet: The Soldier, the Politician, Officeholder and Writer*, p. 8.

11. Joseph G. Dawson III, *Army Generals and Reconstruction Louisiana, 1862–1877*, p. 172.

12. *Ibid.*, p. 238.

13. DiNardo and Nofi, p. 205.

11. John Roy Lynch

1. *Chicago Defender*, November 11, 1939.

2. Adelbert Ames, a graduate of the U.S. Military Academy and a Civil War hero (winner of the Congressional Medal of Honor), was selected by President Grant in 1869 to command the Mississippi military district. Ames was elected governor of Mississippi in 1873. Ames, *Adelbert Ames*.

3. Lynch, *The Facts of Reconstruction*, p. 29.

4. *Journal of the House of Representatives of the State of Mississippi*, Regular session, Jackson, Mississippi, 1873, p. 2055.

5. John Hope Franklin, ed., *The Autobiography of John R. Lynch*, p. xvi.

6. *Congressional Record*, 43rd Congress 2nd Session 1875, p. 4783.

7. *Congressional Record*, 43rd Congress 1st Session 1875, pt. 2: 947.

8. Lynch served in the 43rd, 44th and 47th Congresses.

9. Woodson, *Negro Orators and Their Orations*, p. 282.

10. George A. Sewell and Margaret L. Dwight, *Mississippi Black History Makers*.

11. Harris quotes John W. Burgess, *Reconstruction and the Constitution: 1866–1876*, p. 263.

12. James W. Garner, author of *Reconstruction in Mississippi*, probably the best of the Dunning-school studies of the period, reviewed Lynch's book for the *Mississippi Valley Historical Review*, III (June 1916) 112–113, but he refrained from passing judgment on it, except to comment: "On the whole, the book is a fair and temperate presentation of the case of the reconstructionists."

13. Details of his death and burial are found in the *Chicago Defender*, November 11, 1939.

12. Albert Talmon Morgan

1. T. J. Stiles, *Robber Barons and Radicals: Reconstruction and the Origins of Civil Rights*, p. 13.

2. My major source for the information in this chapter is the personal narrative written by Albert T. Morgan, *Yazoo; Or, On the Picket Line of Freedom in the South*, which he published in 1884.

3. Morgan, pp. 17–19, 25–27, 29–33, 38–39, 47–48, 82–84.

4. *Ibid.*, Introduction.

5. Stiles, Preface, p. xiv.

6. Morgan, p. 448.

7. *Ibid.*, pp. 103, 112–113.

8. Lerone Bennett, Jr., *Black Power U.S.A.: The Human Side of Reconstruction, 1867–1877*, p. 257.

9. Morgan, p. 366.

10. Stiles, Preface, p. xxi.

11. *Ibid.*, p. 80.

12. Morgan, Joseph Logsdon's Introduction.

13. Morgan, pp. 401–414.

14. *Ibid.*, declaration for an invalid pension, Jan. 23, 1879, and affidavit, April 11, 1879, Pension Record.

15. Carolyn V. Shannon, affidavit, October 20, 1923, Pension Records.

16. Stiles, pp. 288–289.

17. http://www.lucyparsons.org

18. Morgan, p. 202.

13. Albert R. Parsons

1. Philip S. Foner, ed., *The Autobiographies of the Haymarket Martyrs*, p. 28.

2. *Appleton's Encyclopedia of American Biography* (New York, 1888–1899), IV, p. 663.

3. William H. Parsons, "Albert R. Parson's Ancestors."

4. Alan Calmer, *Labor Agitator: The Story of Albert R. Parsons.* The bulk of the labor history recounted in this chapter is taken from this remarkable book.

5. Foner, *Autobiographies*, p. 27.

6. Lucy E. Parsons, ed. *Life of Albert R. Parsons*, p. 1.

7. Foner, *Autobiographies*, p. 28.

8. *Ibid.*

9. *Ibid.*

10. *Ibid.*, p. 29.

11. *Ibid.*

12. The Ku Klux Klan aimed, through terror and violence to re-subjugate Negroes and to prevent the development of a democratic South. It was responsible for the murders of thousands of black and white people.

13. The great Chicago fire started on October 8, 1871, in the barn of Catherine O'Leary and before the flames subsided, nearly 100,000 were made homeless and 73 miles of street and 17,500 buildings destroyed. Relief societies were immediately established in Chicago.

14. "Forty Acres and a Mule" was the slogan popularized among the freedmen during and after the Civil War. It aroused their hope that they would obtain land and a mule from the federal government so as not to be at the mercy of the white planters.

15. Foner, *Autobiographies*, p. 51.

16. Waldo R. Browne, *Altgeld of Illinois*, pp. 94–105.

17. Unidentified clipping, Parsons papers.

14. Pinckney Benton Stewart Pinchback

1. Elsie M. Lewis, "The Political Mind of the Negro, 1865–1900," p. 197.

2. George H. Devol, *Forty Years a Gambler on the Mississippi*, pp. 216–217.

3. Simmons, pp. 759–763.

4. Draft of speech to Republican State Convention, June 19, 1867. P. B. S. Pinchback Papers, Moorland-Spingarn Collection, Howard University Library, Washington, D.C.

5. Simmons, p. 321.

6. *New Orleans Republican*, October 10 — November 5, 1869.

7. *Ibid.*, November 22, 1871.

8. Simmons, pp. 539–540.

9. *Ibid.*, p. 541.

10. *New Orleans Times-Democrat*, April 26, 1890.

11. *New Orleans Times*, March 11, 1872.

12. James Haskins, *Pinckney Benton Stewart Pinchback*, p. 258, note 28.

13. *Carpet-Bag Misrule in Louisiana: The Tragedy of the Reconstruction Era*, p. 49.

14. Dawson, pp. 173–180.

15. James W. Loewen, *Lies Across America*, p. 219.

16. *Congressional Record*, 43rd Congress, 1st Session, p. 898.

17. *Congressional Record*, 51st Congress, 2nd Session, p. 78.

18. Samuel Denny Smith, *The Negro in Congress, 1870–1901*, pp.143–144.

15. Robert Smalls

1. *Official Records of the Union and Confederate Navies in the War of the Rebellion*, vol. XII, pp. 821–825.

2. "The Steamer Planter and Her Captain," *Harper's Weekly*, vol. 6 (June 14, 1862) pp. 372–373.

3. *New York Commercial Advertiser*, May 1, 1862.

4. Report, Du Pont to Welles, May 14, 1862, ORN Series 1, 12, 821.

5. *Congressional Globe*, 37th Congress, 2nd session, 1862, 286–287, 2364–2440.

6. Charles Cowley, *The Romance of History in the Black County and the Romance of War in the Career of General Robert Smalls*, pp. 9–10.

7. *Charleston Courier*, September 21, 1866.

8. Maurine Christopher, *America's Black Congressmen*, p. 42.

9. Ragsdale and Treese.

10. *Ibid.*

11. Christopher, p. 53.

12. Rose, p. 403.

13. Edward A. Miller, Jr., *Gullah Statesman: Robert Smalls from Slavery to Congress, 1839–1915*, p. 250.

14. William H. Shirley, Jr., "A Black Republican Congressman during the Democratic Resurgence in South Carolina: Robert Smalls, 1876–1882," p. 54.

16. Albion Winegar Tourgee

1. Otto H. Olsen, *Carpetbagger's Crusade: The Life of Albion Winegar Tourgee*, p. 13.

2. *Ibid.*, p. 21–31.

3. Otto H. Olsen, "Albion W. Tourgee: Carpetbagger," pp. 436–437.

4. *Ibid.*, pp. 437–440.

5. *Ibid.*, pp. 442–443.

6. Otto H. Olsen, "The Ku Klux Klan: A Study in Reconstruction Politics and Propaganda," pp. 348–349.

7. *National Anti-Slavery Standard*, October 19, 1867 (letter signed "Wenckar").

8. Albion W. Tourgee, *A Fool's Errand*, Introduction by George M. Frederickson.

17. George Henry White

1. Christopher, *Black Americans in Congress*, p. 161.

2. *Ibid.*

3. *Congressional Record*, 56th Congress, 2d Session, pp. 1636–1638.

4. Rayford W. Logan writes, "During White's two terms, Negroes were subjected to vilification in Congress the like of which has rarely been equaled except in the early days of Nazi struggle for power in Germany and some recent attacks upon eminent Americans by an irresponsible Senator" (*The Negro in American Life and Thought: The Nadir, 1877–1901*, p. 90). The senator referred to was Senator Joseph R. McCarthy.

5. The reference is to the debates on the reapportionment of the House of Representatives after the census of 1900. Bills were introduced dealing only with the size of the House, but Republican representatives Marlin E. Olmsted of Pennsylvania and Edgar D. Crumpacker of Indiana sought to direct attention to the second section of the Fourteenth Amendment, because of the disenfranchisement of Negroes in Southern states.

6. Christopher, p. 166.

7. Charles F. White, *Who's Who in Colored Philadelphia*, p. 89.

8. Richard R. Wright, Jr., "The Economic Condition of Negroes in the North: Negro Communities in New Jersey," pp. 385–393.

9. *History of Whitesboro*, Cape May County Planning Board, 1973.

10. The Berean School grew out of the Berean Presbyterian Church of Philadelphia. The School was one of several institutions: The Berean Building and Loan, the Seaside Home, the Bureau of Mutual Help, and the Manual Training and Industrial School.

11. John A. Saunders, *100 Years After Emancipation: History of the Philadelphia Negro, 1787–1963*, pp. 141–142.

12. Ragsdale and Treese.

18. The End of Reconstruction

1. Du Bois, *Black Reconstruction in America*.

2. Du Bois, "*Reconstruction and its Benefits.*"

3. Carl Schurz, Report to the President, 1865, p. 40.

4. *Ibid.*, p. 44.

5. *Occasional Papers of the American Negro Academy*, no. 6, p. 10.

6. Don C. Seitz, *The Dreadful Decade.*

7. Bowers.

8. Paul H. Buck, *The Road to Reunion, 1865–1900*, p. 295.

9. Leon F. Litwack, *Trouble in Mind: Black Southerners in the Age of Jim Crow*, Preface p. xiii.

Bibliography

Alexander, Edward Porter. *Memoirs of a Confederate Staff Officer.* Jackson, Tenn., 1958. Originally published in 1907.

Allen, James, Hilton Als, John Lewis, and Leon F. Litwack. *Without Sanctuary: Lynching Photography in America.* Santa Fe, N.M.: Twin Palms, 2000.

Allen, James S. *Reconstruction: A Study in Democracy.* New York: International Publishers, 1937.

Alvord, John W. *"Reports on Schools and Finances of Freedmen."* Washington, D.C.: Bureau of Refugees, Freedmen and Abandoned Lands, 7th Semi-Annual Report, 1868.

Ames, Blanche A. *Adelbert Ames: Broken Oaths and Reconstruction in Mississippi, 1835–1933.* New York: Argosy Antiquarian, 1964.

Aptheker, Herbert. *The Negro in the Civil War.* New York: International Publishers, 1938.

Avary, Myrta L. *Dixie After the War.* New York: Doubleday, Page, 1906.

Ball, Edward. *The Sweet Hell Inside.* New York: William Morrow, 2001.

Ball, W. W. *A Boy's Recollections of the Red Shirt Campaign of 1876 in South Carolina.* Columbia, S.C., 1911.

Barnard, Harry. *Rutherford B. Hayes and His America.* Indianapolis: Bobbs-Merrill, 1954.

Belz, Herman. *Emancipation and Equal Rights.* New York: Norton, 1978.

Bennett, Jr., Lerone. *Before the Mayflower.* Chicago: Johnson Publishing Co., 1982.

_____. *Black Power U.S.A.: The Human Side of Reconstruction, 1867–1877.* Maryland: Penguin Books, 1969.

Bentley, George R. *A History of the Freedmen's Bureau.* Philadelphia: University of Pennsylvania, 1955.

Bergman, Peter M. *The Chronological History of the Negro in America.* New York: Harper & Row, 1969.

Billington, Ray Allen. *The Journal of Charlotte L. Forten.* New York: Dryden Press, 1953.

Blaine, James G. *Twenty Years in Congress.* Norwich, Conn.: Henry Bill Publishing Co., 1884.

Blight, David W. *Race and Reunion: The Civil War in American Memory.* Cambridge, Mass.: Harvard University Press, 2001.

Bolden, Tonya. *And Not Afraid to Dare.* New York: Scholastic Press, 1998.

Bond, Horace Mann. "Social and Economic Forces in Alabama Reconstruction." *Journal of Negro History* 23 (July 1938): 290–348.

Bowers, Claude G. *The Tragic Era.* New York: Blue Ribbon Books, 1929.

Brodie, Fawn, N. *Thaddeus Stevens: Scourge to the South.* New York: Norton, 1959.

Browne, Waldo R. *Altgeld of Illinois.* New York: B. W. Huebsch, 1924.

Brownlow, W. G. *Sketches of the Rise, Progress and Decline of Secession.* Philadelphia: G.W. Childs, 1862.

Bruce, Dickson D., Jr., *Archibald Grimké: Portrait of a Black Independent.* Baton Rouge: Louisiana State University Press, 1993.

Bruce, Robert V. *1877, Year of Violence.* Indianapolis: Bobbs-Merrill, 1959.

Buck, Paul H. *The Road to Reunion, 1865–1900.* New York: Vintage Books, 1937.

Buckmaster, Henrietta. *Freedom Bound.* New York: Macmillan, 1965.

Burgess, John W. *Reconstruction and the Constitution: 1866–1876.* New York: Charles Scribner's Sons, 1909.

Button, John. *The Radicalism Handbook*, Santa Barbara, Calif.: ABC-Clio, 1995.

Calmer, Alan. *Labor Agitator: The Story of Albert R. Parsons.* New York: International Publishers, 1937.

Carpet-Bag Misrule in Louisiana: The Tragedy of the Reconstruction Era. New Orleans: Louisiana State Museum, 1938.

Carter, Hodding. *The Angry Scar.* New York: Doubleday, 1959.

Cate, Wirt A. *Q. C. Lamar, Statesman of Secession and Reunion.* Chapel Hill: University of North Carolina Press, 1935.

Cell, John W. *The Highest Stage of White Supremacy: The Origins of Segregation in South Africa and the American South.* New York: Cambridge University Press, 1982.

Chalmers, David M. *Hooded Americanism.* New York: Doubleday, 1965.

Cheek, William, and Aimee Lee Cheek. *John Mercer Langston and the Fight for Black Freedom, 1829–65.* Urbana: University of Illinois Press, 1989.

Cheek, William F. "A Negro Runs for Congress." *Journal of Negro History* 52, January, 1967.

Child, Lydia Maria. *The Freedmen's Book.* Boston: Ticknor and Fields, 1865.

Christopher, Maurine. *America's Black Congressmen.* New York: Thomas Y. Crowell, 1971.

_____. *Black Americans In Congress.* New York: Thomas Y. Crowell, 1976.

Clay, William L. *Just Permanent Interests.* New York: Amistad Press, 1992.

Coben, Stanley. "Northeastern Business and Radical Reconstruction: A Reexamination." *Mississippi Valley Historical Review* 44 (June 1959): 68.

Coulter, E. Merton. *William G. Brownlow, Fighting Parson of the Southern Highlands.* Chapel Hill: University of North Carolina Press, 1937.

Cowley, Charles. *The Romance of History in the Black County and the Romance of War in the Career of General Robert Smalls.* Lowell, Mass., 1882.

Cromwell, John W. *The Negro in American History.* Washington, D.C.: American Negro Academy, 1914.

Cruden, Robert. *The Negro in Reconstruction.* Englewood Cliffs, N.J.: Prentice-Hall, 1969.

Cullen, Jim. *The Civil War in Popular Culture.* Washington, D.C.: Smithsonian Institution Press, 1995.

Current, Richard N. *Those Terrible Carpetbaggers.* New York: Oxford University Press, 1988.

Daniels, Josephus. *Tar Heel Editor.* Chapel Hill: University of North Carolina Press, 1939.

Dawson, Joseph G., III, *Army Generals and Reconstruction, Louisiana, 1862–1877.* Baton Rouge: Louisiana State University Press, 1982.

De Forrest, John W. *A Union Officer in Reconstruction.* New Haven, Conn.: Yale University Press, 1948.

Devol, George H. *Forty Years a Gambler on the Mississippi.* Austin, TX: Steck-Vaughn, 1967. Originally published in 1887.

DiNardo, R. L., and Albert Nofi, eds. *James Longstreet: The Man, the Soldier, the Controversy.* Conshohocken, Pa.: Combined Publishing, 1998.

Donald, David. *Charles Sumner and the Rights of Man.* New York: Knopf, 1970.

_____. *The Politics of Reconstruction, 1863–1867.* Baton Rouge: Louisiana State University Press, 1965.

Donald, Henderson H. *The Negro Freedmen*. New York: Henry Schuman, 1952.

D'orso, Michael. *Like Judgment Day*. New York: G.P. Putnam's Sons, 1996.

Douglass, Frederick. *Life and Times of Frederick Douglass*. Hartford, 1882. Reprint, New York: Crowell-Collier, 1962.

Dray, Philip. *At the Hands of Persons Unknown: The Lynching of Black America*. New York: Random House, 2002.

Du Bois, W. E. B. *Black Reconstruction in America*. Philadelphia: Albert Saifer Publisher, 1935.

_____. "Reconstruction and Its Benefits," *American Historical Review*, July 1910.

Edelstein, Tilden G. *Strange Enthusiasm*. New Haven, Conn.: Yale University Press, 1968.

Elam, W. C. "A Scalawag." *Southern Magazine* 8, April 1871.

Engs, Robert Francis. *Freedom's First Generation: Black Hampton, Virginia, 1861–1890*. Philadelphia: University of Pennsylvania Press, 1979.

Fischer, Roger A. *The Segregation Struggle in Louisiana 1862–77*. Champaign: University of Illinois Press, 1974.

Flynn, James J. *Negroes of Achievement in Modern America*. New York: Dodd, Mead, 1970.

Foner, Eric. *Freedom's Lawmakers*. New York: Oxford University Press, 1993.

_____. *Reconstruction: America's Unfinished Revolution*. New York: Harper and Row, 1988.

_____. *The Story of American Freedom*. New York: Norton, 1998.

Foner, Philip S., ed. *The Autobiographies of the Haymarket Martyrs*. New York: Humanities Press, 1969.

_____. *The Life and Writings of Frederick Douglass*. 4 vols. New York: International Publishers, 1950–1955.

_____. *Nothing but Freedom, Emancipation and Its Legacy*. Baton Rouge: University of Louisiana Press, 1983.

Foner, Philip S., and George E. Walker, eds. *Proceedings of the Black National and State Conventions, 1865–1900*. Philadelphia: Temple University Press, 1986.

Foner Philip S., and Robert J. Branham, eds. *Lift Every Voice: African American Oratory, 1787–1900*. Tuscaloosa: University of Alabama Press, 1998.

Franklin, John Hope. *The Autobiography of John R. Lynch*. Chicago: University of Chicago Press, 1970.

_____. *Reconstruction after the Civil War*. Chicago: University of Chicago Press, 1961.

Furnas, J. C. *The Road to Harpers Ferry*. New York: William Sloane Associates, 1959.

Garner, James W. *Reconstruction in Mississippi*. New York: Macmillan, 1901.

Genovese, Eugene D. *Roll, Jordon, Roll: The World the Slaves Made*. New York: Random House, 1972.

Gibson, Albert M. *A Political Crime: The History of the Great Fraud*. New York: W.S. Gottsberger, 1885.

Gillette, William. *Retreat from Reconstruction, 1869–1879*. Baton Rouge: Louisiana State University Press, 1979.

Granada, Ray. *Violence: "An Instrument of Policy in Reconstruction Alabama." Alabama Historical Quarterly* 30 (Fall-Winter 1968).

Green, Richard L., ed. *A Salute to Black Abolitionists*. Chicago: Empak Enterprises, 1988.

Green, Shirley. "History of Whitesboro." Whitesboro Historian Foundation, 1998.

Grimké, Archibald H. *Charles Sumner: The Scholar in Politics*. New York: Funk & Wagnalls, 1892.

The Hampton Album. New York: Museum of Modern Art, 1966.

Harris, William C. *The Day of the Carpetbagger: Republican Reconstruction in Mississippi*. Baton Rouge: Louisiana State University Press, 1979.

Harrison, Paul Carter. *Black Light: The African American Hero*. New York: Thunder's Mouth Press, 1993.

Haskins, James. *Pinckney Benton Stewart Pinchback*. New York: Macmillan, 1973.

Haworth, P. L. *The Hayes-Tilden Disputed Election of 1876*. Cleveland: Burroughs, 1906.

Hennessey, Melinda M. "Political Terrorism in the Black Belt: The Eutaw Riot." *Alabama Review* 33 (January 1980): 112–125.

Henry, Robert S. *The Story of Reconstruction*. New York: Konecky & Konecky, 1937.

Hermann, Janet Sharp. *The Pursuit of a Dream*. New York: Oxford University Press, 1981.

Higginson, Mary Thatcher. *Thomas Wentworth Higginson: The Story of His Life*. Boston: Houghton Mifflin, 1914.

Higginson, Thomas Wentworth. *Army Life in a Black Regiment*. Boston: Fields, Osgood, 1870.

_____. *Black Rebellion*. New York: Arno Press, 1969.

Hirschson, Stanley P. *Farewell to the Bloody Shirt*. Bloomington: Indiana University Press, 1962.

Holland, Frederick May. *Frederick Douglass: The Colored Orator*. New York: Funk & Wagnalls, 1891.

Hoover, Dwight W. *Understanding Negro History*. Chicago: Quadrangle Books, 1968.

Hopkins, Pauline E. *Contending Forces*. Carbondale: Southern Illinois University Press, 1978.

Jackson, Luther P. "Free Negroes of Petersburg, Virginia." *Journal of Negro History* 12, July 1927.

Jones, Jacqueline. *Soldiers of Light and Love: Northern Teachers and Georgia Blacks, 1865–1873*. Chapel Hill: University of North Carolina Press, 1980.

Jones, Wilmer L. *After the Thunder*. Dallas: Taylor, 2000.

Justesen, Benjamin R. *George Henry White: An Even Chance in the Race of Life*. Baton Rouge: Louisiana State University Press, 2001.

Keller, Morton. *Affairs of State: Public Life in the Nineteenth Century*. Cambridge, Mass.: Harvard University Press.

Kendrick, Benjamin B. *The Journal of the Joint Committee of Fifteen on Reconstruction*. New York, 1914.

Kennedy, John F. *Profiles in Courage*. New York: Harper & Brothers, 1956.

Kennedy, Stetson. *After Appomattox*. Gainesville: University Press of Florida, 1995.

_____. *Palmetto Country*. New York: Duell, Sloan and Pearce, 1946. Reprint, Tallahassee: Florida A & M University Press, 1989.

Klingman, Peter D. *Josiah Walls*. Gainesville: University of Florida Press, 1976.

Langston, John M. *From the Virginia Plantation to the National Capitol*. Hartford, Conn.: American Pub. Co., 1894.

Lebsock, Suzanne. "Radical Reconstruction and the Property Rights of Southern Women." *Journal of Southern History* 43 (May 1977): 195–216.

Lee, George L. *Interesting People: Black American History Makers*. Jefferson, N.C.: McFarland, 1989.

Lerner, Gerda. *The Grimké Sisters from South Carolina: Rebels Against Slavery*. Boston: Houghton Mifflin, 1967.

Lester, C. Edwards. *Life and Public Services of Charles Sumner*. New York: United States Pub. Co., 1874.

Lewis, Elsie M. "The Political Mind of the Negro, 1865–1900." *Journal of Southern History* XXI, May 1955.

Lincove, David A., ed. *Reconstruction in the United States*. Westport, Conn.: Greenwood Press, 2000.

Lindsey, Howard O. *A History of Black America*. Conn.: Chartwell Books, 1994.

Lingley, Charles Ramsdell. *Since the Civil War*. New York: Century, 1921.

Litwack, Leon F. *Been in the Storm So Long*. New York: Random House, 1979.

_____. *Trouble in Mind: Black Southerners in the Age of Jim Crow*. New York: Alfred A. Knopf, 1998.

_____, and August Meier, eds. *Black Leaders of the Nineteenth Century*, Urbana: University of Illinois Press, 1988.

Lockwood, Lewis, ed. *Two Black Teachers During the Civil War.* New York: Arno Press, 1969.

Loewen, James W. *Lies My Teacher Told Me.* New York: New Press, 1995.

_____. *Lies across America.* New York: New Press, 1999.

Logan, Rayford W. *The Negro in American Life and Thought: The Nadir, 1877–1901.* New York: Dial Press, 1954.

Longstreet, James. *From Manassas to Appomattox: Memoirs of the Civil War in America.*

Longsworth, Polly. *I, Charlotte Forten, Black and Free.* New York: Thomas Y. Crowell, 1970.

Lonn, Ella. *Reconstruction in Louisiana after 1868.* New York: Russell & Russell, 1918.

Lynch, John R. *The Facts of Reconstruction.* New York: Neale Pub. Co., 1913.

_____. "More About the Historical Errors of James Ford Rhodes." *Journal of Negro History* 3, April 1918.

_____. "Some Historical Errors of James Ford Rhodes." *Journal of Negro History* 2, October 1917.

_____. "The Tragic Era." *Journal of Negro History,* 16 January 1931.

Magdol, Edward. *A Right to the Land: Essays on the Freedmen's Community.* Westport, Conn.: Greenwood, 1977.

Malcolmson, Scott L. *One Drop of Blood: The American Misadventure of Race.* New York: Farrar Straus Giroux, 2000.

Mantell, Martin E. *Johnson, Grant, and the Politics of Reconstruction.* New York: Columbia University Press, 1973.

McKitrick, Eric L. *Andrew Johnson and Reconstruction.* Chicago: University of Chicago Press, 1960.

Merriam, George S. *The Negro and the Nation: A History of Slavery and Enfranchisement.* New York: Henry Holt, 1906.

Meyer, Howard N. *Colonel of the Black Regiment.* New York: Norton, 1967.

Miller, Edward A., Jr. *Gullah Statesman: Robert Smalls from Slavery to Congress, 1839–1915.* Columbia: University of South Carolina Press, 1995.

Moore, John Hammond, ed. *The Juhl Letters to the Charleston Courier.* Athens: University of Georgia Press, 1974.

Morgan, Albert I. *Yazoo; or, On the Picket Line of Freedom in the South.* (1884.) Reprint with introduction by Joseph Lodgson, Columbia: University of South Carolina Press, 2000.

Nathans, Elizabeth S. *Losing the Peace: Georgia Republicans and Reconstruction, 1865–1871.* Baton Rouge: Louisiana State University Press, 1968.

Newby, I. A., ed. *The Civil War and Reconstruction, 1850–1877.* New York: Appleton-Century-Crofts, 1971.

Nicolay, John G., and John Hay, eds. *The Complete Works of Abraham Lincoln.* New York: F.D. Tandy, 1894.

Nowlin, William F. *The Negro in American National Politics.* New York: Russell & Russell, 1970.

Nugent, Walter T. K. *Money and American Society, 1865–1880.* New York: Free Press, 1968.

Occasional Papers of the American Negro Academy, No. 6, *Chicago Weekly Inter Ocean.*

Olsen, Otto H. "Albion W. Tourgee: Carpetbagger." *North Carolina Historical Review,* Autumn 1963.

_____. *Carpetbagger's Crusade: The Life of Albion Winegar Tourgee.* Baltimore: Johns Hopkins Press, 1965.

_____. "The Ku Klux Klan: A Study in Reconstruction Politics and Propaganda," *North Carolina Historical Review,* Summer 1962.

_____. "Reconsidering the Scalawags." *Civil War History* 12, December 1966.

Oubre, Claude F. *Forty Acres and a Mule: The Freedmen's Bureau and Black Ownership.* Baton Rouge: Louisiana State University Press, 1978.

Owen, William Miller. *In Camp and Battle with the Washington Artillery of New Orleans.* Gaithersburg, Md., 1982. Originally published in 1885.

Packard, Jerold M. *American Nightmare: The History of Jim Crow.* New York: St. Martin's Press, 2002.

Parsons, Lucy, ed. *Life of Albert R. Parsons: With Brief History of the Labor Movement in America*. Chicago: L.E. Parsons, 1903. Originally published in 1889.

Peabody, Francis G. *Education for Life*. New York: Doubleday, 1918.

Pearson, Elizabeth Ware, ed. *Letters from Port Royal, 1862–1868*. Boston: W. B. Clarke, 1906.

Peek, Ralph L. "Lawlessness in Florida, 1868–1871." *Florida Historical Quarterly* 40, October 1961.

Phillips, Ulrich Bonnell. *The Slave Economy of the Old South*. Baton Rouge: Louisiana State University Press, 1968.

Pierce, E. L. *Memoirs and Letters of Charles Sumner*. Boston: Roberts, 1893.

Pike, James S. *The Prostrate South*. New York: Loring & Mussey, 1935.

Potter, Joan, and Constance Claytor. *African American Firsts*. Elizabethtown, N.Y.: Pinto Press, 1994.

Pullen, John J. *The Twentieth Maine: A Volunteer Regiment in the Civil War*. Philadelphia: Lippincott, 1957.

Rabinowitz, Howard N., ed. *Southern Black Leaders of the Reconstruction Era*. Urbana: University of Illinois Press, 1982.

Rable, George C. *But There Was No Peace: The Role of Violence in the Politics of Reconstruction*. Athens: University of Georgia Press, 1984.

Rachleff, Peter J. *Black Labor in the South: Richmond, Virginia, 1865–1900*. Philadelphia: Temple University Press, 1984.

Ragsdale, Bruce A., and John D. Treese. *Black Americans in Congress, 1870–1989*. Washington, D.C.: U.S. Government Printing Office, 1990.

Reid, George W. "The Post-Congressional Career of George H. White, 1901–1918." *The Journal of Negro History* 61, October 1976.

Reid, Whitelaw. *After the War: A Southern Tour*. Cincinnati, 1866.

Richardson, H. Edward. *Cassius Marcellus Clay*. Lexington: University Press of Kentucky, 1976.

Richardson, Joe M. *The Negro in the Reconstruction of Florida, 1865–1877*. Tallahassee: Florida A & M University Press, 1965.

Rose, Willie Lee. *Rehearsal for Reconstruction: The Port Royal Experiment*. Indianapolis: Bobbs-Merrill, 1964.

Rousseve, Charles B. *The Negro in Louisiana*. New Orleans: Xavier University Press, 1968.

Russell, Dick. *Black Genius and the American Experience*. New York: Carroll & Graf, 1998.

Salley, Columbus. *The Black 100*. New York: Carol Publishing Group, 1993.

Sanger, Donald B., and Thomas R. Hay. *James Longstreet: The Soldier, the Politician, Officeholder and Writer*. Baton Rouge: Louisiana State University Press, 1952.

Saunders, John A. *100 Years After Emancipation: History of the Philadelphia Negro, 1787–1963*. Philadelphia: Tribune Press, 1968.

Schurz, Carl. *Reminiscences*. New York: McClure, 1907.

Scroggs, Jack B. "Southern Reconstruction. A Radical View." *Journal of Southern History* 25, March 1966.

Seitz, Don C. *The Dreadful Decade*. Indianapolis: Bobbs-Merrill, 1926.

Sellin, Thorsten. *Slavery and the Penal System*. New York: Elsevier, 1976.

Sewell, George A., and Margaret L. Dwight. *Mississippi Black History Makers*. Jackson: University Press of Mississippi, 1984.

Shapiro, Herbert. "The Ku Klux Klan During Reconstruction: The South Carolina Episode." *Journal of Negro History* 49, January 1964.

Sharkey, Robert P. *Money, Class, and Party: An Economic Study of Civil War and Reconstruction*. Baltimore: Johns Hopkins Press, 1959.

Sherman, John. *Recollections of Forty Years in the House*. Chicago: The Werner Co., 1895.

Shirley, Jr., William H. "A Black Republican Congressman during the Democratic Resurgence in South Carolina; Robert Smalls 1876–1882," M.A. thesis, University of South Carolina, 1970.

Shofner, Jerrell H. *Nor Is It Over Yet: Florida in the Era of Reconstruction*. Gainesville: University of Florida Press, 1974.

Simkins, Francis B. *The Everlasting South*. Baton Rouge: Louisiana State University Press, 1963.

_____., and Robert H. Woody. *South Carolina during Reconstruction*. Chapel Hill: University of North Carolina Press, 1932.

Simmons, William J. *Men of Mark*. Chicago: Johnson Publishing Company, 1970.

Sims, Patsy. *The Klan*. New York: Dorset Press, 1978.

Singh, Robert. *The Congressional Black Caucus*. Thousand Oaks, Calif.: Sage Publications, 1998.

Singletary, Otis A. *Negro Militia and Reconstruction*. Austin: University of Texas Press, 1957.

Skaggs, W. H. *Southern Obligarchy*. New York: Devin-Adair, 1924.

Sloan, John K. "The Ku Klux Klan and the Alabama Election of 1872," *Alabama Review* 18, April 1965.

Smith, Samuel Denny. *The Negro in Congress, 1870–1901*. Port Washington, N.Y.: Kennikat Press, 1966. Originally published in 1940.

Somers, Dale A. "James P. Newcomb: The Making of a Radical." Southwestern Historical Quarterly 72m (April 1969): 449–469.

Sorrel, Gilbert Moxley. *Recollections of a Confederate Staff Officer*, Jackson, Tenn., 1958. Originally published in 1905.

Stampp, Kenneth M., and Leon F. Litwack, eds. *Reconstruction: An Anthology of Revisionist Writings*. Baton Rouge: Louisiana State University Press, 1969.

Staples, Thomas S. *Reconstruction in Arkansas, 1862–1874*. New York: Columbia University Press, 1923.

Sterling, Dorothy. *Captain of the Planter: The Story of Robert Smalls*. New York: Doubleday, 1958.

_____, ed. *The Trouble They Seen*. Garden City. New York: Doubleday & Company, 1976.

_____. *We Are Your Sisters: Black Women in the Nineteenth Century*. New York: Norton, 1984.

Sternstein, Jerome L., ed. "The Sickles Memorandum: Another Look at the Hayes-Tilden Election Night Conspiracy." *Journal of Southern History* 32 (May 1966): 116–120.

Stewart, James B. *Wendell Phillips: Liberty's Hero*. Baton Rouge: Louisiana State University Press, 1986.

Stewart, Jeffrey C. *1001 Things Everyone Should Know about African American History*. New York: Doubleday, 1996.

Stiles, T. J. *Robber Barons and Radicals: Reconstruction and the Origins of Civil Rights*. New York: Berkeley Publishing Group, 1997.

Still, William. *The Underground Railroad*. Philadelphia: People's Pub. Co., 1879.

Talbot, Edith Armstrong. *Samuel Chapman Armstrong: A Biographical Study*. New York: Doubleday, Page, 1904.

Taylor, A. S. "Negro Congressmen a Generation After." *Journal of Negro History* 7, April 1932.

Tourgee, Albion Winegar. *An Appeal to Caesar*. New York: Fords, Howard & Hulbert, 1884.

_____. *A Fool's Errand*. New York: Fords, Howard & Hulbert, 1879.

_____. *The Invisible Empire*. New York: Fords, Howard & Hulbert, 1880.

Townsend, W.H. *Lincoln and His Wife's Home Town*. Indianapolis, Bobbs-Merrill, 1929.

Trefousse, H. L. *Benjamin Franklin Wade*. New York: Twayne Publishers, 1963.

_____. *The Radical Republicans*. New York: Alfred A. Knopf, 1969.

Trelease, Allen W. *White Terror: The Ku Klux Klan Conspiracy and Southern Reconstruction*. New York: Harper & Row, 1971.

Tunnell, Ted. *Crucible of Reconstruction*. Baton Rouge: Louisiana State University Press, 1984.

Tuttleton, James W. *Thomas Wentworth Higginson*. Boston: Twayne Publishers, 1978.

Underwood, James Lowell, and W. Lewis Burke, eds. *At Freedom's Door*. Columbia: University of South Carolina Press, 2000.

Vaughn, William P. *Schools for All: The Blacks and Public Education in the South, 1865–1877.* Lexington: University Press of Kentucky, 1974.

Wade, Wyn Craig. *The Fiery Cross: The Ku Klux Klan in America.* New York: Simon and Schuster, 1987.

Walker, Clarence E. *A Rock in a Weary Land: The African Methodist Episcopal Church during the Civil War and Reconstruction.* Baton Rouge: Louisiana State University Press, 1982.

Walker, Jonathan. *Trial and Imprisonment of Jonathan Walker, at Pensacola, Florida.* Boston: Anti-Slavery Office, 1845. Reprint, Gainesville: University Press of Florida, 1976.

Warmoth, Henry C. *War, Politics, and Reconstruction: Stormy Days in Louisiana.* New York: Macmillan, 1930.

Washington, Booker T. *The Future of the American Negro.* Boston: Small, Maynard, 1899.

_____. *The Story of the Negro: The Rise of the Race from Slavery.* New York: Doubleday, Page, 1909.

_____. *Up from Slavery.* New York:, Doubleday, Page, 1905.

Welles, Gideon. *Diary of Gideon Welles, Secretary of the Navy under Lincoln and Johnson*, edited by John T. Morse, Jr. 3 vols. Boston: Houghton Mifflin, 1911.

Wells, Anna Mary. *Dear Preceptor: The Life and Times of Thomas Wentworth Higginson.* Boston: Houghton Mifflin, 1963.

Wharton, Vernon L. *The Negro in Mississippi, 1865–1890.* Chapel Hill: University of North Carolina Press, 1947.

White, Charles F. *Who's Who in Colored Philadelphia.* 1912.

Whittier, John Greenleaf. "The Anti-Slavery Convention of 1833." *Atlantic Monthly*, February 1874.

Wiley, B. I. *Southern Negroes, 1861–1865.* New Haven, Conn.: Yale University Press, 1938.

Wilson, Charles Reagan. *Baptized in Blood: The Religion of the Lost Cause, 1865–1920.* Athens: University of Georgia Press, 1980.

Wilson, Theodore B. *The Black Codes of the South.* Tuscaloosa: University of Alabama Press, 1965.

Woldman, Albert A. *Lincoln and the Russians.* Cleveland: World, 1952.

Wood, Forrest G. *Black Scare: The Racist Response to Emancipation and Reconstruction.* Berkeley, University of California Press, 1968.

Woodson, Carter G. *Negro Makers of History.* Washington, D.C.: Associated Publishers, 1942.

_____. *Negro Orators and Their Orations.* Washington, D.C.: Associated Publishers, 1925.

_____. *The Story of the Negro Retold.* Washington, D.C.: Associated Publishers, 1935.

Woodward, C. Vann. *The Burden of Southern History.* Baton Rouge: Louisiana State University Press, 1968.

_____. "On Revising Reconstruction History: Negro Suffrage, White Disfranchisement, and Common Sense." *Journal of Negro History* 51, April 1966.

_____. *Origins of the New South, 1877–1913.* Baton Rouge: Louisiana State University Press, 1951.

_____. *Reunion and Reaction.* New York: Doubleday, 1956.

Wright, Jr., Richard R. "The Economic Condition of Negroes in the North: Negro Communities in New Jersey." *The Southern Workman* 27, July 1908.

Index